SRA Reading Mastery

Signature Edition

Series Guide for the Reading Strand

McGraw Hill • SRA

Columbus, OH

Acknowledgments

SRA/McGraw-Hill gratefully acknowledges the authors of *Reading Mastery Signature Edition*.

Siegfried Engelmann

Elaine C. Bruner

Susan Hanner

Jean Osborn

Steve Osborn

Leslie Zoref

Owen Engelmann

Karen Lou Seitz Davis

51, 172 From A White Heron by Sarah Orne Jewett. Published 1886 Houghton Mifflin Company.

Photo Credits

50 Mauro69/iStock/Getty Images; **172** Mauro69/iStock/Getty Images.

SRAonline.com

 SRA

Send all inquiries to this address:
SRA/McGraw-Hill
4400 Easton Commons
Columbus, OH 43219

ISBN: 978-0-07-612675-0
MHID: 0-07-612675-7

19 20 QLM 20 19 18

The *McGraw-Hill* Companies

Contents

Reading Mastery Signature Edition

Reading Mastery Signature Edition is the sixth edition of *Reading Mastery,* which was originally published in 1969 as *Distar Reading.* The Signature Edition greatly expands and refines the instruction found in previous editions.

The Strands

The Signature Edition consists of three strands for students in Grades K through 5. The strands are (1) Reading and Spelling, (2) Language Arts, and (3) Literature.

The Reading and Spelling strand is scheduled daily and presents core decoding, comprehension, and spelling activities. The Language Arts strand and the Literature strand are designed to complement the Reading strand.

The Language Arts programs are strongly recommended for teachers of at-risk students in Grades K, 1, and 2. These students, particularly, need to become familiar with the language of instruction—the language they will encounter now and later in textbooks.

All three *Reading Mastery Signature Edition* strands have clearly stated goals and objectives.

The **Reading** strand

- addresses all five essential components of reading as identified by Reading First: phonemic awareness, phonics and word analysis, fluency, vocabulary, and comprehension.
- provides spelling instruction to help students make the connection between decoding and spelling patterns.
- develops decoding, word-recognition, and comprehension skills that transfer to other subject areas.

The Reading strand includes six yearlong programs (Grades K–5) and one shorter program (Transition). See page 4 for a complete list of student and teacher materials in the Reading strand.

The **Language Arts** strand

- teaches the oral language skills necessary to understand what is said, written, and read in the classroom.
- helps students communicate ideas and information effectively.
- develops the ability to use writing strategies and processes successfully.

The Language Arts strand includes six yearlong programs (Grades K–5). The main student and teacher materials for each grade are listed below.

Teacher Materials	K	1	2	3	4	5
Language Arts Presentation Book(s)	◆	◆	◆	◆	◆	◆
Teacher's Guide	◆	◆	◆	◆	◆	◆
Answer Key	◆	◆	◆	◆	◆	◆
Student Materials						
Workbook(s)	◆	◆	◆	◆		
Textbook			◆	◆	◆	◆

The **Literature** strand

- supports the Reading strand by offering a wide variety of literary forms and text structures.
- provides frequent opportunities for students to work with comprehension strategies.
- gives ample opportunity for students to read independently.

The Literature strand includes six yearlong programs (Grades K–5). The main student and teacher materials for each grade are listed below.

Teacher Materials	K	1	2	3	4	5
Literature Guide	◆	◆	◆	◆	◆	◆
Student Materials						
Literature Collection	◆	◆				
Literature Anthology			◆	◆	◆	◆

This Series Guide focuses on the Reading strand of *Reading Mastery Signature Edition.* For more information on the Language Arts and Literature strands, consult the *Series Guide for the Language Arts and the Literature Strands.*

Instructional Principles

A few simple principles have guided *Reading Mastery* since its inception in the 1960s, and they have played a large part in its many documented successes.

- The program is designed to teach *every* student how to read.
- All instruction is direct and unambiguous; tasks and activities are specified in detail.
- Every reading skill and strategy in the program is carefully taught in isolation and then applied and reviewed.
- Students receive daily practice in decoding and in applying comprehension strategies.
- Teacher assessment of student performance is continuous, and errors are corrected when they occur.

In the Grade K and Grade 1 programs, students learn *how* to read by using an acclaimed phonics method. In the Grade 2 and Grade 3 programs, students read to learn; they learn a variety of information, concepts, and facts. Finally, in the Grade 4 and Grade 5 programs, students read and interpret literature.

Learning to Read— Grades K and 1

Grade K and Grade 1 focus on learning to read. The Grade K program teaches all the prerequisite skills children need to read. These skills include the phonemic manipulations of blending orally presented words that are presented a sound at a time, of saying orally presented words a sound at a time, and of rhyming.

Children in the Grade K program learn sounds for letters. The words they read are composed entirely of sounds they have learned. There are no "sight words." Children begin to read words after they have learned common sounds of six letters.

The stories the children read are composed entirely of words they have learned. For early word-reading in both word lists and stories, students sound out each word and then identify it. Because the words are familiar, students are far less likely to make decoding errors and more likely to make sense out of what they are reading.

To facilitate initial word-reading, a special font is used. The font makes it possible for children to distinguish between long vowel sounds (ā, ē, ī, ō, ū, ȳ) and short vowel sounds. The font shows th, sh, ch, ing, er, wh, and qu as joined letters that make a single sound. Silent letters are set in smaller type and are not pronounced. These prompts permit students to decode words such as hēre, whēre and wēre as perfectly regular words, without learning "phonics rules." The special font is maintained throughout Grade K and part of Grade 1. After students become more fluent decoders, the special font is systematically replaced by a standard font.

In Grades K and 1, students learn to attend to key story details as well as oral and written directions. Deductive reasoning skills are specifically taught. Students connect to stories by predicting story pictures and events and by drawing their own story illustrations. They soon learn—through these and other techniques—how to comprehend the texts they decode.

Stories are designed so that students do not see pictures before reading stories. Instead, students read a story and predict what would be in a picture of that story. Students then see the picture as a confirmation of what they have read. A special activity in Grades K and 1 teaches children basic reading-comprehension skills. The activity, called "Read the Items," is something like "Simon Says." Students first read a rule such as, "If the teacher says go, stand up." Then students apply the rule. You try to "fool" students by saying things like, "Do it" or "Stand up." Students do not stand up until you say, "Go." Through these and similar activities, students receive daily practice in reading carefully, following directions precisely, and applying what they read.

Fast Cycle, an accelerated *Reading Mastery* program that combines Grade K and Grade 1 into a single year, is available for students of above-average ability. For more details on this program and an accelerated schedule, see page 20.

Reading to Learn— Grades 2 and 3

Grade 2 and Grade 3 focus on reading to learn. The emphasis shifts from learning how to decode and comprehend to actually using these skills as tools for learning from written material, not from what somebody says. Grade 2 can be used with Transition, a short program specifically designed to help low-achieving students make the transition from Grade 1 to Grade 2. (For more information on Transition, see page 22.)

The stories and factual articles in Grade 2 and Grade 3 teach students about diverse places in the world, about different eras—from the age of the dinosaurs to the present—and about important historical events. Students learn facts and rules about living near the North Pole, diving deep in the ocean, migrating with a flock of geese, traveling through outer space, and taking a journey through the human body. The engaging stories transform science rules and historical events into experiences that set the stage for conventional content-area reading. They also provide students with a strong foundation of common information in different content areas.

Understanding Literature— Grades 4 and 5

In Grade 4 and Grade 5, students extend what they have learned about reading and begin serious analysis and interpretation of literature. Students focus on not only the content of literature selections but also the ways in which the content is presented. This emphasis introduces students to new styles of writing, new sentence forms, and new vocabulary. It also involves new comprehension skills for interpreting different types of literature.

Students in Grade 4 and Grade 5 read abridged versions of classic novels, along with full-length short stories, poems, myths, folktales, biographies, and factual articles. Through daily writing activities, they compare different writers and analyze specific details of plots, characters, and themes. In addition to answering questions about the material they read, students also complete various comprehension activities that teach specific concepts and strategies. They identify contradictions, interpret figurative language, and draw inferences; they also interpret maps, graphs, and forms. These extended writing activities sharpen student understanding of characters' perspectives and motives and of underlying themes.

Reading Strand Overview

The Reading strand includes six yearlong programs (Grades K–5) plus the shorter Transition (Tr) program between Grades 1 and 2. The main student and teacher materials for each grade are listed below.

Teacher Materials	K	1	Tr	2	3	4	5
Reading Presentation Book(s)	◆	◆	◆	◆	◆	◆	◆
Spelling Presentation Book	◆	◆		◆	◆	◆	◆
Teacher's Guide*	◆	◆	◆	◆	◆	◆	◆
Answer Key*	◆	◆	◆	◆	◆	◆	◆
Curriculum-Based Assessment and Fluency Teacher Handbook	◆	◆		◆	◆	◆	◆
Skills Profile Chart**	◆	◆		◆	◆	◆	◆
Activities across the Curriculum				◆	◆	◆	◆
Audio CD with sound pronunciation guide	◆						
Student Materials							
Storybook(s)	◆	◆					
Textbook(s)			◆	◆	◆	◆	◆
Workbook(s)	◆	◆	◆	◆	◆	◆	◆
Curriculum-Based Assessment and Fluency Student Book	◆	◆		◆	◆	◆	◆
Independent Reader Library (optional)	◆	◆					
Seatwork Blackline Masters (optional)	◆	◆					

* In Transition, the Teacher's Guide and the Answer Key appear in the Reading Presentation Book.

** In Grades 2–5, blackline masters of the Skills Profile Chart appear in the Teacher's Guide.

Teacher Materials

Reading Presentation Books (Grades K–5 and Transition) contain presentation scripts for every lesson. The scripts tell you (the teacher) what to say and do. The scripts also specify students' answers. Many scripts give specific procedures for correcting students' mistakes. Reduced student pages provide an easy reference to what students are reading. Planning pages at every fifth lesson offer an overview of the upcoming vocabulary, skills, and stories.

Spelling Presentation Books (Grades K–5) contain spelling lessons that are presented after the reading activities are completed.

Teacher's Guides (Grades K–5 and Transition) explain each level in detail and provide specific teaching techniques for many types of exercises. The guides also contain correction procedures, suggestions for classroom management, placement tests, and other helpful material.

Answer Keys (Grades K–5 and Transition) contain answer keys for the student Workbooks and Textbooks.

Curriculum-Based Assessment and Fluency Teacher Handbooks (Grades K–5) contain instructions for administering the curriculum-based assessments that appear in the student assessment books. These assessments measure student mastery of skills and concepts taught in the program. The teacher handbook also includes record-keeping charts and remedial exercises.

Skills Profile Charts (Grades K–5) can be used to track each student's mastery of skills taught in the programs. For Grades K and 1, the charts are available as separate folders. For Grades 2–5, the charts appear as blackline masters in the Teacher's Guides.

Activities across the Curriculum (Grades 2–5) connects the Reading strand to science, social studies, geography, art, music, and other content areas. The activities and blackline masters in this component provide new contexts for using comprehension, writing, and research skills.

Audio CD (Grade K) reviews correct sound pronunciation and presents sample exercises for Grade K.

Student Materials

Storybooks (Grades K and 1) and **Textbooks** (Grades 2–5 and Transition) are hardbound, full-color books containing the illustrated stories, novels, poems, information passages, and vocabulary words that students read. The Textbooks for Grades 2–5 also contain comprehension and skill activities that students complete on lined paper.

Workbooks (Grades K–5 and Transition) are softbound consumable books containing questions and exercises that students complete during each lesson. Students answer Workbook questions in the Workbook.

Curriculum-Based Assessment and Fluency Student Books (Grades K–5) are softbound consumable books containing the curriculum-based assessments that students take periodically throughout the program.

Independent Reader Libraries (Grades K and 1) are optional stories that provide additional independent practice after specific lessons. The text of each story consists of words students have already learned.

Seatwork Blackline Masters (Grades K and 1) are optional daily written activities that are coordinated with the reading instruction. Students can complete these activities independently.

Teacher-Directed Activities

Every lesson in the Reading strand begins with teacher-directed activities. The main activities include:

Prereading Exercises (Grades K and 1 and Transition) Students learn letter sounds and readiness skills for decoding and comprehension, such as following directions.

Word Practice (Grades K–5 and Transition) Students read lists of words aloud, both in unison and individually. These words will later appear in the reading selections.

Vocabulary Exercises (Grades 2–5) Students learn the meanings of difficult words that will later appear in the reading selections.

Skill Exercises (Grades K–5 and Transition) You introduce the skill exercises contained in students' Workbooks and Textbooks.

Group Reading (Grades K–5 and Transition) Students take turns reading aloud from their Storybooks or Textbooks.

Comprehension Questions (Grades K–5 and Transition) Both during and after the group reading, you present comprehension questions about the material students read.

Individual Reading Fluency Checkouts (Grades K–5 and Transition) In selected lessons, you measure each student's decoding rate and accuracy.

Workcheck (Grades K–5 and Transition) You check students' independent work.

Spelling (Grades K–5) You conduct spelling activities after the reading lesson is completed.

Independent Student Activities

Every lesson in the Reading strand includes activities that students complete independently. The independent work includes:

Silent Reading (Grades K–5 and Transition) Students read stories, questions, and exercises silently.

Paired Reading (Grades 2–5) Pairs of students orally read a story to each other.

Story Items (Grades K–5 and Transition) Students answer written questions about the stories.

Skill Items (Grades K–5 and Transition) Students complete exercises that teach specific decoding, comprehension, literary, and study skills.

Vocabulary Items (Grades 2–5) Students use new vocabulary words to complete sentences and solve crossword puzzles.

Review Items (Grades K–5 and Transition) Students review previously taught skills and vocabulary.

Fact Games (Grades 2–4) Students play cooperative learning games that involve facts they have learned.

Special Projects (Grades 2–5) Students complete cross-curricular activities that relate to their reading selections, such as writing song lyrics, building a model, and researching a specific topic.

Writing Assignments (Grades 2–5) Students write stories, essays, and poems on assigned topics.

Grade K Reading Strand

The Reading strand for *Reading Mastery Signature Edition,* Grade K, contains 160 daily lessons that teach basic decoding and comprehension skills. Decoding is taught through an explicit phonics method that stresses letter sounds and blending. Students practice decoding by reading word lists and stories, both aloud and silently. Comprehension activities include answering questions about pictures, following directions, and responding to questions about the stories.

Materials

The following teacher and student materials are available for Grade K:

Teacher Materials

- *Reading Presentation Books* (3)
- *Spelling Presentation Book*
- *Teacher's Guide*
- *Answer Key*
- *Curriculum-Based Assessment and Fluency Teacher Handbook*
- *Skills Profile Chart*
- *Audio CD* demonstrating how to pronounce the sounds and how to present exercises

Student Materials

- *Storybook*
- *Workbooks* (3)
- *Curriculum-Based Assessment and Fluency Student Book*
- *Independent Reader Library* (optional)
- *Seatwork Blackline Masters* (optional)

Comprehensive Program Materials

- *Reading Mastery Signature Edition,* Grade K Language Strand
- *Reading Mastery Signature Edition,* Grade K Literature Strand

The Storybook for Grade K contains original stories written especially for the program. There are both realistic and fantasy stories about animals and people.

Sample Activities (first half of program)

(To view a complete sample lesson from Grade K, turn to page 100.)

In the first half of Grade K, students master decoding and comprehension readiness skills, learn individual letter sounds, and learn how to read regularly spelled words.

The following exercises from Lesson 34 are typical of those found in the first half of the program. Exercise 1 (shown below) prepares students for decoding by teaching them how to pronounce specific sounds. First you say a sound; then students say the sound in unison. You use a simple signal to make sure students respond together. After the group has mastered the sound, individual students say the sound.

Exercise 1 also prepares students for comprehension by teaching them how to follow directions.

This is an oral task. Pronounce **c** as in **tack**.

PRONUNCIATION
EXERCISE 1

Children say the sounds

a. You're going to say some sounds. When I hold up my finger, say (pause) **c.** Get ready. (Hold up one finger.) *c.*

b. Next sound. Say (pause) **ĭĭĭ.** Get ready. (Hold up one finger.) *ĭĭĭ.*

c. Next sound. Say (pause) **nnn.** Get ready. (Hold up one finger.) *nnn.*

d. (Repeat *c* for sounds **c, ĭĭĭ,** and **nnn.**)

e. (Call on individual children to do *a, b,* or *c.*)

f. Good saying the sounds.

Reading Presentation Book, Lesson 34

Exercise 2 teaches students how to read the short vowel **i.** First you hold the Presentation Book so students can see the large **i.** Next you touch under the **i** and say the letter's sound: **ĭĭĭ.** Then students say the sound in unison as you touch under the letter. Students practice saying the sound until every student has mastered it. Finally, you call on individual students to say the sound.

A new letter sound is introduced every few lessons. The special font makes the differences between letters obvious to students. For example, **b** and **d** are not mirror images, and **a** and **d** are easily distinguished from each other.

In Grade K, students learn every lowercase letter, as well as the sound combinations **th, sh, ch, iñg, er, oo, wh,** and **qu,** and the word **I.** Long and short vowels are treated as separate letters. For example, short *a* (as in *mat*) is taught in Lesson 1, and it always looks like this: **a.** Long *a* (as in *mate*) is taught in Lesson 58, and it always has a macron over it: **ā.** In Grade 1, students learn other ways of distinguishing between long and short vowels, and the macron is no longer used.

SOUNDS
EXERCISE 2

Introducing the new sound i as in **if**

a. (Touch the first ball of the arrow for **i.**) Here's a new sound. My turn to say it. Get ready. (Move quickly to the second ball. Hold.) **iii.**

b. (Return to the first ball.) My turn again. Get ready. (Move quickly to the second ball. Hold.) **iii.**

c. (Return to the first ball.) My turn again. Get ready. (Move quickly to the second ball. Hold.) **iii.**

d. (Return to the first ball.) Your turn. Get ready. (Move quickly to the second ball. Hold.) *iii.* Yes, *iii.*

e. (Return to the first ball.) Again. Get ready. (Move quickly to the second ball. Hold.) *iii.* Yes, *iii.*

f. (Repeat *e* until firm.)

g. (Call on individual children to do *d*.)

h. Good saying **iii.**

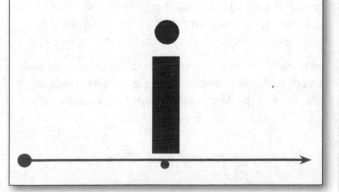

Reading Presentation Book, Lesson 34

In Exercise 13, students learn how to read a regularly spelled word: **am.** First students identify the individual letter sounds in the word. Then they sound out the word. Finally, they read the word by "saying it fast."

This simple and effective sounding-out procedure allows students to read hundreds of regularly spelled words.

EXERCISE 13

Children say the sounds, then sound out the word

a. (Touch the first ball of the arrow for **am.**) You're going to sound it out. (Point to the ball for **a.**) What sound are you going to say first? (Touch the ball.) *aaa.* Yes, **aaa.**

• (Point to the ball for **m.**) What sound are you going to say next? (Touch the ball.) *mmm.* Yes, **mmm.**

b. (Return to the first ball.) Everybody, when I move my finger, say the sounds **aaammm.** Don't stop between the sounds. Get ready. (Move quickly under each sound. Hold.) *Aaammm.*

c. (Return to the first ball.) Again. Sound it out. Get ready. (Move quickly under each sound. Hold.) *Aaammm.*

d. (Repeat *c* until firm.)

e. (Return to the first ball.) Say it fast. (Slash.) *Am.*

• Yes, **am.** You read the word **am.** Do you know who I (pause) **am?**

f. (Call on individual children to do *c* and *e*.)

Reading Presentation Book, Lesson 34

After students finish the Presentation Book activities, they complete Workbook activities. These exercises develop and expand the skills taught in the Presentation Book. First you go over the exercises with the students; then they complete the exercises on their own.

In the exercises shown below, students follow pictured directions, copy letters, pair letters with objects, and complete a picture.

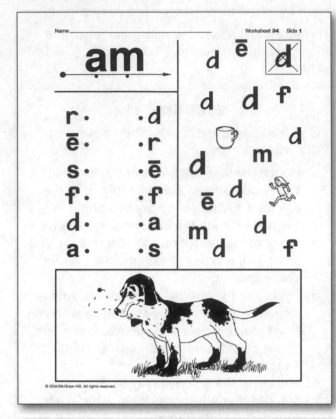

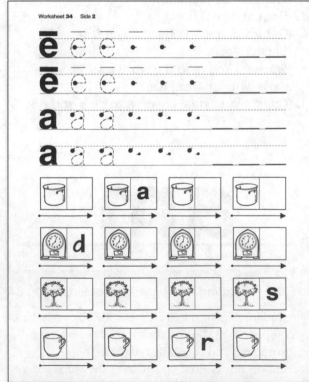

Workbook, Lesson 34

Sample Activities (second half of program)

In the second half of Grade K, students read complete stories, answer comprehension questions, and learn how to read many irregular words. They also learn several sound combinations.

In the exercise from Lesson 113 shown below, you present the sound combination **ch.** The two letters that make up this sound are connected by a heavy black line. This unique font is used for all sound combinations in Grade K. In Grade 1, students learn other means of recognizing sound combinations, and the letters are separated.

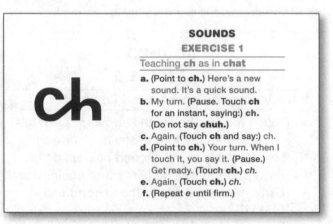

SOUNDS
EXERCISE 1
Teaching **ch** as in **chat**

a. (Point to **ch.**) Here's a new sound. It's a quick sound.
b. My turn. (Pause. Touch **ch** for an instant, saying:) **ch.** (Do not say **chuh.**)
c. Again. (Touch **ch** and say:) ch.
d. (Point to **ch.**) Your turn. When I touch it, you say it. (Pause.) Get ready. (Touch **ch.**) ch.
e. Again. (Touch **ch.**) ch.
f. (Repeat *e* until firm.)

Reading Presentation Book, Lesson 113

In the second half of the program, students continue to learn new regularly spelled words. They also learn how to read irregular words, how to read words "the fast way," and how to read words in lists. The Presentation Book exercises shown on the next page are typical.

In Exercise 12 of Lesson 89, students sound out and read the word **late.** The *e* is smaller than the other letters in the word. Students have already learned the rule "When a word has a little sound, you don't say the sound." This rule allows students to sound out words with silent letters. In Grade 1, students learn other means of identifying silent letters, so the smaller letters become regular size.

In Exercise 14, students read two rhyming words: **wish** and **dish.** Because **dish** is so similar to **wish,** students are able to read the new word without first sounding it out.

After you read the words on this page, you'll get to read the words the fast way.

EXERCISE 12

Children sound out the word and tell what word

a. (Touch the ball for **lāte.**) Sound it out.
b. Get ready. (Touch **l, ā, t** as the children say *lllāāāt.*)
• (If sounding out is not firm, repeat *b.*)
c. What word? (Signal.) *Late.* Yes, **late.**

EXERCISE 13

Children sound out the word and tell what word

a. (Touch the ball for **sand.**) Sound it out.
b. Get ready. (Touch **s, a, n, d** as the children say *sssaaannnd.*)
• (If sounding out is not firm, repeat *b.*)
c. What word? (Signal.) *Sand.* Yes, **sand.**

EXERCISE 14

Children rhyme with **wish**

a. (Touch the ball for **wish.**) Sound it out.
b. Get ready. (Touch **w, i, sh** as the children say *wwwiiishshsh.*)
• (If sounding out is not firm, repeat *b.*)
c. What word? (Signal.) *Wish.* Yes, **wish.**
d. (Quickly touch the ball for **dish.**) This word rhymes with (pause) **wish.** Get ready. (Signal. Move your finger quickly along the arrow.) *Dish.*
e. What word? (Signal.) *Dish.* Yes, **dish.**

EXERCISE 15

Children read the words the fast way

a. Now you get to read the words on this page the fast way.
b. (Touch the ball for **lāte.** Pause three seconds.) Get ready. (Move your finger quickly along the arrow.) *Late.*
c. (Repeat *b* for each word on the page.)

EXERCISE 16

Individual test

(Call on individual children to read one word the fast way.)

lāte

sand

wish

dish

Reading Presentation Book, Lesson 89

In Exercise 15, students read all the words on the page "the fast way." When students read words the fast way, they simply read the words without sounding them out. Finally, in Exercise 16, individual students take turns reading the words.

In Exercise 17 of Lesson 95, students read an irregular word: **was.** First students sound out the word. Then you tell students how to say the word correctly. Finally, students practice reading the word.

A new irregular word is introduced every few lessons. The program teaches more than 50 irregular words.

EXERCISE 17

Children sound out an irregular word (**was**)

a. (Touch the ball for **was.**) Sound it out.
b. Get ready. (Quickly touch each sound as the children say *wwwaaasss.*)

To Correct
If the children sound out the word as **wwwuuuzzz**
1. (Say:) You've got to say the sounds I touch.
2. (Repeat *a* and *b* until firm.)

c. Again. (Repeat *b* until firm.)
d. That's how we <u>sound out</u> the word. Here's how we <u>say</u> the word. **Was.** How do we <u>say</u> the word? (Signal.) *Was.*
e. Now you're going to <u>sound out</u> the word. Get ready. (Touch each sound as the children say *wwwaaasss.*)
f. Now you're going to <u>say</u> the word. Get ready. (Signal.) *Was.*
g. (Repeat *e* and *f* until firm.)
h. Yes, this word is **was.** When I gave him five dollars, he **was** happy.

was

Reading Presentation Book, Lesson 95

Beginning in Lesson 91, students read entire stories in their Storybook. These stories are written with words the students have already learned. Initially, the stories are only a few sentences long. By the end of Grade K, however, students are reading longer stories that are serialized over a span of lessons.

STORY 115

lots of cars

a man on a farm has lots of cars. hē has ōld cars. hē has littlₑ cars.

arₑ his cars fōr gōₐts? nō.

56

STORY 115

arₑ his cars fōr shēēp? nō. arₑ his cars fōr cows? nō.

his cars arₑ fōr cops. hē has lots of cop cars.

57

Storybook, Lesson 115

The story-reading activities for Lesson 115 are shown below and on the next page. In Exercise 21, you read the title of the story. Students learn that the title tells what the story is going to be about. In Exercise 22, students read the entire story the fast way, without sounding out any words. After students finish this first reading, they review any words that gave them trouble. In Exercise 23, you ask individual students to read a sentence from the story.

STORYBOOK

STORY 115
EXERCISE 21

Teacher introduces the title

a. (Pass out Storybook.)
b. Open your book to page 56. ✔
c. (Hold up your reader. Point to the title.) These words are called the title of the story. These words tell what the story is about. I'll read the title the fast way.
d. (Point to the words as you read:) Lots of cars.
e. Everybody, what is this story about? (Signal.) *Lots of cars.* Yes, **lots of cars.**
• This story is going to tell something about **lots of cars.**

EXERCISE 22

First reading—children read the story the fast way

(Have the children reread any sentences containing words that give them trouble. Keep a list of these words.)
a. Everybody, touch the title of the story and get ready to read the words in the title the fast way.
b. First word. ✔
• (Pause three seconds.) Get ready. (Tap.) *Lots.*
c. Next word. ✔
• (Pause three seconds.) Get ready. (Tap.) *Of.*
d. (Repeat c for the word **cars.**)
e. (After the children have read the title, ask:) What's this story about? (Signal.) *Lots of cars.* Yes, **lots of cars.**
f. Everybody, touch the first word of the story. ✔
g. Get ready to read this story the fast way.
h. First word. (Pause three seconds.) Get ready. (Tap.) *A.*
i. Next word. ✔
• (Pause three seconds.) Get ready. (Tap.) *Man.*
j. (Repeat i for the remaining words in the first sentence. Pause at least three seconds between taps. The children are to identify each word without sounding it out.)
k. (Repeat h through j for the next two sentences. Have the children reread the first three sentences until firm.)
l. (The children are to read the remainder of the story the fast way, stopping at the end of each sentence.)
m. (After the first reading of the story, print on the board the words that the children missed more than one time. Have the children sound out each word one time and tell what word.)
n. (After the group's responses are firm, call on individual children to read the words.)

EXERCISE 23

Individual test

a. Look at page 56. I'm going to call on individual children to read a whole sentence the fast way.
b. (Call on individual children to read a sentence. Do not tap for each word.)

Reading Presentation Book, Lesson 115

In Exercise 24, students read the story again, as you ask literal and interpretive comprehension questions.

Most of your questions can be answered by specific words in the story. Students answer these questions in unison, at your signal. Some questions, however, require students to make personal judgments or predictions. These questions are answered by individual students.

Storybook, Lesson 115

In Exercise 25, after students finish the story, they predict what a picture of the story will look like. Then they turn the page and look at a picture of the story. You present comprehension questions about the picture. Later, students draw their own picture of the story.

EXERCISE 24

Second reading—children read the story the fast way and answer questions

a. You're going to read the story again the fast way and I'll ask questions.
b. Starting with the first word of the title. ✔
• Get ready. (Tap.) *Lots.*
c. (Tap for each remaining word. Pause at least three seconds between taps. Pause longer before words that gave the children trouble during the first reading.)
d. (Ask the comprehension questions below as the children read.)

After the children read:	You say:
Lots of cars.	What's this story about? (Signal.) *Lots of cars.*
A man on a farm has lots of cars.	What does he have? (Signal.) *Lots of cars.*
He has little cars.	What kind of cars does he have? (Signal.) *Old cars and little cars.*
Are his cars for goats?	What do you think? *The children respond.* Let's read and find out.
No.	Are they for goats? (Signal.) *No.*
He has lots of cop cars.	What kind of cars does he have? (Signal.) *Cop cars.*

EXERCISE 25

Picture comprehension

a. What do you think you'll see in the picture? *The children respond.*
b. Turn the page and look at the picture.
c. (Ask these questions:)
  1. Do you see lots of cop cars? *Yes.*
  2. What would you do if you had all those cop cars? *The children respond.*
  3. How do you know he lives on a farm? *The children respond.*

Reading Presentation Book, Lesson 115

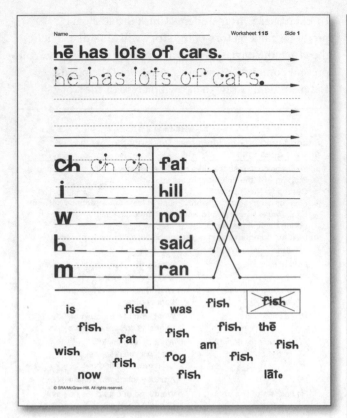

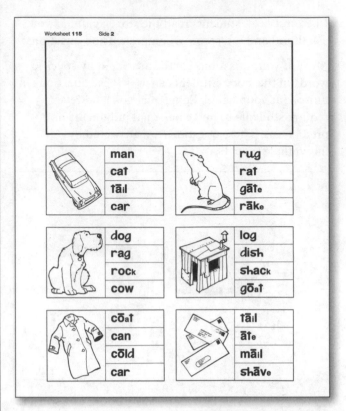

Workbook, Lesson 115

In the four pages of Workbook activities for Lesson 115, students copy letters and sentences, match words, follow pictured directions, and associate words with pictures. You explain all the Workbook exercises before students complete them. Students also draw a picture of the day's story in the blank space on page 2. The other pages (not shown) contain a story presented several days earlier in the Storybook. These pages, which appear every fifth lesson, help parents or guardians understand how their child's reading is progressing.

Lesson 115 also includes an individual fluency checkout (Exercise 33), in which you check each student's ability to read for rate and accuracy. As the group is working independently, you call on individual students to read the day's story aloud. Students earn stars if they read the entire story in less than two minutes, while making no more than three errors.

INDIVIDUAL CHECKOUT: STORYBOOK
EXERCISE 33

2-minute individual fluency checkout: rate/accuracy—whole story from title

a. As you are doing your worksheet, I'll call on children one at a time to read the **whole story.** Remember, you get two stars if you read the story in less than two minutes and make no more than three errors.
b. (Call on a child. Tell the child:) Start with the title and read the story carefully the fast way. Go. (Time the child. Tell the child any words the child misses. Stop the child as soon as the child makes the fourth error or exceeds the time limit.)
c. (If the child meets the rate-accuracy criterion, record two stars on your chart for lesson 115. Congratulate the child. Give children who do not earn two stars a chance to read the story again before the next lesson is presented.)
49 words/**2 min** = 25 wpm [**3 errors**]

Reading Presentation Book, Lesson 115

The spelling lessons begin after lesson 50. After the class finishes the main reading lesson, you present activities from the *Spelling Presentation Book*. Ideally, spelling is scheduled at a time other than the reading period. However, spelling can be presented at the end of the reading lesson if sufficient time is available during the block designated for reading.

The spelling activities reinforce the decoding skills taught in the reading lessons. Students write answers for spelling activities on lined paper, so no additional student materials are required. Sample spelling activities for Spelling Lesson 66 appear in the next column.

SPELLING LESSON 66

WORD WRITING
EXERCISE 1

Children write **dan, on**

a. You're going to write the word **dan.** Think about the sounds in (pause) **dan** and write the word. ✔

To Correct

1. Say the sounds in **dan.** (Signal.) *daaannn.*
2. Say the sounds the hard way. (Signal.) *d* (pause) *aaa* (pause) *nnn.*
3. Write the word **dan.** ✔

b. (Repeat step *a* for **on.**)

EXERCISE 2

Children write **we**

a. You're going to write the word **we.** Listen. **We.** Saying the sounds in (pause) **we** the hard way. Get ready. (Signal for each sound as the children say:) *www* (pause) *ēēē.* (The children are to pause two seconds between the sounds.)
- (Repeat until firm.)
b. Everybody, write the word (pause) **we.** ✔

EXERCISE 3

Children write **in, sun, he, it, at**

a. You're going to write the word **in.** Think about the sounds in (pause) **in** and write the word. ✔
b. (Repeat step *a* for the following: **sun, he, it, at.**)

Spelling Presentation Book, Lesson 66

Grade 1 Reading Strand

The Reading strand for *Reading Mastery Signature Edition,* Grade 1, contains 160 daily lessons that expand basic reading skills. Students in Grade 1 learn strategies for decoding difficult words and for answering interpretive comprehension questions. They also learn basic reasoning skills, such as making inferences and drawing conclusions. The daily reading selections include fantasy and realistic fiction.

Materials

The following teacher and student materials are available for Grade 1:

Teacher Materials

- *Reading Presentation Books* (3)
- *Spelling Presentation Book*
- *Teacher's Guide*
- *Answer Key*
- *Curriculum-Based Assessment and Fluency Teacher Handbook*
- *Skills Profile Folder*

Student Materials

- *Storybooks* (2)
- *Workbooks* (3)
- *Curriculum-Based Assessment and Fluency Student Book*
- *Independent Reader Library* (optional)
- *Seatwork Blackline Masters* (optional)

Comprehensive Program Materials

- *Reading Mastery Signature Edition,* Grade 1 Language Arts Strand
- *Reading Mastery Signature Edition,* Grade 1 Literature Strand

The Storybooks for Grade 1 contain original stories written especially for the program, as well as adaptations of famous children's stories. Many of the stories are serialized over a span of lessons.

Sample Activities

(To view a complete sample lesson from Grade 1, turn to page 109.)

Each lesson in Grade 1 begins with word-practice exercises that appear in the *Reading Presentation Book.* In the first part of the program, you present individual sounds and words, and students read them aloud. Later in the program, you present lists of words that students read aloud.

In Lessons 1–47, the unique *Reading Mastery* font is used in the program materials. In Lessons 48–92, the special font is gradually phased out and replaced by a standard font. During this transition period, students learn the final-e rule and other guides for reading words in standard font. They also learn every capital letter. In Lessons 93–160, standard font is used in all student and teacher materials.

The following sample activities appear in Lesson 97. The lesson begins with four separate word lists. The list in Exercise 1 (shown below) contains new words that are difficult to decode, as well as words that students have already learned. The new words are printed in red. First you read the new words; then students spell then. Finally, students read the new words. After students have mastered the new words, they read the entire list.

Students read all the words in unison. When you point to a word, students look over the word and get ready to read it. Then they read the word in unison as you slash under the word with a finger.

In Exercise 2, students read words that contain various sound combinations, word endings, or root words. These word elements are underlined in each word. Students first read the underlined part; then they read the entire word.

These words with underlined parts teach students an important decoding strategy. The underlines demonstrate that many unfamiliar words contain familiar parts. By identifying these familiar parts, students are able to decode unfamiliar words.

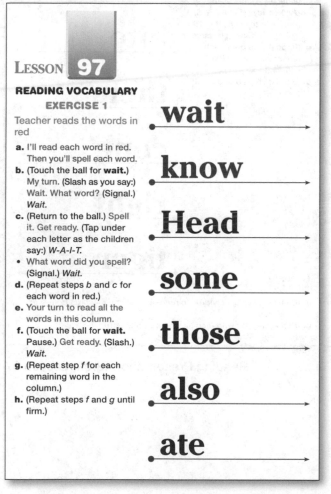

Reading Presentation Book, Lesson 97

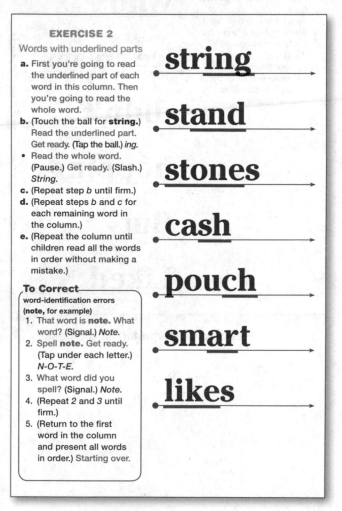

Reading Presentation Book, Lesson 97

In Exercise 3, students read words they have already learned or new words that are easy to decode. You point to each word; then students read the word when you slash under it with a finger.

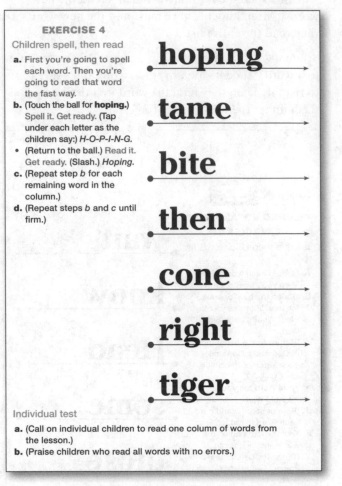

EXERCISE 3

Read the fast way

a. You're going to read all the words in this column the fast way.
b. (Touch the ball for **Let's.** Pause.) Get ready. (Slash.) *Let's.*
c. (Repeat step *b* until firm.)
d. (Repeat steps *b* and *c* for each remaining word in the column.)
e. (Repeat the column until the children read all the words in order without making mistakes.)

Let's

who

ice cream

didn't

hopping

But

Liked

Reading Presentation Book, Lesson 97

In Exercise 4, students spell each word before reading it. This procedure not only promotes accurate spelling, but also teaches students to examine words carefully.

When the group finishes reading all the lists, individual students take turns reading one list each.

EXERCISE 4

Children spell, then read

a. First you're going to spell each word. Then you're going to read that word the fast way.
b. (Touch the ball for **hoping.**) Spell it. Get ready. (Tap under each letter as the children say:) *H-O-P-I-N-G.*
• (Return to the ball.) Read it. Get ready. (Slash.) *Hoping.*
c. (Repeat step *b* for each remaining word in the column.)
d. (Repeat steps *b* and *c* until firm.)

hoping

tame

bite

then

cone

right

tiger

Individual test

a. (Call on individual children to read one column of words from the lesson.)
b. (Praise children who read all words with no errors.)

Reading Presentation Book, Lesson 97

STORYBOOK

STORY 97

EXERCISE 5

Reading—decoding

a. (Pass out Storybook 2.)

b. Everybody, open your reader to page 38.

c. Remember, if the group reads all the way to the red 5 without making more than five errors, we can go on.

d. Everybody, touch the title of the story. ✔

e. If you hear a mistake, raise your hand. Remember, children who do not have their place lose their turn. (Call on individual children to read two or three sentences. Do not ask comprehension questions. Tally all errors.)

To Correct

word-identification errors (**from,** for example)

1. That word is **from.** What word? *From.*
2. Go back to the beginning of the sentence and read the sentence again.

f. (If the children make more than five errors before they reach the red 5: when they reach the 5 return to the beginning of the story and have the children reread to the 5. Do not ask comprehension questions. Repeat step *f* until firm, and then go on to step *g*.)

g. (When the children read to the red 5 without making more than five errors: read the story to the children from the beginning to the 5. Ask the specified comprehension questions. When you reach the 5, call on individual children to continue reading the story. Have each child read two or three sentences.

Ask the specified comprehension questions.)

The Tame Tiger Who Liked Ice Cream[1]

There once was a tame tiger. This tiger did not bite children.[2] He didn't eat goats or sheep.[3] He said, "I like ice cream.[4] So I will go to town and get some."

But the tiger didn't have any cash.[5] He said, "I will fill my pouch with round stones. I hope that the man at the ice cream store likes round stones."[6]

So the tiger filled his pouch with round stones. Then he walked to town. He went up to the man at the ice cream stand.

"I don't have any cash," the tiger said. "But I have a pouch filled with pretty round stones."[7]

"Let's see them," the man said.

So the tiger showed the man his stones. The man said, "I like those stones. They are pretty."[8]

The tiger gave the pouch to the man. ⑤ Then the tiger said, "I want a big cone, and I want some string."[9]

The man said, "What will you do with a big cone and some string?"

"Wait and see," the tiger said. What do you think the tiger did?[10] He ate the ice cream from the cone.[11] Then he put the big cone on his head with a string.[12]

The tiger said, "I love ice cream and I love hats. I ate the ice cream and now I have the best hat in town."[13]

The man at the ice cream stand said, "That tiger is very tame. He is also very smart."

The end

---

[1] What is this story going to be about? (Signal.) *The tame tiger who liked ice cream.*
- A tiger is an animal with stripes.
[2] Did this tiger bite children? (Signal.) *No.* Right. He was tame.
[3] I wonder what he did eat? Let's read some more.
[4] Now we know. What does he eat? (Signal.) *Ice cream.*
[5] What didn't he have? (Signal.) *Cash.* What's cash? (The children respond.) Right. He didn't have any money.
[6] What does the tiger want to do with the round stones? (The children respond.)
[7] Does he have cash? (Signal.) *No.*
- What does he have? (Signal.) *Pretty round stones.*
[8] Did the man like those stones? (Signal.) *Yes.*
[9] What did the tiger say? (Signal.) *I want a big cone, and I want some string.*
[10] What do you think? (The children respond.)
- Let's keep reading.
[11] What's the first thing the tiger did? (Signal.) *He ate the ice cream.*
[12] What's the next thing he did? (Signal.) (The children respond.)
[13] How did he get that hat? (The children respond.) Right. He made it from the cone and string.

After the word-practice exercises are completed, you direct students as they read aloud from their Storybooks (the pages are reproduced in your Presentation Book). During this group reading, you monitor students' decoding accuracy and present comprehension questions.

Students begin the group reading by reading the first part of the story within a specified decoding error limit. The first part of the story extends from the title to the circled 5. You call on individual students to read two or three sentences each. Students must practice reading the first part of the story until they can read up to the circled 5 while making no more than five decoding errors.

After the group reads the first part of the story within the error limit, you reread the first part to the group and present the comprehension questions. Numbers are placed within your reproduced Storybook pages to indicate where you present the questions. The actual questions are printed under the reproduced pages.

When you finish rereading the first part of the story, students take turns reading the rest of the story, as you present more comprehension questions. These questions teach both literal and interpretive comprehension skills. In Lesson 97, for example, students relate titles to story content, answer literal questions, identify the meanings of common words, and predict narrative outcomes.

After students finish reading the story, they complete written exercises in their Workbooks. In the exercises for Lesson 97, students answer questions about the story, follow written directions, and complete deductions. They also read a short passage and answer questions about the passage.

You explain new Workbook exercises to the students. In Lesson 97, for example, you explain the deductions exercise. Students do the remaining exercises on their own.

WORKSHEET 97

DEDUCTIONS

The children will need pencils.

EXERCISE 7

Picture deductions

a. (Pass out Worksheet 97 to each child.)

b. (Hold up side 2 of your worksheet and touch the sentence in the box in the deductions exercise.)

c. Everybody, touch this sentence on your worksheet. ✔

d. (Call on a child.) Read the sentence in the box. *All the big horses are tired.*

e. Everybody, say that rule. (Signal.) *All the big horses are tired.*

• (Repeat until firm.)

f. You know that some of the horses in the picture are tired. What kind of horses are those? (Signal.) *All the big horses.*

• Everybody, touch a horse you know is tired. ✔

g. You don't know about the horses that are not big. Everybody, touch a horse you don't know about. ✔

h. (Call on a child.) Read the instructions below the box. *Circle every horse that is tired.*

i. Everybody, what are you going to do? (Signal.) *Circle every horse that is tired.* Yes, circle every horse that you know is tired.

j. Do it. ✔

INDEPENDENT ACTIVITIES
EXERCISE 8

Summary of independent activities

Everybody, now you'll do your worksheet. Remember to do all parts of the worksheet and to read all the parts carefully.

Reading Presentation Book, Lesson 97

Name_____   Worksheet **97**   Side **1**

1. The tiger was _____ .
   lame   old   tame   time

2. Did he bite children? _____

3. What did he like to eat? _____
   ice   ice bits   ice cream   ice skates

4. Did the tiger have any cash? _____

5. What was in his pouch? _____
   stops   cones   stones   rocks

6. Did the man like the stones? _____

7. Who said, "What will you do with a big cone and some string"? _____

8. Who said, "Wait and see"? _____

9. The tiger made the cone into a h_____ .

The boy felt cold in the rain.

1. Make a box around the word that tells how the boy felt.

2. Make a box around the words that tell where the boy is.

3. Make a line over the words that tell who felt cold.

Worksheet **97**   Side **2**

One day, the boss left a note for Sid. Here is what that note said: "Tape my cane with a bit of white tape. The white tape is in the tape can."
Do you think Sid did what the note said? Yes, he did. After he looked at the note, he got the white tape and taped the cane.

1. Who left the note for Sid? _____

2. The note told Sid to _____ a cane.

3. Where was the white tape? _____
   in the tap can   in the tape can

4. Sid got the tape and taped the _____ .

All the big horses are tired.

Circle every horse that is tired.

Workbook, Lesson 97

After the class finishes the main reading lesson, you present activities from the *Spelling Presentation Book*. Depending on the amount of time available, spelling can be presented at the end of the reading lesson or at another time of day.

The spelling activities reinforce the decoding skills taught in the reading program. Students write answers for spelling activities on lined paper, so no additional student materials are required. Students spell by sounds until Spelling Lesson 90. Thereafter, they spell by letter names. Sample activities for Spelling Lesson 97 appear below.

EXERCISE 1
WORD COMPLETION

a. (Write on the board:)

> 1. _ap
> 2. h_t
> 3. sh_t

b. Copy the board. ✔
c. Word 1 is supposed to be **cap.** What word? (Signal.) *Cap.*
• A letter is missing for **cap.** What letter? (Signal.) *C.*
• Write it in the blank. ✔
d. Word 2 is supposed to be **hut.** What word? (Signal.) *Hut.*
• A letter is missing for **hut.** What letter? (Signal.) *U.*
• Write it in the blank. ✔
e. Word 3 is supposed to be **shot.** What word? (Signal.) *Shot.*
• A letter is missing for **shot.** What letter? (Signal.) *O.*
• Write it in the blank. ✔
f. Get ready to spell the words you just wrote.
g. Look at word 1. What word? (Signal.) *Cap.*
• Spell **cap.** Get ready. (Signal.) *C-A-P.*
• Fix it if it's not spelled right.
h. (Repeat step *g* for **2. hut, 3. shot.**)

EXERCISE 2
SENTENCE COPYING

Children are responsible for copying capital letters.

a. (Write on the board:)

> **What are we to do?**

• I'll read the sentence on the board: **What are we to do?**
b. Spell **What.** Get ready. (Signal.) *W-H-A-T.*
• Spell **are.** Get ready. (Signal.) *A-R-E.*
• Spell **we.** Get ready. (Signal.) *W-E.*
• Spell **to.** Get ready. (Signal.) *T-O.*
• Spell **do.** Get ready. (Signal.) *D-O.*
c. Copy this sentence on lined paper.
d. (Pause, then check and correct.)
• Read the sentence you just copied. Get ready. (Signal.) *What are we to do?*

EXERCISE 3
SPELLING REVIEW

a. Get ready to spell and write some words.
b. Word 1 is **stop.** What word? (Signal.) *Stop.*
• Spell **stop.** Get ready. (Signal.) *S-T-O-P.*
• Write it. ✔
c. Word 2 is **swim.** What word? (Signal.) *Swim.*
• Spell **swim.** Get ready. (Signal.) *S-W-I-M.*
• Write it. ✔
d. (Repeat step *c* for **3. ran, 4. wish.**)
e. I'll spell each word.
• Put an **X** next to any word you missed and write that word correctly.
• (Spell each word twice. Write the words on the board as you spell them.)

Spelling Presentation Book, Lesson 97

Reading Mastery Fast Cycle

Reading Mastery Fast Cycle (available in *Reading Mastery Classic Edition*) is an accelerated beginning-reading program for students of average or above-average ability. Fast Cycle is a one-year program that covers the same material presented in Grades K and 1, but with less repetition. Fast Cycle is also appropriate for students who enter first grade without going through the Grade K program. After completing Fast Cycle, students should be placed in Grade 2.

Fast Cycle presents exercises from Grades K and 1 on an accelerated schedule. For example, in Grade K, a new letter is generally introduced in every fourth lesson. In Fast Cycle, a new letter is generally introduced in every second lesson.

The table on the next page shows an alternative to the *Classic Edition* Fast Cycle program. The table shows *Signature Edition* lessons that may be skipped to achieve an accelerated schedule that closely parallels the Fast Cycle schedule. This schedule is effective for average or above-average learners.

The Placement Test for Grade K can be used to determine if students should be placed in Fast Cycle. The test appears on pages 86 and 87 of this guide.

Materials

The following teacher and student materials are available for Fast Cycle:

Teacher Materials

- *Reading Presentation Books* (4)
- *Spelling Presentation Book*
- *Teacher's Guide*
- *Teacher's Take-Home Book and Answer Key*
- *Skills Profile Folder*
- *Cassette* demonstrating how to pronounce the sounds and how to present tasks from the program
- *Benchmark Testing and Management Handbook* (optional)
- *Assessment Manual* (optional)

Student Materials

- *Storybooks* (2)
- *Take-Home Books* (4)
- *Benchmark Test Books* (optional)

Accelerated Instruction Schedule

Grade K Schedule

Teach Lesson	Skip Lessons	Teach Lesson	Skip Lessons	Teach Lesson	Skip Lessons	Teach Lesson	Skip Lessons
	1–11		49		83		119
12		50–51		84		120	
	13		52–53		85		121
14		54		86		122	
	15		55		87–89		123–124
16		56		90–91		125–126	
	17–18		57		92		127
19		58		93–94		128	
	20–21		59		95		129
22–23		60–62		96		130	
	24		63		97		131
25–27		64		98		132	
	28		65		99		133–134
29		66–67		100		135	
	30		68		101		136
31		69		102		137–138	
	32		70		103		139
33		71		104–106		140	
	34		72		107		141
35–36		73		108		142	
	37		74		109		143–144
38–39		75–76		110		145–147	
	40		77		111		148–149
41–42		78		112		150	
	43		79		113–114		151
44–45		80		115–116		152	
	46–47		81		117		153–154
48		82		118		155–158	159–160

Grade 1 Schedule

Teach Lesson	Skip Lessons	Teach Lesson	Skip Lessons	Teach Lesson	Skip Lessons	Teach Lesson	Skip Lessons
	1–10		39		59–75		127–132
11–12		40–46		76–94		133–137	
	13–22		47		95–96		138–145
23		48–49		97		146–160	
	24–32		50		98–102		
33–38		51–58		103–126			

Transition

The Transition program can be used between Grade 1 and Grade 2. Transition is primarily intended for low-performing students who have trouble moving between Grade 1—which emphasizes learning to read—and Grade 2, which emphasizes reading to learn. Transition offers these students 35 lessons of additional practice with decoding and comprehension. Transition can also be used as supplementary material for all students at the beginning of Grade 2. The program is especially useful for students who haven't read much during summer vacation.

Materials

Transition includes the following teacher and student materials:

- *Teacher Presentation Book* (includes teacher's guide, lesson presentation scripts, and answer key)
- Student *Textbook*
- Student *Workbook*

The Textbook contains high-interest stories written especially for the program. The stories cumulatively review all the sounds and words taught in Transition.

Sample Activities

(To view a complete sample lesson from Transition, turn to page 119.)

Each lesson in Transition begins with word-practice exercises, and many lessons include sound-combination exercises as well. You direct students to read lists of words or sound combinations that appear in their Textbook.

A sound-combination exercise from Lesson 5 appears in the next column. The exercise teaches or reviews seven sound combinations: **aw, gh, ge, ce, ch, qu,** and **ou.** More than 20 sound combinations are taught or reviewed in Transition.

EXERCISE 1

Sounds

a. Open your textbook to lesson 5. Find the celery. ✔
- (Teacher reference:)

aw	gh	ge	ce	ch	qu	ou

- You'll spell each combination, then tell me the sound it makes.
b. Spell the first combination. Get ready. (Tap 2 times.) *A-W.* The sound for that combination is **awe.**
- What's the sound? (Signal.) *awe.*
c. Spell the next combination. Get ready. (Tap 2 times.) *G-H.* That combination has no sound at all.
- What's the sound? (Signal.) *(No response.)* **G-H** doesn't make a sound.
d. Spell the next combination. Get ready. (Tap 2 times.) *G-E.* The sound for that combination is **j.**
- What's the sound? (Signal.) *j.*
e. Spell the next combination. Get ready. (Tap 2 times.) *C-E.* The sound for that combination is **sss.**
- What's the sound? (Signal.) *sss.*
f. Spell the next combination. Get ready. (Tap 2 times.) *C-H.*
- What's the sound? (Signal.) *ch.*
g. Spell the next combination. Get ready. (Tap 2 times.) *Q-U.* The sound for that combination is **koo.**
- What's the sound? (Signal.) *koo.*
h. Spell the last combination. Get ready. (Tap 2 times.) *O-U.*
- What's the sound? (Signal.) *ow.*

Teacher Presentation Book, Lesson 5

For the word-practice exercises, students read several types of word lists, including lists of familiar words, lists of words with underlined parts, lists of rhyming words, and lists of words that you or the students spell before reading. Students usually read each list twice. For the first reading, they address the common features of words in the list, such as underlined parts, rhymes, or spelling. For the second group reading, students read all the words in the list "the fast way."

In the lists of words with underlines, the underlined parts can be sound combinations (such as **point** or **slic̲e̲s̲**), syllables (such as **pouncing**), or familiar words embedded in longer words (such as **any̲where**). Exercises 1, 3, and 6 in the sample Transition lesson on pages 120–122 illustrate lists of words with underlined parts.

Exercise 5 of the sample Transition lesson presents rhyming pairs. The pairing suggests that if word parts are spelled the same, the sounds for those parts are probably—but not always—the same.

After the word-practice activities, students read their Textbook story aloud. They read the story twice. For the first reading, the emphasis is on decoding. The group has to read the entire story while staying within a decoding error limit. If the group exceeds the limit, they either reread the sentences that had mistakes or reread the entire story.

In the first-reading exercise for the sample Transition lesson ("Rolla Slows Down"), the error limit is six. After the group reads the title, you call on individual students to read one or two sentences each. Meanwhile, the other students follow along and help you track decoding errors.

For the second reading of the story (Exercise 8), the emphasis is on comprehension. Once again, students take turns reading the story aloud, but you ask comprehension questions after every few sentences. The comprehension questions are embedded in your Presentation Book copy of the story, and the students' responses are specified.

After students finish the second reading of the Textbook story, they complete Textbook and Workbook activities. Some of these activities relate to the story they have just read. Students write answers to questions about the story or finish sentences that correspond to story events. In other activities, students match words with definitions or descriptions; pictures with sentences or descriptions; or story characters with quotes. Students also follow rules for circling and crossing out displayed words or pictures, drawing missing pictures, and writing missing words. For their lined-paper activities, students read short passages from their Textbook independently and write answers to questions about those passages.

You generally introduce a particular type of Workbook activity when it first appears. Thereafter, students complete the activity independently.

Grade 2 Reading Strand

The Reading strand for *Reading Mastery Signature Edition,* Grade 2, contains 145 daily lessons that emphasize reasoning and study skills. Students in Grade 2 learn how to apply rules in various contexts and how to interpret maps, graphs, and time lines. The program also introduces many complex sentence forms and a range of vocabulary activities. The daily reading selections include realistic fiction, fantasy, and factual articles.

Materials

The following teacher and student materials are available for Grade 2:

Teacher Materials

- *Reading Presentation Books* (3)
- *Spelling Presentation Book*
- *Teacher's Guide*
- *Answer Key*
- *Curriculum-Based Assessment and Fluency Teacher Handbook*
- *Activities across the Curriculum*

Student Materials

- *Textbooks* (3)
- *Workbooks* (3)
- *Curriculum-Based Assessment and Fluency Student Book*

Comprehensive Program Materials

- *Reading Mastery Signature Edition,* Grade 2 Language Arts Strand
- *Reading Mastery Signature Edition,* Grade 2 Literature Strand

The Textbooks for Grade 2 contain stories and comprehension passages written especially for the program. Most of the stories are serialized over a span of lessons, and many stories incorporate science facts and rules. A partial listing of the Textbook contents appears below.

- **A Tricky Toad Named Goad**—A toad has amusing adventures in which she tricks people.
- **Nancy Learns About Being Small**—A girl becomes very small and learns important facts about common objects.
- **Herman Travels the World**—A fly goes around the world on a jet. Students use maps to follow the jet's progress.
- **Linda and Kathy Alone on an Island**—Two shipwrecked girls struggle to survive on an island.
- **Bertha and Her Nose**—A girl with a great sense of smell helps an investigator capture a group of polluters.
- **Andrew Dexter's Dreams**—A bank teller gets superhuman powers and is hired by a football team.
- **The Time Machine**—Two boys find a time machine and go back and forth in time.
- **Comprehension Passages**—Short passages that provide background information for the stories.

Sample Activities

(To view a complete sample lesson from Grade 2, turn to page 130.)

Students begin most lessons in Grade 2 by working on model sentences that contain selected vocabulary words. Then students read different types of word lists. The following activities from lessons 52 and 16 are typical.

Exercise 1 in Lesson 52 introduces a new model vocabulary sentence. Students first read the sentence on a page in the back of their Textbooks. Then they learn what the sentence means, practice saying the sentence, and respond to exercises about the meanings of specific words in the sentence.

VOCABULARY SENTENCES
LESSONS 51–100

13. The smoke swirled in enormous billows.
14. The occasional foul smell was normal.
15. They constructed an enormous machine.
16. She survived until she was rescued.
17. The soldiers protected their equipment.
18. Lawyers with talent normally succeed.
19. A dozen typists approached the stairs.
20. The job required a consultant.
21. The adults huddled around the fire.
22. The customer bought a valuable gift.
23. They had reasons for interrupting her talk.
24. He frequently argued about the championship.

Textbook, page 397

EXERCISE 1

Vocabulary

a. **Find page 397 in your textbook.** ✔
- Touch sentence 13. ✔
- This is a new vocabulary sentence. It says: The smoke swirled in enormous billows. Everybody, read that sentence. Get ready. (Signal.) *The smoke swirled in enormous billows.*
- Close your eyes and say the sentence. Get ready. (Signal.) *The smoke swirled in enormous billows.*

- Again. Say the sentence. Get ready. (Signal.) *The smoke swirled in enormous billows.*
- (Repeat until firm.)

b. When smoke **swirls,** it spins around as it drifts. If you mix chocolate syrup in milk, you'll see swirls of brown and white. What's a word that means **spun around?** (Signal.) *Swirled.*

c. Things that are **enormous** are very, very large. What's another way of saying **The building was very, very large?** (Signal.) *The building was enormous.*

d. **Billows** are large clouds or waves that are swelling up.

e. Listen to the sentence again: The smoke swirled in enormous billows.
- Everybody, say that sentence. Get ready. (Signal.) *The smoke swirled in enormous billows.*
- (Repeat until firm.)

f. What word means that the smoke spun around and around? (Signal.) *Swirled.*
- What word means **very, very large?** (Signal.) *Enormous.*
- What word tells you that the clouds were swelling up? (Signal.) *Billows.*
- (Repeat step f until firm.)

Reading Presentation Book, Lesson 52

After students finish working on the vocabulary sentence, they read aloud the word lists that appear at the beginning of their Textbook lesson (part A).

There are three types of word lists in Grade 2. The first type consists of words that are difficult to decode, such as those in column 1 on the next page. In Exercise 2, you read these words aloud. Then students read the words aloud and spell them.

The second type of list consists of words that have a common sound, a common ending, or another common feature. In Lesson 52, column 2 contains words with endings, and column 3 lists compound words. For column 2, you explain the common feature; then students read the words. For column 3, students first read the underlined part, then the whole word. For each unfamiliar word (such as *frisky*), you explain the meaning. Sample teacher presentations for these lists appear in the next column.

The third type of list consists of words that are easy to decode or that students have already learned. You simply direct students to read these lists.

After students finish reading all the columns, individual students take turns reading one to three words each.

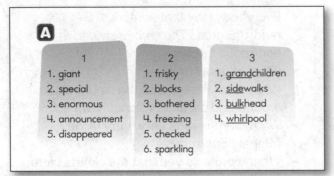

Textbook, Lesson 52

EXERCISE 2

Reading Words

Column 1

a. Find lesson 52 in your textbook. ✔
- Touch column 1. ✔

- (Teacher reference:)

1. giant	4. announcement
2. special	5. disappeared
3. enormous	

b. Word 1 is **giant.** What word? (Signal.) *Giant.*
- Spell **giant.** Get ready. (Tap for each letter.) *G-I-A-N-T.*
c. Word 2 is **special.** What word? (Signal.) *Special.*
- Spell **special.** Get ready. (Tap for each letter.) *S-P-E-C-I-A-L.*

Column 2

i. Find column 2. ✔
- (Teacher reference:)

1. frisky	4. freezing
2. blocks	5. checked
3. bothered	6. sparkling

- All these words have endings.
j. Word 1. What word? (Signal.) *Frisky.*
- **Frisky** means **playful** or **full of energy.** What's another way of saying **The cats were playful?** (Signal.) *The cats were frisky.*
k. Word 2. What word? (Signal.) *Blocks.*
- (Repeat for words 3–6.)
l. Let's read those words again.
- Word 1. What word? (Signal.) *Frisky.*
- (Repeat for words 2–6.)
m. (Repeat step l until firm.)

Column 3

n. Find column 3. ✔
- (Teacher reference:)

1. <u>grand</u>children	3. <u>bulk</u>head
2. <u>side</u>walks	4. <u>whirl</u>pool

- All these words are compound words. The first part of each word is underlined.
o. Word 1. What's the underlined part? (Signal.) *grand.*
- What's the whole word? (Signal.) *Grandchildren.*
p. Word 2. What's the underlined part? (Signal.) *side.*
- What's the whole word? (Signal.) *Sidewalks.*
q. Word 3. What's the underlined part? (Signal.) *bulk.*
- What's the whole word? (Signal.) *Bulkhead.*
r. Word 4. What's the underlined part? (Signal.) *whirl.*
- What's the whole word? (Signal.) *Whirlpool.*
s. Let's read those words again.
- Word 1. What word? (Signal.) *Grandchildren.*
- (Repeat for words 2–4.)
t. (Repeat step s until firm.)

Reading Presentation Book, Lesson 52

The final vocabulary exercise in Lesson 52 reviews the model sentence that was introduced at the beginning of the lesson. Students say the sentence and answer questions about word meanings.

EXERCISE 3

Vocabulary Review

a. Here's the new vocabulary sentence: The smoke swirled in enormous billows.
- Everybody, say that sentence. Get ready. (Signal.) *The smoke swirled in enormous billows*.
- (Repeat until firm.)
- What word means **very, very large?** (Signal.) *Enormous*.

b. What word tells you that the clouds were swelling up? (Signal.) *Billows*.
- What word means that the smoke spun around and around? (Signal.) *Swirled*.

Reading Presentation Book, Lesson 52

After students complete the vocabulary and word-reading exercises, they usually read their Textbook stories aloud. Many stories are preceded by comprehension passages that present background information about the stories. Students make use of this information as they read the stories.

The following group-reading activities from Lesson 16 are typical.

Students begin by reading the comprehension passage aloud. Individual students take turns reading two or three sentences each. As students read the passage, you present comprehension questions from the Presentation Book that teach various comprehension, reference, and study skills.

B More Facts About Toads and Frogs

Toads and frogs are members of the same family. But toads are different from frogs. Here are some facts about how toads and frogs are different:
- Toads have skin that is rough and covered with warts.
- No toads have teeth, but some frogs have teeth.
- The back legs of toads are not as big or strong as the back legs of frogs.

Textbook, Lesson 16

EXERCISE 3

Story Background

a. Find part B in your textbook. ✔
- The information passage gives some facts about toads and frogs.
b. Everybody, touch the title. ✔
- (Call on a student to read the title.) *[More Facts About Toads and Frogs.]*
- Everybody, what's the title? (Signal.) *More Facts About Toads and Frogs*. **ND**
c. (Call on individual students to read the passage, each student reading two or three sentences at a time.)

More Facts About Toads and Frogs

Toads and frogs are members of the same family. But toads are different from frogs. Here are some facts about how toads and frogs are different:

Toads have skin that is rough and covered with warts.

- Everybody, what is a toad's skin covered with? (Signal.) *Warts*. **ND**
- Warts are like rough bumps. Everybody, do **frogs** have skin that is rough and covered with warts? (Signal.) *No*. **C/C**

No toads have teeth, but some frogs have teeth.

- Everybody, listen to that fact again: No toads have teeth, but some frogs have teeth.
- Say that fact. Get ready. (Signal.) *No toads have teeth, but some frogs have teeth*.
- (Repeat until firm.) **RF/R**
- Do any toads have teeth? (Signal.) *No*. **RF/R**
- Do any frogs have teeth? (Signal.) *Yes*. **RF/R**

The back legs of toads are not as big or strong as the back legs of frogs.

- Everybody, whose back legs are stronger, toads' or frogs'? (Signal.) *Frogs'*. **DC**
- So which animal could jump farther, a toad or a frog? (Signal.) *A frog*. **DI**

Reading Presentation Book, Lesson 16

After students finish the comprehension passage, they read the main story aloud within the decoding error limit that is specified in your Presentation Book. As students read, you present comprehension questions from the Presentation Book, which contains a reproduction of the story. These questions emphasize interpretive comprehension skills, reasoning skills, and study skills. In Lesson 16, students compare and contrast, recall facts and rules, draw conclusions, and make predictions.

C Goad Uses Her First Trick

Goad lived near Four Mile Lake. Down the road from the lake was a town. The name of that town was Toadsville. It was named Toadsville because so many people who visited the town had come to hunt for a big, smart, fast toad. And in the evening you could find hundreds of people sitting around Toadsville talking about Goad. First they would talk about some of the traps that had been made to catch Goad. Then they would tell how Goad escaped. One of their favorite stories is the one of the great big net.

Five hunters from Alaska had come to Four Mile Lake with a net that was nearly a mile wide. They waited until Goad was on a hill where there were no trees, just some white rocks. Then they flew over the hill in a plane and dropped the great big net over the hill. ✶ Goad was under the net. The five hunters rushed to the place where Goad had last been seen. But there was no Goad. There was some grass and five large white rocks. The hunters removed the net and began to go over every centimeter of the ground.

Textbook, Lesson 16

EXERCISE 4
Story Reading

a. Find part C in your textbook. ✔
- We're going to read this story two times. First you'll read it out loud and make no more than 6 errors. Then I'll read it and ask questions.
b. Everybody, touch the title. ✔
- (Call on a student to read the title.) *[Goad Uses Her First Trick.]*
- Everybody, what's Goad going to do in this story? (Signal.) *Her first trick.* ⓟ
c. (Call on individual students to read the story, each student reading two or three sentences at a time.)

- (**Correct errors:** Tell the word. Direct the student to reread the sentence.)
- (If the group makes more than 6 errors, direct the students to reread the story.)

d. (After the group has read the selection making no more than 6 errors:)
Now I'll read the story and ask questions.

Goad Uses Her First Trick

Goad lived near Four Mile Lake. Down the road from the lake was a town. The name of that town was Toadsville. It was named Toadsville because so many people who visited the town had come to hunt for a big, smart, fast toad.

- Everybody, who is that big, smart, fast toad? (Signal.) *Goad.* ⓐᴘᴋ

And in the evening you could find hundreds of people sitting around Toadsville talking about Goad. First they would talk about some of the traps that had been made to catch Goad. Then they would tell how Goad escaped. One of their favorite stories is the one of the great big net.

- How could you use a great big net to catch a toad? (Call on a student. Idea: *Drop it on top of the toad*.) ⓓɪ

Reading Presentation Book, Lesson 16

After students finish reading the main story, they work independently in the Workbook and Textbook. The independent work for Lesson 16 (shown below) includes items about the comprehension passage and the main story, skill items, and review items.

The comprehension-passage items and main-story items are based on the questions you presented during the group reading. Students recall narrative details, classify objects, and explain causes and effects. Story items in other lessons involve different skills, such as sequencing events, inferring details, and interpreting motives.

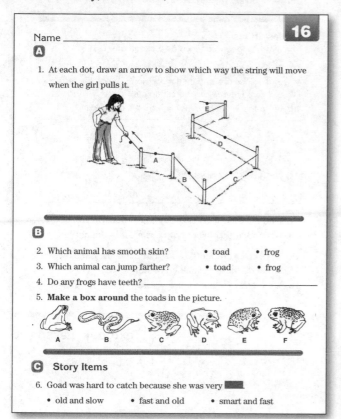

Name _____ **16**

A

1. At each dot, draw an arrow to show which way the string will move when the girl pulls it.

B

2. Which animal has smooth skin?   • toad   • frog
3. Which animal can jump farther?   • toad   • frog
4. Do any frogs have teeth? _____
5. **Make a box around** the toads in the picture.

A   B   C   D   E   F

C Story Items

6. Goad was hard to catch because she was very ▆▆▆.
   • old and slow   • fast and old   • smart and fast

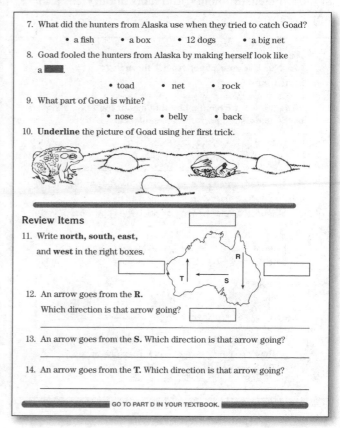

7. What did the hunters from Alaska use when they tried to catch Goad?
   • a fish   • a box   • 12 dogs   • a big net
8. Goad fooled the hunters from Alaska by making herself look like a ▆▆▆.
   • toad   • net   • rock
9. What part of Goad is white?
   • nose   • belly   • back
10. **Underline** the picture of Goad using her first trick.

Review Items

11. Write **north, south, east,** and **west** in the right boxes.

12. An arrow goes from the **R.** Which direction is that arrow going?

13. An arrow goes from the **S.** Which direction is that arrow going?

14. An arrow goes from the **T.** Which direction is that arrow going?

▬▬▬▬ GO TO PART D IN YOUR TEXTBOOK. ▬▬▬▬

Workbook, Lesson 16

The skill items teach vocabulary and reasoning skills, such as using vocabulary words and making comparisons. The review items review previously taught facts and skills.

In Lesson 16, students review map-reading skills, standard measurements, and facts about fleas and apple trees.

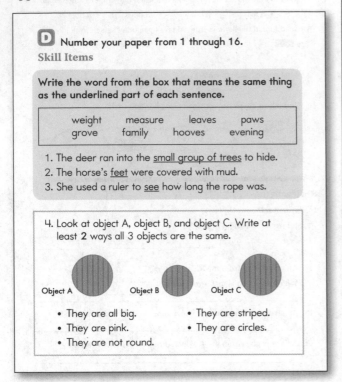

D Number your paper from 1 through 16.

Skill Items

Write the word from the box that means the same thing as the underlined part of each sentence.

weight	measure	leaves	paws
grove	family	hooves	evening

1. The deer ran into the <u>small group of trees</u> to hide.
2. The horse's <u>feet</u> were covered with mud.
3. She used a ruler to <u>see</u> how long the rope was.

4. Look at object A, object B, and object C. Write at least **2** ways all 3 objects are the same.

Object A   Object B   Object C

- They are all big.
- They are pink.
- They are not round.
- They are striped.
- They are circles.

The workers propped up the cage with steel bars.
5. What 2 words refer to supporting something?
6. What word names a strong metal?
7. What objects were made of a strong metal?
8. What object was propped up?

Review Items
9. Which is longer, an inch or a centimeter?

10. Some of the lines in the box are one inch long. Some of the lines are one centimeter long. Write the letter of every line that is one centimeter long.
11. Write the letter of every line that is one inch long.

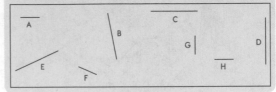

12. Where do the fleas in flea circuses usually come from?
13. What's the first thing that fleas must be taught?

14. What color are the flowers that apple trees make?
15. When do those flowers come out?
16. What grows in each place where there was a flower?

Textbook, Lesson 16

After the class finishes the main reading lesson, you present activities from the *Spelling Presentation Book*. Depending on the amount of time available, spelling can be presented at the end of the reading lesson or at another time of day.

The spelling activities reinforce the decoding skills taught in the reading program. Students write answers for spelling activities on lined paper, so no additional student materials are required. Sample activities for Spelling Lesson 16 appear below.

Patterns

> *Note:* Pronounce the *sound* **a** like the *letter* **A**.

a.   (Write on the board:)

ay

- If you hear the sound **A** at the end of a word, that part is probably spelled **A-Y**.
- Here are some words that have the combination **A-Y: say, may, play, stay, bay.**

b.   You're going to write words on lined paper. Number your paper from 1 through 5. ✔

c.   Word 1 is **play.** What word? (Signal.) *Play.*
- Write the word **play.** ✔

d.   Word 2 is **day.** What word? (Signal.) *Day.*
- Write the word **day.** ✔

e.   Word 3 is **say.** What word? (Signal.) *Say.*
- Write the word **say.** ✔

f.   Word 4 is **may.** What word? (Signal.) *May.*
- Write the word **may.** ✔

g.   Word 5 is **stay.** What word? (Signal.) *Stay.*
- Write the word **stay.** ✔

h.   Check your work. Make an **X** next to any word you got wrong.

i.   Word 1. Spell **play.** Get ready. (Tap for each letter.) *P-L-A-Y.*
- (Repeat for: **2. day, 3. say, 4. may, 5. stay.**)

Consonant Patterns

a.   Listen to these word endings: **-ack, -ick, -ock, -uck.**

b.   Say those endings with me. Get ready. (Signal.) *-ack, -ick, -ock, -uck.*

c.   By yourselves. Say those endings. Get ready. (Signal.) *-ack, -ick, -ock, -uck.*
- (Repeat steps b and c until firm.)

d.   Listen: **lock.** Is the ending **-ack, -ick, -ock,** or **-uck?** (Signal.) *Yes.*

e.   Listen: **stuck.** Is the ending **-ack, -ick, -ock,** or **-uck?** (Signal.) *Yes.*

f.   Listen: **lake.** Is the ending **-ack, -ick, -ock,** or **-uck?** (Signal.) *No.*

g.   Listen: **rock.** Is the ending **-ack, -ick, -ock,** or **-uck?** (Signal.) *Yes.*

h.   Listen: **look.** Is the ending **-ack, -ick, -ock,** or **-uck?** (Signal.) *No.*

i.   Listen: **trick.** Is the ending **-ack, -ick, -ock,** or **-uck?** (Signal.) *Yes.*

j.   Listen: **bike.** Is the ending **-ack, -ick, -ock,** or **-uck?** (Signal.) *No.*

Reading Vocabulary

a.   (Write on the board:)

remove

- The word **remove** is one of your vocabulary words.
- **Remove** means you **get rid of** something or take it away.

b.   Everybody, look at **remove** and spell it. Get ready. (Tap for each letter.) *R-E-M-O-V-E.*
- Spell it again. Get ready. (Tap for each letter.) *R-E-M-O-V-E.*

c.   (Erase the board.)
- Spell **remove** without looking. Get ready. (Signal.) *R-E-M-O-V-E.*
- Now write **remove** on your lined paper. ✔

d.   Check your work. Make an **X** if you spelled **remove** wrong. **Remove** is spelled (pause) R-E-M-O-V-E. ✔

e.   Turn your paper over and spell **remove** again. Get ready. (Signal.) *R-E-M-O-V-E.*
- **Remove** will be in your vocabulary exercises and on some of your spelling tests.

Grade 3 Reading Strand

The Reading strand for *Reading Mastery Signature Edition,* Grade 3, contains 140 daily lessons that emphasize problem-solving skills and reading in the content areas. Students in Grade 3 evaluate problems and solutions, learn facts about the world, and complete research projects. Many of the daily reading selections incorporate facts from science and social studies.

Materials

The following teacher and student materials are available for Grade 3:

Teacher Materials

- *Reading Presentation Books* (2)
- *Spelling Presentation Book*
- *Teacher's Guide*
- *Answer Key*
- *Curriculum-Based Assessment and Fluency Teacher Handbook*
- *Activities across the Curriculum*

Student Materials

- *Textbooks* (2)
- *Workbooks* (2)
- *Curriculum-Based Assessment and Fluency Student Book*

Comprehensive Program Materials

- *Reading Mastery Signature Edition,* Grade 3 Language Arts Strand
- *Reading Mastery Signature Edition,* Grade 3 Literature Strand

The Textbooks for Grade 3 contain stories, factual articles, and comprehension passages written especially for the program. All of the stories are serialized over a span of lessons, and most incorporate science facts and rules. A partial listing of the *Textbook* contents appears below.

- **Old Henry and Tim**—An imaginative story about two geese who help each other during their annual migration
- **Oomoo, Oolak, and a Polar Bear**—A realistic story about Alaskan Eskimos
- **Leonard the Inventor**—A realistic story about a boy who invents an energy-saving device
- **A Trip Through the Solar System**—A science-fiction story about a trip to Jupiter
- **Waldo the Animal Trainer**—A realistic story about a boy who trains animals
- **Susie and Denali**—A realistic adventure about a young girl and her sled dog
- **Go Anywhere–See Anything**—An imaginative story about two children who can go anywhere and see anything
- **Comprehension Passages**—Short passages that provide background information for the stories
- **Factual Articles**—Articles about people and the world

Sample Activities

(To view a complete sample lesson from Grade 3, turn to page 143.)

Students begin most lessons in Grade 3 by working on model sentences that contain selected vocabulary words. Then students read different types of word lists. The following activities from Lesson 43 are typical.

Exercise 1 introduces a new model vocabulary sentence. Students first read the sentence on a page in the back of their Textbooks. Then they learn what the sentence means, practice saying the sentence, and respond to exercises about the meanings of specific words. In Exercise 2 (not shown), students review a previous vocabulary sentence.

VOCABULARY SENTENCES

Lessons 1—70

1. The horses became restless on the dangerous route.
2. Scientists do not ignore ordinary things.
3. She actually repeated that careless mistake.
4. The smell attracted flies immediately.
5. The rim of the volcano exploded.
6. The new exhibit displayed mysterious fish.
7. She automatically arranged the flowers.
8. They were impressed by her large vocabulary.
9. He responded to her clever solution.
10. The patent attorney wrote an agreement.
11. The applause interrupted his speech.
12. She selected a comfortable seat.
13. Without gravity, they were weightless.
14. She demonstrated how animals use oxygen.
15. Lava erupted from the volcano's crater.
16. The incredible whales made them anxious.
17. The boring speaker disturbed the audience.

Textbook, page 352

Vocabulary

a. **Find the vocabulary sentences on page 352 in your textbook.** ✔
- Touch sentence 10. ✔
- This is a new vocabulary sentence. It says: The patent attorney wrote an agreement. Everybody, say that sentence. Get ready. (Signal.) *The patent attorney wrote an agreement.*
- Close your eyes and say the sentence. Get ready. (Signal.) *The patent attorney wrote an agreement.*
- (Repeat until firm.)

b. A **patent** is a license that says that only one person can make a particular product. New inventions are patented so that not everybody can make the product.

c. A patent **attorney** is a lawyer whose special job is getting patents for new inventions.

d. The sentence says the patent attorney wrote an **agreement.** An agreement is a paper that tells what two people promise to do. If people make an agreement, they shouldn't break the agreement. They should keep their promises.

e. Listen to the sentence again: The patent attorney wrote an agreement. Everybody say that sentence. Get ready. (Signal.) *The patent attorney wrote an agreement.*

f. Everybody, what word means **lawyer?** (Signal.) *Attorney.*
- What word names a license for somebody to be the only person who can make a product? (Signal.) *Patent.*
- What do we call a lawyer whose special job is getting patents for new inventions? (Signal.) *Patent attorney.*
- What word means **a promise made by people?** (Signal.) *Agreement.*
- (Repeat step f until firm.)

Reading Presentation Book, Lesson 43

After students finish working on the vocabulary sentences, they read aloud the word lists that appear at the beginning of their Textbook lesson, in part A. In Lesson 43, for example, students read three columns of words.

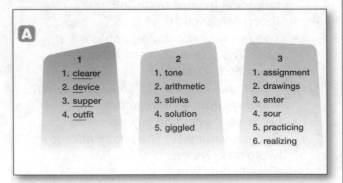

Textbook, Lesson 43

There are three types of word lists in Grade 3: lists of words that are difficult to decode, lists of words with common features (such as column 1 above), and lists of words that are easy to decode or that students have already learned (such as columns 2 and 3 above).

The teacher presentation material for columns 1 and 2 appears below. For both columns, you direct students as they read the words in unison. For each unfamiliar word (such as *tone*), you explain the meaning. When students finish reading all the columns, individual students take turns reading one to three words each.

EXERCISE 3

Reading Words

Column 1

a. Find lesson 43 in your textbook. ✔
• Touch column 1. ✔
• (Teacher reference:)

1. clearer	3. supper
2. device	4. outfit

• All these words have more than one syllable. The first part of each word is underlined.
b. Word 1. What's the underlined part? (Signal.) *clear*.
• What's the whole word? (Signal.) *Clearer*.
• Spell **clearer.** Get ready. (Tap for each letter.) *C-L-E-A-R-E-R*.
c. Word 2. What's the underlined part? (Signal.) *de*.
• What's the whole word? (Signal.) *Device*.
• Spell **device.** Get ready. (Tap for each letter.) *D-E-V-I-C-E*.

Column 2

h. Find column 2. ✔
• (Teacher reference:)

1. tone	4. solution
2. arithmetic	5. giggled
3. stinks	

i. Word 1. What word? (Signal.) *Tone*.
• Your tone of voice tells what you are feeling. I can say "What are you doing?" so it sounds like a question or so it sounds like I'm scolding you. Which tone of voice do you want to hear? (Call on a student. Student preference.)
• (Say "What are you doing?" using the selected tone of voice.)
j. Word 2. What word? (Signal.) *Arithmetic*.
• (Repeat for words 3–5.)
k. Let's read those words again.
• Word 1. What word? (Signal.) *Tone*.
• (Repeat for words 2–5.)
l. (Repeat step k until firm.)

Reading Presentation Book, Lesson 43

After students finish reading the word lists, they read the Textbook story. (In some lessons—but not Lesson 43—students read a comprehension passage before reading the story. The comprehension passage provides background information for the story.)

Students read the first part of each story aloud within the decoding error limit that is specified in your Presentation Book. As students read, you present comprehension questions from the Presentation Book, which contains a reproduction of the story. After students complete their oral reading, they read the rest of the story silently. You present another group of comprehension questions at the end of the silent reading.

The comprehension questions in Grade 3 emphasize reasoning skills and character analysis. In Lesson 43, for example, students evaluate problems and solutions, predict outcomes, interpret a character's feelings, and predict a character's actions.

B — A Good Idea

The next evening, after supper, it happened. Leonard had no warning that it would happen. But it did. Everything in his mind suddenly came together and he had the idea for a great invention.

Here's how it happened: After supper, he went to his room to get a pencil. He was going to make some more drawings of ideas for inventions. When he started back to the kitchen, Grandmother Esther hollered at him, "Turn off the light in your room. Remember to save energy."

Leonard turned around, went back to his room, turned off the light, and stood there in the dark room. He felt the idea coming into his head. It got bigger and clearer and . . . "Hot dog!" he shouted. He shouted, "What an idea for an invention! Hot dog!"

He ran into the kitchen. "I've got it. What an idea! This is the best idea anybody ever had for an invention!"

His mother smiled. "I'll bet it's a machine that makes up a list of things you need at the store."

"Stop talking about that stupid machine," Grandmother Esther yelled from the other room. She ran into the kitchen. She was wearing her exercise outfit.

Grandmother Esther asked, "What's your idea, Leonard?"

Textbook, Lesson 43

Story Reading

a. Find part B in your textbook. ✔
- The error limit for group reading is 11 errors. Read carefully.

b. Everybody, touch the title. ✔ (ND)
- (Call on a student to read the title.) *[A Good Idea.]*
- Everybody, what's the title? (Signal.) *A Good Idea.*
- (Call on individual students to read the story, each student reading two or three sentences at a time. Ask the specified questions as the students read.)

- (**Correct errors:** Tell the word. Direct the student to reread the sentence.)
- (If the group makes more than 11 errors, direct the students to reread the story.)

A Good Idea

The next evening, after supper, it happened. Leonard had no warning that it would happen. But it did. Everything in his mind suddenly came together and he had the idea for a great invention.

- What happened that evening? (Call on a student. Idea: *Leonard got an idea for a great invention*.) (ND)
- Everybody, did Leonard know that this would happen? (Signal.) *No.* (ND)

Here's how it happened: After supper, he went to his room to get a pencil. He was going to make some more drawings of ideas for inventions. When he started back to the kitchen, Grandmother Esther hollered at him, "Turn off the light in your room. Remember to save energy."

Leonard turned around, went back to his room, turned off the light, and stood there in the dark room. He felt the idea coming into his head. It got bigger and clearer and . . . "Hot dog!" he shouted.

Leonard said, "Let me explain how it's going to work. It's dark outside. And it's dark in the living room of your house. But when you walk through the door to the living room, the light goes on automatically. The light stays on as long as you're in the living room. But when you leave the living room, the light goes off."

Leonard's mother shook her head. "That sounds far too difficult."

Grandmother Esther said, "It sounds difficult to you because you don't know how the electric eye works."

"The electric eye?" Leonard's mother asked.

Leonard said, "Here's how it works, Mom. There's a little beam of light that goes across the doorway to the living room. When you enter the room, you break the beam. When you break that ☀ beam, the light turns on. Then when you leave the room, you break the beam and the light goes off."

"Oh, my," Leonard's mother said. He could tell from her tone of voice that she didn't understand what he said.

"Good thinking," Grandmother Esther said, and slapped Leonard on the back. "That's a fine idea for an invention, a fine idea."

"Thank you," Leonard said.

Grandmother Esther made a sour looking face. Slowly she said, "There's one big problem with being a good inventor. You have to think of all the things that could go wrong."

210   Lesson 43

"What could go wrong?" Leonard asked.

Grandmother Esther explained. "When you break the beam one time, the light goes on. When you break the beam the next time, the light goes off. When you break the beam the next time, the light goes on."

"Right," Leonard said.

"That's the problem," Grandmother Esther said. "What if two people walk into a dark room? When the first one goes into the room, the light will go on. Now the second person goes into the room. What happens to the light?"

"It goes off," Leonard said very sadly. He shook his head. "Now both people are in the dark, and my invention stinks."

"Wrong!" Grandmother Esther shouted. "Both people are in the dark, but your invention does not stink. Every invention has problems. An inventor has to look at these problems and try to solve them. But you must remember that inventing something is more than just getting an idea. You must work on that idea until it is a good idea. Then you must take that good idea and make it into a good invention. Just because there's a problem doesn't mean that you give up. You've got a great idea."

Leonard's mother said, "I have a great idea for an invention. It's a machine that . . ."

"Not now," Grandmother Esther said. "We're close to a _real_ invention."

Leonard said, "I'll just have to think about the problem and try to figure out how to solve it."

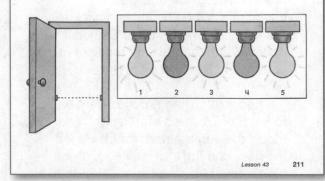

Lesson 43   211

Textbook, Lesson 43

He shouted, "What an idea for an invention! Hot dog!"

He ran into the kitchen. "I've got it. What an idea! This is the best idea anybody ever had for an invention!"

His mother smiled. "I'll bet it's a machine that makes up a list of things you need at the store."

"Stop talking about that stupid machine," Grandmother Esther yelled from the other room. She ran into the kitchen. She was wearing her exercise outfit.

- Look at the picture on the next page. ✔
- What is Grandmother Esther wearing? (Call on a student. Ideas: *Her exercise outfit; purple sweatsuit*.) ⓋⒶ

Grandmother Esther asked, "What's your idea, Leonard?"

Leonard said, "Let me explain how it's going to work. It's dark outside. And it's dark in the living room of your house. But when you walk through the door to the living room, the light goes on automatically. The light stays on as long as you're in the living room. But when you leave the living room, the light goes off."

- Leonard explained how the invention would work. Listen to that part again:

  Leonard said, "Let me explain how it's going to work. It's dark outside. And it's dark in the living room of your house. But when you walk through the door to the living room, the light goes on automatically. The light stays on as long as you're in the living room. But when you leave the living room, the light goes off."

- What happens when you walk **into** the room? (Call on a student. Idea: *The light goes on*.) ⓃⒹ

- What happens when you **leave** the room? (Call on a student. Idea: *The light goes off*.) (ND)
- What kind of thing could make the lights go on and off automatically? (Call on a student. Idea: *An electric eye*.) (APK)

Leonard's mother shook her head. "That sounds far too difficult."

Grandmother Esther said, "It sounds difficult to you because you don't know how the electric eye works."

- Everybody, did Grandmother Esther know how Leonard was thinking of making the lights go on and off? (Signal.) *Yes*. (DC)
- What was he going to use? (Signal.) *An electric eye*. (DI)

"The electric eye?" Leonard's mother asked.

Leonard said, "Here's how it works, Mom. There's a little beam of light that goes across the doorway to the living room. When you enter the room, you break the beam. When you break that ◄ beam, the light turns on. Then when you leave the room, you break the beam and the light goes off."

"Oh, my," Leonard's mother said. He could tell from her tone of voice that she didn't understand what he said.

"Good thinking," Grandmother Esther said, and slapped Leonard on the back. "That's a fine idea for an invention, a fine idea."

"Thank you," Leonard said.

- Everybody, do you think she feels that the electric eye invention is the right idea? (Signal.) *Yes*. (ND)

Grandmother Esther made a sour looking face. Slowly she said, "There's one big problem with being a good inventor. You have to think of all the things that could go wrong."

"What could go wrong?" Leonard asked.

Grandmother Esther explained. "When you break the beam one time, the light goes on. When you break

the beam the next time, the light goes off. When you break the beam the next time, the light goes on."

"Right," Leonard said.

"That's the problem," Grandmother Esther said. "What if two people walk into a dark room? When the first one goes into the room, the light will go on. Now the second person goes into the room. What happens to the light?"

"It goes off," Leonard said very sadly. He shook his head. "Now both people are in the dark, and my invention stinks."

- What happens when the first person enters the room? (Call on a student. Idea: *The light goes on*.) (ND)
- What happens when the second person enters the room? (Call on a student. Idea: *The light goes off*.) (ND)
- Everybody, is that the way Leonard wants it to work? (Signal.) *No*. (ND)
- Read the rest of the story to yourself and be ready to answer some questions. Remember, Leonard has just said that he thinks his invention stinks. Raise your hand when you're finished.

"Wrong!" Grandmother Esther shouted. "Both people are in the dark, but your invention does not stink. Every invention has problems. An inventor has to look at these problems and try to solve them. But you must remember that inventing something is more than just getting an idea. You must work on that idea until it is a good idea. Then you must take that good idea and make it into a good invention. Just because there's a problem doesn't mean that you give up. You've got a great idea."

Leonard's mother said, "I have a great idea for an invention. It's a machine that . . ."

"Not now," Grandmother Esther said. "We're close to a <u>real</u> invention."

Leonard said, "I'll just have to think about the problem and try to figure out how to solve it."

After students finish reading the story, they work independently in their Workbooks and Textbooks. The independent work for Lesson 43 includes story items, skill items, and review items. In other lessons, students play fact games or complete special projects.

The story items are based on the comprehension questions presented during the group reading. In Lesson 43, for example, students recall narrative details, evaluate problems and solutions, and use rules to predict outcomes. For the skill items, students use vocabulary words to write complete sentences. For the review items, students review facts about prehistoric eras, animal behavior, and geographic locations.

Ⓐ Story Items

1. Leonard got his idea for a great invention when Grandmother Esther told him to do something. What did she tell him to do?
_____

Leonard's original invention had problems.

2. What does the light in a dark room do when you walk into the room?
_____

3. What does the light do when you leave the room?
_____

4. Let's say two people walk into a dark room. What happens to the light in the room when the first person enters?
_____

5. What happens to the light when the second person enters?
_____

6. What will Leonard use to make the lights work automatically?
_____

7. Did Leonard's mother understand how his invention would work?
_____

8. Grandmother Esther told Leonard that every invention has
_____

9. So what does the inventor have to do?
   • quit   • solve the problems   • hide the problems

Here's the rule about an electric eye: **Each time the beam of light is broken, the light changes.** Shade the bulbs that are off for each problem. The first problem is already done for you.

10. The light is off. The beam is broken 4 times.

Is the light **on** or **off** at the end? _____

11. Here's another problem. The light is off. The beam is broken 8 times.

   a. Shade the bulbs that are off.

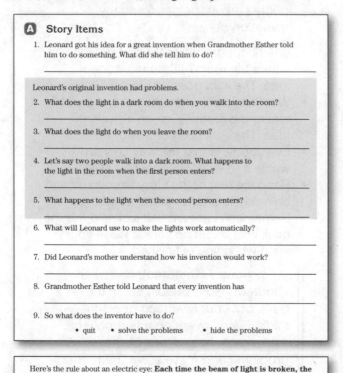

   b. Is the light **on** or **off** at the end? _____

12. Here's another problem. The light is off. The beam is broken 3 times.

   a. Shade the bulbs that are off.

   b. Is the light **on** or **off** at the end? _____

Workbook, Lesson 43

Ⓒ Number your paper from 1 through 24.
Skill Items

Use the words in the box to write complete sentences.

device	outfit	solution	entered
impressed	mentioned	responded	vocabulary

1. They were ▨▨ by her large ▨▨.
2. He ▨▨ to her clever ▨▨.

Review Items

Here's how an electric eye at a store works.
3. When somebody walks in the door, the body stops the beam of light from reaching the ▨▨.
4. When the body stops the beam, what does the device do next?
5. What does that tell the shopkeeper?

6. Write the letter of the layer that went into the pile first.
7. Write the letter of the layer that went into the pile next.
8. Write the letter of the layer that went into the pile last.
9. Write the letter of the layer that we live on.
10. What's the name of layer C?

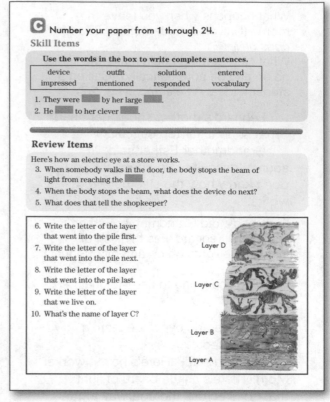

11. Name the country that is just north of the United States.
12. Which letter shows where the United States is?
13. Which letter shows where Canada is?

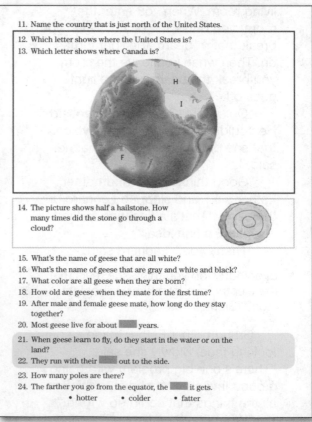

14. The picture shows half a hailstone. How many times did the stone go through a cloud?

15. What's the name of geese that are all white?
16. What's the name of geese that are gray and white and black?
17. What color are all geese when they are born?
18. How old are geese when they mate for the first time?
19. After male and female geese mate, how long do they stay together?
20. Most geese live for about ▨▨ years.
21. When geese learn to fly, do they start in the water or on the land?
22. They run with their ▨▨ out to the side.
23. How many poles are there?
24. The farther you go from the equator, the ▨▨ it gets.
   • hotter   • colder   • fatter

Textbook, Lesson 43

After the class finishes the main reading lesson, you present activities from the *Spelling Presentation Book*. Depending on the amount of time available, spelling can be presented at the end of the reading lesson or at another time of day.

The spelling activities reinforce the decoding skills taught in the reading program. Students write answers for spelling activities on lined paper, so no additional student materials are required. Sample activities for Spelling Lesson 43 appear below.

EXERCISE 1
Sentence Variations

a. Get ready to write on lined paper.
- You are going to write a sentence made up of words you know how to spell. Put the right end mark at the end of the sentence.
b. The sentence is: **The graceful sailboats are sleek and green.**
- Say that sentence. Get ready. (Signal.) *The graceful sailboats are sleek and green.*
- (Repeat until firm.)
c. Write it. ✔
d. Get ready to check your spelling. Put an **X** next to any word you missed.
e. Spell **The.** Get ready. (Signal.) *T-H-E.*
- Check it. ✔
f. Spell **graceful.** Get ready. (Signal.) *G-R-A-C-E-F-U-L.*
- Check it. ✔
- (Repeat for: **sailboats, are, sleek, and, green.**)
g. What end mark did you put at the end of the sentence? (Signal.) *A period.*
- Check it. ✔
h. Fix any words you missed.

EXERCISE 2
Prefix Introduction

a. (Write on the board:)

> 1. un + happy =
>
> 2. un + lucky =
>
> 3. un + kind =

- In these words, the prefix **un** means: **opposite.**
b. What does **un** mean? (Signal.) *Opposite.*
c. So what word means **the opposite of happy?** (Signal.) *Unhappy.*
d. What word means **the opposite of lucky?** (Signal.) *Unlucky.*
- What word means **the opposite of kind?** (Signal.) *Unkind.*
- Number your paper from 1 to 3. ✔
e. Add the prefix **un** to make new words. Write just the new words. ✔
f. Check your work. Make an **X** next to any word you got wrong.
g. Word 1. Spell **unhappy.** Get ready. (Tap for each letter.) *U-N-H-A-P-P-Y.*
- (Repeat for: **2. unlucky, 3. unkind.**)

EXERCISE 3
Vocabulary and Spelling Review

a. What word means **right now?** (Signal.) *Immediately.*
b. Spell **immediately.** Get ready. (Tap for each letter.) *I-M-M-E-D-I-A-T-E-L-Y.*
- Spell it again. Get ready. (Tap for each letter.) *I-M-M-E-D-I-A-T-E-L-Y.*
c. Now you're going to spell some other words.
d. Word 2 is **sweeter.** Spell **sweeter.** Get ready. (Tap for each letter.) *S-W-E-E-T-E-R.*
e. Word 3 is **unhappy.** Spell **unhappy.** Get ready. (Tap for each letter.) *U-N-H-A-P-P-Y.*
f. Word 4 is **choice.** Spell **choice.** Get ready. (Tap for each letter.) *C-H-O-I-C-E.*

Spelling Presentation Book, Lesson 43

Grade 4 Reading Strand

The Reading strand for *Reading Mastery Signature Edition,* Grade 4, contains 120 daily lessons that emphasize literary analysis and extended writing. Students in Grade 4 read classic and modern fiction, poetry, and prose, and they learn how to analyze characters, settings, plots, and themes. The daily writing assignments focus on literary interpretation and critical thinking. Other program activities include making outlines, inferring word meaning from context, and using reference materials.

Materials

The following teacher and student materials are available for Grade 4:

Teacher Materials

- *Reading Presentation Books* (2)
- *Spelling Presentation Book*
- *Teacher's Guide*
- *Answer Key*
- *Curriculum-Based Assessment and Fluency Teacher Handbook*
- *Activities across the Curriculum*

Student Materials

- *Textbooks* (2)
- *Workbook*
- *Curriculum-Based Assessment and Fluency Student Book*

Comprehensive Program Materials

- *Reading Mastery Signature Edition,* Grade 4 Language Arts Strand
- *Reading Mastery Signature Edition,* Grade 4 Literature Strand

The Textbooks for Grade 4 contain both classic and modern literature. Students read two abridged novels, as well as short stories, folktales, myths, factual articles, biographies, and poetry. A partial listing appears below.

- **Abridged Novels** by L. Frank Baum *(The Wonderful Wizard of Oz)* and Mark Twain *(The Prince and the Pauper)*
- **Short Stories** by well-known children's writers, including Jack London, Rudyard Kipling, and Hans Christian Andersen
- **Folktales and Myths,** including "Beauty and the Beast" and "The Golden Touch"
- **Factual Articles** about endangered species, Tudor England, the Yukon, animal migration, and other topics
- **Biographies** of Jackie Robinson, Jane Addams, and Mark Twain
- **Poetry** by Kathryn and Byron Jackson, Langston Hughes, and Harry Behn

Sample Activities

(To view a complete sample lesson from Grade 4, turn to page 155.)

Students begin every lesson in Grade 4 by reading in their Textbooks. The following activities from Lesson 76 are typical.

In part A, you direct students as they read different types of word lists aloud. The lists in Lesson 76 include words that are hard to decode, compound words, and word practice.

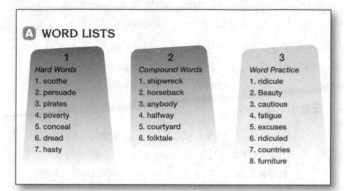

A WORD LISTS

1	2	3
Hard Words	*Compound Words*	*Word Practice*
1. soothe	1. shipwreck	1. ridicule
2. persuade	2. horseback	2. Beauty
3. pirates	3. anybody	3. cautious
4. poverty	4. halfway	4. fatigue
5. conceal	5. courtyard	5. excuses
6. dread	6. folktale	6. ridiculed
7. hasty		7. countries
		8. furniture

Textbook, Lesson 76

EXERCISE 1

Hard Words

1. Everybody, find column 1. ✔
   - The words in this column are hard words from your textbook stories.

1. soothe	5. conceal
2. persuade	6. dread
3. pirates	7. hasty
4. poverty	

2. Word 1 is **soothe.** Everybody, what word? (Signal.) *Soothe.*
   - (Repeat for every word in the column.)
3. Let's read these words again.
4. Word 1. Everybody, what word? (Signal.) *Soothe.*
   - (Repeat for every word in the column.)
5. (Repeat the column until firm.)

EXERCISE 2

Compound Words

1. Everybody, find column 2. ✔
   - All these compound words consist of two short words.

1. shipwreck	4. halfway
2. horseback	5. courtyard
3. anybody	6. folktale

2. Word 1. Everybody, what's the first short word? (Signal.) *Ship.*
   - Everybody, what's the compound word? (Signal.) *Shipwreck.*
   - (Repeat for every word in the column.)
3. (Repeat the column until firm.)

EXERCISE 3

Word Practice

1. Everybody, find column 3. ✔
   - We're going to practice these words.

1. ridicule	5. excuses
2. Beauty	6. ridiculed
3. cautious	7. countries
4. fatigue	8. furniture

2. Word 1. Everybody, what word? (Signal.) *Ridicule.*
   - (Repeat for every word in the column.)
3. (Repeat the column until firm.)

Reading Presentation Book, Lesson 76

In part B, students read sentences that contain boldface vocabulary words. Students use context clues to determine the meaning of these words.

B VOCABULARY FROM CONTEXT

1. There was nothing within a hundred miles of this lonely, **desolate** place.
2. She was good at talking people into doing things, but she could not **persuade** anybody to go to the beach with her.
3. The old house was frightening, and the sounds within it **terrified** me.
4. She seemed to be kind, but she was really very **selfish** and thought of nobody but herself.
5. He was so upset that nothing we could do would comfort or **soothe** him.
6. At first he was wealthy, but then he lost all his wealth and found himself in **poverty**.

Textbook, Lesson 76

Vocabulary From Context

1. Everybody, find part B. ✔
• These sentences use the words you just read.
2. We're going to use the rest of the sentence to figure out the meaning of the word in bold type.

Sentence 1

1. There was nothing within a hundred miles of this lonely, **desolate** place.

1. (Call on a student to read the sentence.)
• What could **desolate** mean? (Ideas: *Gloomy; barren; uninhabited.*)

Sentence 2

2. She was good at talking people into doing things, but she could not **persuade** anybody to go to the beach with her.

1. (Call on a student to read the sentence.)
• What could **persuade** mean? (Idea: *Convince.*)

Sentence 3

3. The old house was frightening, and the sounds within it **terrified** me.

1. (Call on a student to read the sentence.)
• What could **terrified** mean? (Idea: *Greatly frightened.*)

Sentence 4

4. She seemed to be kind, but she was really very **selfish** and thought of nobody but herself.

1. (Call on a student to read the sentence.)
• What could **selfish** mean? (Idea: *Concerned only with herself.*)

Sentence 5

5. He was so upset that nothing we could do would comfort or **soothe** him.

1. (Call on a student to read the sentence.)
• What could **soothe** mean? (Ideas: *Relax; make him feel better.*)

Reading Presentation Book, Lesson 76

In part C, students read a Story Background passage that conveys important information about the story for Lesson 76, "Beauty and the Beast." The passage explains that the story is a folktale and describes differences between folktales and myths. You ask questions from the Presentation Book as individual students take turns reading the passage aloud.

C STORY BACKGROUND

Folktales

The next story you will read is a folktale called "Beauty and the Beast." Like myths, folktales are old stories that people told aloud before someone wrote them down. But folktales are usually much newer than myths. The myths you have just read, for example, take place about three thousand years ago. In comparison, "Beauty and the Beast" takes place just a few hundred years ago.

Another difference is that myths usually include gods and goddesses, but folktales do not. Instead, folktales often have witches, wizards, or other kinds of magic.

"Beauty and the Beast" is one of the most famous folktales of all time. Many movies have been made of the story, and many writers have retold it in their own words. The story comes from France, a large country in Europe.

Textbook, Lesson 76

Story Background

1. Everybody, find part C. ✔
2. (Call on individual students to read two or three sentences each.)
3. (After students complete each section, ask the questions for that section.)

Folktales

The next story you will read is a folktale called "Beauty and the Beast." Like myths, folktales are old stories that people told aloud before someone wrote them down. But folktales are usually much newer than myths. The myths you have just read, for example, take place about three thousand years ago. In comparison, "Beauty and the Beast" takes place just a few hundred years ago.

Another difference is that myths usually include gods and goddesses, but folktales do not. Instead, folktales often have witches, wizards, or other kinds of magic.

- Who were the gods in the myths you have read? (Ideas: *Zeus, Hermes; the stranger in "The Golden Touch."*) APK
- Who can name some folktales that have witches or wizards? (Ideas: *Cinderella; Sleeping Beauty; Snow White; Hansel and Gretel.*) APK

"Beauty and the Beast" is one of the most famous folktales of all time. Many movies have been made of the story, and many writers have retold it in their own words. The story comes from France, a large country in Europe.

- How many of you have seen a movie of "Beauty and the Beast"? (Have students raise their hands.) APK
- The version you will read is different from the movie versions.

Reading Presentation Book, Lesson 76

In part D, students read the first chapter of "Beauty and the Beast." They read the first part of the chapter aloud, within a specified error limit. Individual students take turns reading a few sentences each. During this oral reading, you ask the comprehension questions specified in your Presentation Book. Then students read the rest of chapter silently. You ask more comprehension questions when everyone has finished reading.

D READING

Beauty and the Beast
Chapter 1

Once upon a time there lived a merchant who was enormously rich. The merchant had six sons and six daughters, and he would let them have anything they wanted.

But one day their house caught fire and burned to the ground, with all the splendid furniture, books, pictures, gold, silver, and precious goods it contained. Yet this was only the beginning of their misfortune. Shortly after the fire, the merchant lost every ship he had upon the sea, either because of pirates, shipwrecks, or fire. Then he heard that the people who worked for him in distant countries had stolen his money. At last, he fell into great poverty.

All the merchant had after those misfortunes was a little cottage in a desolate place a hundred miles from the town in which he used to live. He moved into the cottage with his children. They were in despair at the idea of leading such a different life. The cottage stood in the middle of a dark forest, and it seemed to be the most dismal place on earth.

The children had to cultivate the fields to earn their living. They were poorly clothed, and they missed the comforts and amusements of their earlier life. Only the youngest daughter tried to be brave and cheerful. She had also been sad at first, but she soon recovered her good nature. She set to work to make the best of things. But when she tried to persuade her sisters to join her in dancing and singing, they ridiculed her and said that this miserable life was all she was fit for. But she was far prettier and more clever than they were. She was so lovely that she was called Beauty.

After two years, their father received news that one of his ships, which he had believed to be lost, had come safely into port with a rich cargo. All the sons and daughters at once thought their poverty would be over, and they wanted to set out directly for the town. But their father was more cautious, so he decided to go by himself. Only Beauty had any doubt that they would soon be rich again. The other daughters gave their father requests for so many jewels and dresses that it would have taken a fortune to buy them. But Beauty did not ask for anything. Her father noticed her silence and said, "And what shall I bring for you, Beauty?"

"The only thing I wish for is to see you come home safely," she answered.

This reply angered her sisters, who thought she was accusing them of asking for costly things. But her father was pleased. Still, he told her to choose something.

"Well, dear Father," she said, "since you insist upon it, I want you to bring me a rose. I have not seen one since we came here, and I love them very much." ✦

So the merchant set out on horseback and reached the town as quickly as possible. But when he got there, he found out that his partners had taken the goods the ship had brought. So he found himself poorer than when he had left the cottage. He had only enough money to buy food on his journey home. To make matters worse, he left town during terrible weather. The storm was so bad that he was exhausted with cold and fatigue before he was halfway home. Night came on, and the deep snow and bitter frost made it impossible for the merchant's horse to carry him any further.

The merchant could see no houses or lights. The only shelter he could find was the hollow trunk of a great tree. He crouched there all night long. It was the longest night he had ever known. In spite of his weariness, the howling of the wolves kept him awake. And when the day broke, he was not much better off, for falling snow had covered up every path, and he did not know which way to turn.

At last, he made out some sort of path, and he started to follow it. It was rough and slippery, so he kept falling down. But the path soon became easier, and it led him to a row of trees that ended at a splendid castle. It seemed very strange to the merchant that no snow had fallen in the row of trees. Stranger still, the trees were fruit trees, and they were covered with apples and oranges. ★

The merchant walked down the row of trees and soon reached the castle. He called, but nobody answered. So he opened the door and called again. Then he climbed

Textbook, Lesson 76

Reading Aloud

1. Everybody, find part D. ✔
 • The error limit for this lesson is 10.
2. (Call on individual students to read two or three sentences each.)
3. (After students complete each section, ask the questions for that section.)

Beauty and the Beast
Chapter 1

Once upon a time there lived a merchant who was enormously rich. The merchant had six sons and six daughters, and he would let them have anything they wanted.

 • What do merchants do? (Idea: *Buy and sell things.*) **APK**
 • How many children did the merchant have in all? (Response: *Twelve.*) **DC**
 • How do you think those children might behave if they got everything they wanted? (Ideas: *They might be spoiled; they might be ungrateful.*) **H**

But one day their house caught fire and burned to the ground, with all the splendid furniture, books, pictures, gold, silver, and precious goods it contained. Yet this was only the beginning of their misfortune. Shortly after the fire, the merchant lost every ship he had upon the sea, either because of pirates, shipwrecks, or fire. Then he heard that the people who worked for him in distant countries had stolen his money. At last, he fell into great poverty.

 • Name some things that went wrong for the merchant. (Ideas: *His house burned down; he lost all his ships; the people who worked for him stole his money.*) **R**
 • How rich was the merchant after all this misfortune? (Ideas: *He wasn't rich; he was poor.*) **C/E**

Reading Presentation Book, Lesson 76

up a flight of steps and walked through several splendid rooms. The pleasant warmth of the air refreshed him, and he suddenly felt very hungry; but there seemed to be nobody in this huge palace who could give him anything to eat.

The merchant kept wandering through the deep silence of the splendid rooms. At last, he stopped in a room smaller than the rest, where a bright fire was burning next to a couch. The merchant thought this room must be prepared for someone, so he sat down to wait. But very soon he fell into a heavy sleep.

His extreme hunger wakened him after several hours. He was still alone, but a good dinner had been set on a little table. The merchant had eaten nothing for an entire day, so he lost no time in beginning his meal, which was delicious. He wondered who had brought the food, but no one appeared.

After dinner, the merchant went to sleep again. He woke completely refreshed the next morning. There was still no sign of anybody, although a fresh meal of cakes and fruit was sitting on the little table at his elbow. The silence began to terrify the merchant, and he decided to search once more through the rooms. But it was no use. There was no sign of life in the palace. Not even a mouse could be seen.

Textbook, Lesson 76

All the merchant had after those misfortunes was a little cottage in a desolate place a hundred miles from the town in which he used to live. He moved into the cottage with his children. They were in despair at the idea of leading such a different life. The cottage stood in the middle of a dark forest, and it seemed to be the most dismal place on earth.

The children had to cultivate the fields to earn their living. They were poorly clothed, and they missed the comforts and amusements of their earlier life. Only the youngest daughter tried to be brave and cheerful. She had also been sad at first, but she soon recovered her good nature. She set to work to make the best of things. But when she tried to persuade her sisters to join her in dancing and singing, they ridiculed her and said that this miserable life was all she was fit for. But she was far prettier and more clever than they were. She was so lovely that she was called Beauty.

- Why do you think working was especially hard for these children? (Idea: *Because they were used to having servants do all the work.*) (MJ)
- What's the title of this story? (Response: *Beauty and the Beast.*) (NE)
- Who do you think one of the main characters will be? (Response: *Beauty.*) (P)
- Who will the other main character be? (Response: *The Beast.*) (P)

After two years, their father received news that one of his ships, which he had believed to be lost, had come safely into port with a rich cargo. All the sons and daughters at once thought their poverty would be over, and they wanted to set out directly for the town. But their father was more cautious, so he decided to go by himself. Only Beauty had any doubt that they would soon be rich again. The other daughters gave their father requests for so many jewels and dresses that it would have taken a fortune to buy them. But Beauty did not ask for anything. Her father noticed her silence and said, "And what shall I bring for you, Beauty?"

Reading Presentation Book, Lesson 76

After students finish reading the story, they work independently in their Textbooks and Workbooks. In the Textbook exercises for Lesson 76, students write the main idea of a paragraph (part E), answer interpretive comprehension questions about the story (part F), and write a poem (part G).

Students write the answers to Workbook exercises in the Workbook itself. In Lesson 76, they answer literal comprehension questions about the story (part A), use vocabulary words in context (part B), sequence story events (part C), and review material from earlier lessons in the program (parts D and E).

E MAIN IDEA

For each paragraph, write a sentence that tells the complete main idea.

1. Saturday finally arrived. Janet took her camera out of her closet. Then she went outside to look for her friends. When she had found everybody, she told them to stand together on her porch. She looked through her camera and told everybody to stand closer together. Finally, she said, "Smile," and pressed the button on the camera. The camera went "click," and some of Janet's friends made faces.

2. William liked rowing boats. Last spring, William visited Swan Lake. He rented a rowboat for the whole day. He hopped into the boat and started to pull the oars. The boat started across the lake. William could see the boat rental place getting farther and farther away. William kept rowing. He looked at people fishing and at birds flying near the water. He had fun seeing how fast he could row. After a long time, he came to the opposite side of the lake.

F COMPREHENSION

Write the answers.
1. Why were most of the merchant's children greedy and spoiled?
2. Name at least three ways that Beauty was different from her sisters.
3. Why do you think Beauty asked her father for a rose?
4. Why did the merchant get lost on the way home?
5. Name at least three strange things about the palace.

G WRITING

What objects do you think are beautiful?
• Pick an object that you think is beautiful, such as a flower, a painting, or a river. Then write a poem about the object. Describe what the object looks like and tell why you think it's beautiful.

Textbook, Lesson 76

A STORY DETAILS

Write the answers.
1. At the beginning of the story, how rich was the merchant?

2. How many children did the merchant have?

3. What happened to his house?

4. What kind of house did the family move into?

5. Before her father left for town, what did Beauty ask him to bring back?

6. What kinds of things did the other children ask for?

7. Where did the merchant sleep during the storm?

8. What was strange about the row of trees the merchant found?

9. Why was the palace so silent?

B VOCABULARY

Write the correct words in the blanks.

shrewd	calculate
witty	century
appetite	secure
inhabitant	sympathy
discontented	defeat

1. Lillian was so _____ with her job that she quit.
2. The wise man made many _____ decisions.
3. A _____ is a long time.
4. The experts could not _____ the number of stars in the sky.
5. She was glad to see the food because she had an enormous _____
6. The cat was _____ from dogs as long as it stayed inside the house.
7. After the child fell, her mother held her and showed great _____

C SEQUENCING

Put the following events in the correct order by numbering them from 1 to 5.

____ The merchant found a palace.

____ The merchant spent the night in a tree.

____ The merchant moved to a cottage.

____ The merchant's house burned down.

____ The merchant went back to the town.

D RELATED FACTS

Write which Greek god each statement describes. Choose *Hermes*, *Poseidon*, or *Zeus*.

1. The god of the sky

2. The god of the ocean

3. The god of travelers

E STORY REVIEW

Write whether each statement describes *The Miraculous Pitcher* or *The Golden Touch*.

1. Zeus appeared in this story.

2. The main character was a king.

3. One of the characters had a magic staff.

4. One of the characters was changed into a statue.

5. The story showed how evil greed can be.

6. The story showed why you should be kind to strangers.

Workbook, Lesson 76

After the class finishes the main reading lesson, you present activities from the *Spelling Presentation Book*. Depending on the amount of time available, spelling can be presented at the end of the reading lesson or at another time of day.

The spelling activities reinforce the decoding skills taught in the reading program. Students write answers for spelling activities on lined paper, so no additional student materials are required. Sample activities for Spelling Lesson 76 appear below.

EXERCISE 1
Word Introduction

Note: Pronounce the sound /ē/ like the letter name **E**.

a. (Write on the board:)

> chief
> niece
> grief
> brief
> thief

b. Get ready to read these words.
- In each of these words, the sound /ē/ is spelled **i-e.**
- First word: **chief.** What word? (Signal.) *Chief.*
c. Next word: **niece.** What word? (Signal.) *Niece.*
- (Repeat for: **grief, brief, thief.**)
d. Now spell those words.
- Spell **chief.** Get ready. (Signal.) *C-H-I-E-F.*
e. Spell **niece.** Get ready. (Signal.) *N-I-E-C-E.*
- (Repeat for: **grief, brief, thief.**)
f. (Erase the board.)
- Spell the words without looking.
g. Spell **chief.** Get ready. (Signal.) *C-H-I-E-F.*
h. Spell **niece.** Get ready. (Signal.) *N-I-E-C-E.*
- (Repeat for: **grief, brief, thief.**)

EXERCISE 2
Word Building

a. (Write on the board:)

> **1. re + cover + ing =**
> **2. re + cite + al =**
> **3. slug + ish + ly =**
> **4. waste + ful + ness =**
> **5. dis + tract + ed =**
> **6. mis + quote + ing =**

b. You're going to write the words that go after the equal signs.
- Some of these words follow the final **e** rule. Be careful.
- Number your paper from 1 to 6. ✔
c. Word 1: Write **recovering** on your paper. ✔
d. Do the rest of the words on your own. ✔
e. Check your work. Make an **X** next to any word you got wrong.
f. Word 1. Spell **recovering.** Get ready. (Tap for each letter.) *R-E-C-O-V-E-R-I-N-G.*
- (Repeat for: **2. recital, 3. sluggishly, 4. wastefulness, 5. distracted, 6. misquoting.**)

EXERCISE 3
Prompted Review

a. (Write on the board:)

> **1. athlete**
> **2. danger**
> **3. studies**
> **4. tensely**
> **5. suddenly**
> **6. recovering**

b. Word 1 is **athlete.** Spell **athlete.** Get ready. (Signal.) *A-T-H-L-E-T-E.*
c. Word 2 is **danger.** Spell **danger.** Get ready. (Signal.) *D-A-N-G-E-R.*
d. (Repeat step c for: **3. studies, 4. tensely, 5. suddenly, 6. recovering.**)
e. (Erase the board.)
- Now spell those words without looking.
f. Word 1 is athlete. Spell **athlete.** Get ready. (Signal.) *A-T-H-L-E-T-E.*

Spelling Presentation Book, Lesson 76

Grade 5 Reading Strand

The Reading strand for *Reading Mastery Signature Edition,* Grade 5, contains 120 daily lessons that focus on literary language, reasoning strategies, and varied writing activities. The reading selections include classic and modern fiction, poetry, and prose. Students in Grade 5 interpret complex sentence forms, figurative language, and literary irony; they also identify contradictions and faulty logic. In addition, students write essays, dialogues, short stories, and poems.

Materials

The following teacher and student materials are available for Grade 5:

Teacher Materials

- *Reading Presentation Books* (2)
- *Spelling Presentation Book*
- *Teacher's Guide*
- *Answer Key*
- *Curriculum-Based Assessment and Fluency Teacher Handbook*
- *Activities across the Curriculum*

Student Materials

- *Textbooks* (2)
- *Workbook*
- *Curriculum-Based Assessment and Fluency Student Book*

Comprehensive Program Materials

- *Reading Mastery Signature Edition,* Grade 5 Language Arts Strand
- *Reading Mastery Signature Edition,* Grade 5 Literature Strand

The Textbooks contain both classic and modern literature. Students read abridged novels and novellas, as well as short stories, a folktale, a myth, factual articles, poetry, biographies, and a play. A partial listing appears below.

- **Abridged Novels and Novellas** by Mark Twain *(Tom Sawyer),* Homer *(The Odyssey),* Frances Hodgson Burnett *(Sara Crewe),* and Jack London (*The Cruise of the* Dazzler)
- **Short Stories** by well-known writers, including Robert McCloskey, O. Henry, Guy de Maupassant, and Sarah Orne Jewett
- **Folktales and Myths,** including "The Table, the Donkey, and the Stick" and "Persephone"
- **Factual Articles** about American history, the apprentice system, and San Francisco Bay
- **Biographies** of Harriet Tubman and Jack London
- **Poetry** by Walt Whitman, William Wordsworth, and Ernest Thayer

Sample Activities

(To view a complete sample lesson from Grade 5, turn to page 166.)

Students begin every lesson in Grade 5 by reading in their Textbooks. The following activities from Lesson 57 are typical.

In part A, you direct students as they read different types of word lists aloud. The lists in Lesson 57 include hard words, word practice, and new vocabulary.

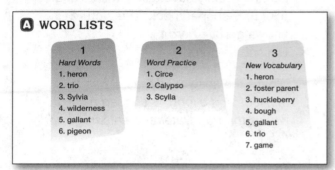

A WORD LISTS

1
Hard Words
1. heron
2. trio
3. Sylvia
4. wilderness
5. gallant
6. pigeon

2
Word Practice
1. Circe
2. Calypso
3. Scylla

3
New Vocabulary
1. heron
2. foster parent
3. huckleberry
4. bough
5. gallant
6. trio
7. game

Textbook, Lesson 57

EXERCISE 1

Hard Words

1. Look at column 1.
   - These are hard words from your textbook stories.

1. heron	**4. wilderness**
2. trio	**5. gallant**
3. Sylvia	**6. pigeon**

2. Word 1 is **heron.** Everybody, what word? (Signal.) *Heron.*
   - (Repeat this procedure for every word in the column.)
3. Let's read the words again.
4. Word 1. Everybody, what word? (Signal.) *Heron.*
   - (Repeat this procedure for every word in the column.)
5. (Repeat the column until firm.)

EXERCISE 2

Word Practice

1. Look at column 2.
   - We're going to practice these words.

1. Circe	**3. Scylla**
2. Calypso	

2. Word 1. Everybody, what word? (Signal.) *Circe.*
   - (Repeat this procedure for every word in the column.)
3. (Repeat the column until firm.)

EXERCISE 3

New Vocabulary

1. Look at column 3.
   - First we'll read the words in this column. Then we'll read their definitions.

1. heron	**5. gallant**
2. foster parent	**6. trio**
3. huckleberry	**7. game**
4. bough	

2. Word 1. Everybody, what word? (Signal.) *Heron.*
   - (Repeat this procedure for every word in the column.)
3. (Repeat the column until firm.)

Reading Presentation Book, Lesson 57

In part B, students read vocabulary definitions aloud and practice using the vocabulary words in context.

B VOCABULARY DEFINITIONS

1. **heron**—*Herons* are birds that wade through water and eat frogs and fish. Herons usually have tall, thin legs and a long, S-shaped neck. The picture shows a *white heron*.
   • Describe a heron.
2. **foster parent**—A *foster parent* is somebody who brings up a child but is not the child's real parent.
   • What do we call somebody who brings up a child but is not the child's real parent?
3. **huckleberry**—A *huckleberry* is a small purple or black berry that grows on bushes.
   • What is a huckleberry?
4. **bough**—A *bough* of a tree is a branch of the tree.
   • What is a branch of a tree?
5. **gallant**—Somebody who is *gallant* is brave and noble.
   • What's another way of saying *He was a noble warrior*?
6. **trio**—A *trio* is a group of three.
   • What's another way of saying *A group of three went to the river*?
7. **game**—Wild animals that are hunted are called *game*.
   • What do we call wild animals that are hunted?

Textbook, Lesson 57

Vocabulary Definitions

1. Everybody, find part B. ✔
   • These are definitions for the words you just read.
2. (For each word, call on a student to read the definition and the item. Then ask the student to complete the item.)

1. **heron**—*Herons* are birds that wade through water and eat frogs and fish. Herons usually have tall, thin legs and a long, S-shaped neck. The picture shows a *white heron*.
   • Describe a heron.

   • What's the answer? (Ideas: *It has tall, thin legs and a long, S-shaped neck; it wades through water and eats frogs and fish.*)

2. **foster parent**—A *foster parent* is somebody who brings up a child but is not the child's real parent.
   • What do we call somebody who brings up a child but is not the child's real parent?

   • What's the answer? (Response: *A foster parent.*)

3. **huckleberry**—A *huckleberry* is a small purple or black berry that grows on bushes.
   • What is a huckleberry?

   • What's the answer? (Idea: *A small purple or black berry that grows on bushes.*)

4. **bough**—A *bough* of a tree is a branch of the tree.
   • What is a branch of a tree?

   • What's the answer? (Response: *A bough.*)

5. **gallant**—Somebody who is *gallant* is brave and noble.
   • What's another way of saying *He was a noble warrior*?

   • What's the answer? (Response: *He was a gallant warrior.*)

Reading Presentation Book, Lesson 57

In part C, students read Part 1 of "A White Heron," a classic short story by Sarah Orne Jewett. The story includes a focus question that draws attention to a central theme. You can choose to have students read the first half of the story aloud or silently; the second part is always read silently. After students finish reading the story, you ask comprehension questions. You then have the option of asking pairs of students to reread the second half of the story to each other.

C READING

A White Heron
by Sarah Orne Jewett*
Part 1

Focus Question: How did Sylvia feel about living on her foster mother's farm?

The woods were filled with shadows one June evening, but a bright sunset still glimmered faintly among the trunks of the trees. A girl named Sylvia was driving a cow from the pasture to her home. Sylvia had spent more than an hour looking for the cow and had finally found her hiding behind a huckleberry bush.

Sylvia and the cow were going away from the sunset and into the dark woods. But they were familiar with the path, and the darkness did not bother them.

Sylvia wondered what her foster mother, Mrs. Tilley, would say because they were so late. But Mrs. Tilley knew how difficult it was to find the cow. She had chased the beast many times herself. As she waited, she was only thankful that Sylvia could help her. Sylvia seemed to love the out-of-doors, and Mrs. Tilley thought that being outdoors was a good change for an orphan girl who had grown up in a town.

The companions followed the shady road. The cow took slow steps, and the girl took very fast ones. The cow stopped at the brook to drink, and Sylvia stood still and waited. She let her bare feet cool themselves in the water while the great twilight moths struck softly against her. She waded on through the brook as the cow moved away, and she listened to the waterbirds with pleasure.

There was a stirring in the great boughs overhead. They were full of little birds that seemed to be wide awake and going about their business. Sylvia began to feel sleepy as she walked along. However, it was not much farther to the house, and the air was soft and sweet.

She was not often in the woods so late as this. The darkness made her feel as if she were a part of the gray shadows and the moving leaves. She was thinking how long it seemed since she had first come to her foster mother's farm a year ago. Sylvia wondered if everything was still going on in the noisy town just the same as when she had lived there. ◆

It seemed to Sylvia that she had never been alive at all before she came to live at her foster mother's farm. It was a beautiful place to live, and she never wished to go back to the town. The thought of the children who used to chase and frighten her made her hurry along the path to escape from the shadows of the trees.

* Adapted for young readers

Textbook, Lesson 57

EXERCISE 6
Focus Question

1. Everybody, find part C. ✔
2. What's the focus question for today's lesson? (Response: *How did Sylvia feel about living on her foster mother's farm?*)

EXERCISE 7
Reading Aloud (Optional)

1. We're going to read aloud to the diamond.
- (Call on individual students to read several sentences each.)

A White Heron
by Sarah Orne Jewett
Part 1
Focus Question: How did Sylvia feel about living on her foster mother's farm?

The woods were filled with shadows one June evening, but a bright sunset still glimmered faintly among the trunks of the trees. A girl named Sylvia was driving a cow from the pasture to her home. Sylvia had spent more than an hour looking for the cow and had finally found her hiding behind a huckleberry bush.

Sylvia and the cow were going away from the sunset and into the dark woods. But they were familiar with the path, and the darkness did not bother them.

Sylvia wondered what her foster mother, Mrs. Tilley, would say because they were so late. But Mrs. Tilley knew how difficult it was to find the cow. She had chased the beast many times herself. As she waited, she was only thankful that Sylvia could help her. Sylvia seemed to love the out-of-doors, and Mrs. Tilley thought that being outdoors was a good change for an orphan girl who had grown up in a town.

The companions followed the shady road. The cow took slow steps, and the girl took very fast ones. The cow stopped at the brook to drink, and Sylvia stood still and waited. She let her bare feet cool themselves in the water while the great twilight moths struck softly against her.

Suddenly, she was horror-struck to hear a clear whistle not very far away. It was not a bird's whistle. It sounded more like a boy's. Sylvia stepped aside into the bushes, but she was too late. The whistler had discovered her, and he called out in a cheerful voice, "Hello, little girl, how far is it to the road?"

Trembling, Sylvia answered quietly, "A long distance."

She did not dare to look at the tall young man, who carried a gun over his shoulder. But Sylvia came out of the bushes and again followed the cow, while the young man walked alongside her.

"I have been hunting for some birds," the stranger said kindly, "and I have lost my way. Don't be afraid," he added gallantly. "Speak up and tell me what your name is and whether you think I can spend the night at your house and go out hunting early in the morning." ★

Sylvia was more alarmed than before. Would her foster mother blame her for this? She hung her head, but she managed to answer "Sylvia" when her companion again asked her name.

Mrs. Tilley was standing in the doorway when the trio came into view. The cow gave a loud moo as if to explain the situation.

Mrs. Tilley said, "Yes, you'd better speak up for yourself, you naughty old cow! Where'd she hide herself this time, Sylvia?" But Sylvia kept silent.

The young man stood his gun beside the door and dropped a heavy gamebag next to it. Then he said good evening to Mrs. Tilley. He repeated his story and asked if he could have a night's lodging.

"Put me anywhere you like," he said. "I must be off early in the morning, before day, but I am very hungry indeed. Could you give me some milk?"

"Dear sakes, yes," said Mrs. Tilley. "You might do better if you went out to the main road, but you're welcome to what we've got. I'll milk the cow right now, and you make yourself at home. Now step round and set a plate for the gentleman, Sylvia!"

Sylvia promptly stepped. She was glad to have something to do, and she was hungry herself.

Textbook, Lesson 57

"Put me anywhere you like," he said. "I must be off early in the morning, before day, but I am very hungry indeed. Could you give me some milk?"

"Dear sakes, yes," said Mrs. Tilley. "You might do better if you went out to the main road, but you're welcome to what we've got. I'll milk the cow right now, and you make yourself at home. Now step round and set a plate for the gentleman, Sylvia!"

Sylvia promptly stepped. She was glad to have something to do, and she was hungry herself.

- How did Sylvia feel about living on her foster mother's farm? (Ideas: *She loved being outdoors; the farm made her feel alive.*) ⒹⒸⒺ
- Why didn't Sylvia like the town? (Ideas: *The other children made fun of her; it was noisy and crowded.*) ⒹⒸⒺ
- Why do you think Sylvia didn't dare to look at the young man? (Ideas: *She was afraid of him; he was a stranger; she was shy.*) ⒹⒸⒺ
- How do you think Sylvia feels about hunting? Explain your answer. (Ideas: *She probably doesn't like hunting because she loves living things; she probably doesn't like hunting because guns are noisy.*) ⒹⒸⒺ
- What do you think will happen in the next part of the story? (Ideas: *The stranger will ask Sylvia to go hunting with him; the stranger will rob Sylvia and her foster mother.*) Ⓟ

EXERCISE 9

Paired Practice (Optional)

1. Now you'll read in pairs.
- Whoever read second the last time will read first today.
- Remember to start at the diamond and switch at the star.
2. (Observe students and answer questions as needed.)

After students finish reading the story, they work independently in their Textbooks and Workbooks. In the Textbook exercises for Lesson 57, students make inferences (part D), complete deductions (part E), review vocabulary words (part F), answer interpretive comprehension questions (part G), and write an essay (part H).

Students write the answers to Workbook exercises in the Workbook itself. In Lesson 57, they answer literal comprehension questions about the story (part A), use vocabulary words in context (part B), identify different types of figurative language (part C), complete deductions (part D), distinguish characters by trait (part E), and make comparisons (part F).

D INFERENCE

Write the answers for items 1–8.

You have to answer different types of questions about the passages you read. Some questions are answered by words in the passage. Other questions are *not* answered by words in the passage. You have to figure out the answer by making a deduction.

The following passage includes both types of questions.

More about Ecology

Two hundred years ago, many people were not concerned with ecology. They believed there was no end to the different types of wildlife, so they killed wild animals by the hundreds of thousands. When we look back on these killings, we may feel shocked. But for the people who lived two hundred years ago, wild animals seemed to be as plentiful as weeds.

Because of these killings, more than a hundred types of animals have become extinct since 1800. An animal is extinct when there are no more animals of that type.

One type of extinct animal is the passenger pigeon. At one time, these birds were so plentiful that flocks of them used to blacken the sky. Now the passenger pigeon is gone forever. Think of that. You will never get to see a living passenger pigeon or any of the other animals that have become extinct. The only place you can see those animals is in a museum, where they are stuffed and mounted.

1. Are house cats extinct?
2. Is that question answered by **words** or a **deduction?**
3. What extinct animal is mentioned in the passage?
4. **Words** or **deduction?**
5. How many types of animals have become extinct since 1800?
6. **Words** or **deduction?**
7. The dodo bird is extinct. How many animals of that type are alive today?
8. **Words** or **deduction?**
Write the answers about the deductions.

E DEDUCTIONS

Oliver believed that if he studied, he would pass the test. Oliver studied for the test.
1. So, what did Oliver believe would happen?

Nadia believed that if you ate an apple a day you would stay healthy. Nadia ate an apple every day.
2. So, what did Nadia believe would happen?

F VOCABULARY REVIEW

unprecedented
maneuver
devoted
spurn
endured
regard

For each item, write the correct word.
1. When you move skillfully, you ▮▮▮▮.
2. When you consider something, you ▮▮▮ it.
3. Something that has never occurred before is ▮▮▮.

G COMPREHENSION

Write the answers.
1. How did Sylvia feel about living on her foster mother's farm?
2. Why didn't Sylvia like the town?
3. Why do you think Sylvia didn't dare to look at the young man?
4. How do you think Sylvia feels about hunting? Explain your answer.
5. What do you think will happen in the next part of the story?

H WRITING

Where would you rather live, on a farm or in a town?

Write an essay that explains your answer. Try to answer the following questions:
• What are the advantages of living on a farm?
• What are the disadvantages of living on a farm?
• What are the advantages of living in a town?
• What are the disadvantages of living in a town?
• Where would you rather live? Why?
Make your essay at least sixty words long.

A STORY DETAILS

Write or circle the answers.

1. Sylvia was ___ who lived on a farm.
   • a vacationer • a farmhand • an orphan

2. Where had Sylvia lived before coming to the farm?

3. Sylvia thought she had never been ___ at all before coming to the farm.
   • scared • alive • punished

4. Which place did Sylvia enjoy more, the town or the farm?

5. How had the children in town treated Sylvia?

6. What was the young man doing in the woods?

7. Was Sylvia bold or shy?

8. What was the name of the person who owned the farm?

9. That person was Sylvia's ___.
   • employer • mother • foster parent

B VOCABULARY

Write the correct words in the blanks.

regarded	suitable
appealed	humiliating
unprecedented	maneuvered

1. The starving boy _____ to the sympathy of the crowd.
2. They _____ the criminal as a dangerous person.
3. He _____ the shopping cart past the fallen cans.
4. The pitcher made an _____ number of strikeouts.

C FIGURATIVE LANGUAGE

For each statement, write *simile, metaphor,* or *exaggeration.*

1. Her face was like a pale star.

2. The apartment was a prison.

3. The day was like a dream.

D DEDUCTIONS

Complete each deduction.

Every element has an atomic weight. Argon is an element.

1. What's the conclusion about argon?

Horses eat grass. A palomino is a horse.

2. What's the conclusion about a palomino?

E CHARACTER TRAITS

Write whether each phrase describes *Sylvia, Mrs. Tilley,* or *the stranger.*

1. Very shy

2. Whistled loudly

3. An orphan

4. Owned a farm

5. Felt like a part of the woods

6. Hunted for animals

F COMPARISONS

Write *Odyssey* if the event occurred in *The Odyssey.* Write *Yarn* if the event occurred in "Mystery Yarn."

1. Telemachus was one of the suitors.

2. Telemachus helped defeat the suitors.

3. The suitors took a test that involved unwinding string.

4. The suitors took a test that involved a bow and arrow.

After the class finishes the main reading lesson, you present activities from the *Spelling Presentation Book*. Depending on the amount of time available, spelling can be presented at the end of the reading lesson or at another time of day.

The spelling activities reinforce the decoding skills taught in the reading program. Students write answers for spelling activities on lined paper, so no additional student materials are required. Sample activities for Spelling Lesson 57 appear below.

EXERCISE 1

Word Introduction

a. (Write on the board:)

> tragic
> comic
> critic
> medic
> pulse
> magic

b. Get ready to read these words.
*   First word: **tragic.** What word? (Signal.) *Tragic.*
c. Next word: **comic.** What word? (Signal.) *Comic.*
*   (Repeat for: **critic, medic, pulse, magic.**)
d. Now spell those words.
*   Spell **tragic.** Get ready. (Signal.) *T-R-A-G-I-C.*
e. Spell **comic.** Get ready. (Signal.) *C-O-M-I-C.*
*   (Repeat for: **critic, medic, pulse, magic.**)
f. (Erase the board.)
*   Spell the words without looking.
g. Spell **tragic.** Get ready. (Signal.) *T-R-A-G-I-C.*
h. Spell **comic.** Get ready. (Signal.) *C-O-M-I-C.*
*   (Repeat for: **critic, medic, pulse, magic.**)
i. Get ready to write those words.
j. First word: **tragic.** Write it. ✔
*   (Repeat for: **comic, critic, medic, pulse, magic.**)

EXERCISE 2

Word Building

a. (Write on the board:)

> 1. de + fer + ment = _____
> 2. pro + duct + ion = _____
> 3. style + ish + ly = _____
> 4. rhythm + s = _____
> 5. pro + tect + ive = _____
> 6. re + act + ive +ly = _____

b. You're going to write the words that go in the blanks.
*   Number your paper from 1 to 6. ✔
c. Word 1. Write **deferment** on your paper. ✔
d. Do the rest of the words on your own. ✔
e. Check your work. Make an **X** next to any word you got wrong.
f. Word 1. Spell **deferment.** Get ready. (Tap for each letter.) *D-E-F-E-R-M-E-N-T.*
*   (Repeat for: **2. production, 3. stylishly, 4. rhythms, 5. protective, 6. reactively.**)

EXERCISE 3

Spelling Review

a. Get ready to spell some words.
b. Word 1 is **thoughtlessly.**
*   What word? (Signal.) *Thoughtlessly.*
*   Spell **thoughtlessly.** Get ready. (Signal.) *T-H-O-U-G-H-T-L-E-S-S-L-Y.*
c. Word 2 is **stretcher.**
*   What word? (Signal.) *Stretcher.*
*   Spell **stretcher.** Get ready. (Signal.) *S-T-R-E-T-C-H-E-R.*
d. (Repeat step c for: **3. photographing, 4. retained, 5. reception, 6. music.**)
e. (Give individual turns on: **1. thoughtlessly, 2. stretcher, 3. photographing, 4. retained, 5. reception, 6. music.**)

Spelling Presentation Book, Lesson 57

Testing and Management

The Signature Edition of *Reading Mastery* includes two types of tests: placement tests and curriculum-based assessments. You use the placement tests to determine each student's initial placement in the program. You use the assessments to measure student progress within the program. Each assessment includes administration instructions, student testing material, record-keeping charts, and remedial exercises.

Placement Tests

Students should generally be placed in the level of *Reading Mastery Signature Edition* that corresponds with their grade level. To ensure accurate placement, however, you should administer the appropriate placement test(s). There are six placement tests, one for each grade. The Grade K test can also be used to determine which students should be placed in Fast Cycle. Similarly, the Grade 2 test can be used to determine which students should be placed in Transition.

The placement tests should be administered at the beginning of the school year. The results will provide you with

- information about each student's decoding skills (Grades K–5) and comprehension skills (Grades 1–5).
- a means of identifying which students should be placed in another level of *Reading Mastery Signature Edition*.
- guidelines for grouping students.

Copies of the placement tests and accompanying instructions appear on pages 84–99 of this guide as well as in the *Teacher's Guide* for each level. These pages may be reproduced for classroom use.

Assessments and Mastery Tests

Reading Mastery Signature Edition is designed so that each student's reading skills are constantly evaluated. Decoding skills, for example, are periodically measured through rate-and-accuracy fluency checkouts. For these timed checkouts, the student reads a passage aloud as you record the student's decoding errors. Comprehension, reference, and study skills are measured through the daily independent work. Because the independent work is directly related to other program material, it serves as a continuous test of each student's skill mastery. You check the independent work every day and record each student's performance.

In-program mastery tests are used in Grades K–3. These criterion-referenced tests are scheduled intermittently in Grade K, after every fifth lesson in Grade 1, and after every tenth lesson in Grades 2 and 3. Each test item measures student mastery of a specific skill taught in *Reading Mastery*.

In addition to these in-program evaluations, *Reading Mastery Signature Edition* includes separate *Curriculum-Based Assessment and Fluency* books for teachers and students in Grades K–5. These books contain curriculum-based assessments and fluency checkouts, as well as remedial exercises for students who perform poorly on the tests. Like the in-program test items, each assessment item measures student mastery of a specific skill taught in *Reading Mastery*.

The remedial exercises are designed to help students who score less than 80% on the assessments. Each assessment has its own set of remedial exercises. The exercises provide a general review of the tested skills, using examples different from those on the assessment. There is a specific remedial exercise for every tested skill.

Grouping the Students

Reading Mastery can be presented either to small groups of students or to the entire class. In general, Grades K to 3 should be presented to small groups of students, while Grades 4 and 5 can be presented to the entire class.

Small-group instruction offers several advantages. If you use small-group instruction, students can be grouped according to their ability levels: above-average, average, or below-average. This homogeneous grouping allows you to spend more time with the below-average students, who need the most help. You can use the placement test results as a guideline for the initial grouping of students.

Small-group instruction also allows you to monitor individual performance more closely. In small groups, individual students have more opportunities to read aloud and to answer your questions. Students in small groups also get a better view of displays in the Presentation Book. This is particularly important in Grades K, 1, and Transition, where you often point to pictures, words, and letters in the Presentation Book.

Small-group instruction is simple with *Reading Mastery* because you can teach one group of students while other groups are doing their independent work. Ideally, for Grades K and 1, the class should be divided into three groups: above-average, average, and below-average. The below-average group should be the smallest. For Grades 2 and 3, the class can be divided into just two groups: one for below-average students and another for the rest of the class. Grades 4 and 5 are usually presented to the entire class, but they can also be presented to small groups.

Scheduling the Reading Period

Generally, one lesson of *Reading Mastery* should be presented on each day of the school year. Every lesson is divided into four parts: group instruction, independent work, workcheck, and spelling. The group instruction usually requires 30 minutes; the independent work, between 20 and 30 minutes; the workcheck, 10 minutes. Students should complete the independent work immediately after finishing the group instruction. If necessary, however, they can complete the independent work later in the day or even as homework. The spelling lesson, which should be presented at another time of day, if possible, takes about 10 to 15 minutes per lesson. If you have two reading groups and plan to present spelling lessons to the entire class, present the spelling lesson that corresponds to the reading lesson of the lower group.

The following chart shows one possible schedule for reading lessons in a class with two groups of students.

	Group A	Group B
8:45–9:15	group instruction	
9:15–9:45	independent work	group instruction
9:45–10:15	workcheck	independent work
10:15–10:25		workcheck
2:15-2:30	spelling lesson	spelling lesson

Motivating the Students

Reading Mastery is designed so that every student can succeed. Each lesson consists of a series of exercises. Students are able to succeed on every exercise, and their success is consistently rewarded. As soon as students learn a new skill in one exercise, they apply that skill in another exercise and review it in still another. This constant application and review provides a consistent reward for learning. Students are motivated to learn each new skill because they know that they will soon be using the skill.

The programs also provide additional incentives for learning. In Grades K and 1, for example, students can earn stars for reading well. In selected lessons, you call on individual students to read a story aloud. The students earn stars if they are able to read within a specific rate and error limit. You keep a permanent record of these stars.

Teaching Techniques

Successful implementation of *Reading Mastery* involves many factors, including classroom arrangement, correct use of the *Presentation Books,* adequate pacing, proper signals, consistent praise, effective correction procedures, and teaching to mastery. The following sections explain these factors in detail.

Arranging the Classroom

The classroom should be arranged differently for the different grades. In Grades K and 1, you usually present the program to small groups of students. The group you are teaching should be seated in a small semicircle in front of you. Students should sit on chairs, not at desks, and you should be within touching distance of every student. Every student in the group must be able to see the pictures or words that you present from the Presentation Book. The lowest performers in the group should be seated directly in front of you, where you can monitor them closely.

Grades 2 and 3 are usually presented to somewhat larger groups of students. The group you are teaching should face you. Students may sit at their desks or on chairs arranged in a semicircle. The group can be arranged in any form as long as all students are facing you. The lowest performers should be seated directly in front of you.

Grades 4 and 5 are usually presented to the entire class. The class should be facing you, and students should be at their desks. The lowest performers should be seated directly in front of you.

Using the Presentation Books

The Presentation Books contain complete scripts for presenting every lesson in *Reading Mastery.* The scripts are carefully written so that all instruction is clear and unambiguous. The program will be most effective if you follow the scripts closely.

The *Presentation Books* use several typefaces and other scripting conventions.

- Blue type indicates what you say.
- **Bold blue type indicates words you emphasize.**
- **(Black type in parentheses indicates what you do.)**
- *Black italic type indicates students' answers.*
- Questions that require an exact group response are followed by a signal and the response. For example: Everybody, what word? **(Signal.)** *Motor.*
- For questions with variable answers posed to individual students, the student's response is enclosed in parentheses and preceded by the word *Idea.* For these questions, accept any answers that express the correct idea, no matter what the phrasing. For example: **Why do you think Ron will be the main character in this story? (Idea:** *Because his name is in the title.***)**

Pacing the Lesson

Present the daily lessons at a lively pace. Fast pacing

- **generates student interest.** Students are likely to pay attention if the lesson is presented at a lively pace.
- **encourages student achievement.** With fast pacing, students cover more material and receive more practice.
- **keeps students thinking.** If a lesson is presented slowly, students' attention may wander. With fast pacing, students are constantly thinking, and they are unlikely to become distracted.
- **reduces management problems.** With fast pacing, students are involved in their work and unlikely to misbehave.

To set a fast pace, you should move quickly, but don't rush students into making mistakes. Experience will show you the pace that is appropriate for each group. Always read over the material before presenting it. Fast pacing is easier if you do not have to refer to the Presentation Book for every word.

Using Signals

For many of the exercises in *Reading Mastery,* students must answer aloud and in unison. This group response is particularly important because

■ every student must initiate a response.

■ every student is able to practice the exercise.

■ you can monitor every student.

■ you can hear any incorrect answers and correct them immediately.

For students to answer simultaneously, you must use a signal. The signal eliminates the problem of one student leading the rest of the group.

There are two basic types of signals: visual and audible. Visual signals are used when students are looking at you or at the Presentation Book. You signal students by making some type of hand motion, such as quickly dropping your hand, touching a word or picture, or slashing under a word.

Audible signals are used when students are reading word lists, stories, or skill exercises in their Storybooks or Textbooks. You use audible signals in these situations because students are looking at what they are reading, not at you. You can use a tap, clap, or finger snap as an audible signal.

Use the following procedure for both visual and audible signals:

1. Ask the specified question.

2. Pause for about one second.

3. Signal visually or audibly.

4. Listen to the group response and correct any errors.

5. Move quickly to the next question.

The one-second pause in step 2 is very important. The pause clearly separates the question from the signal and ensures that every student sees or hears the signal. The pause should always last for about one second. When the pause is of a consistent length, the group is able to answer more effectively.

Praising the Students

Students will work harder if they receive praise for their work. Each lesson provides many opportunities for praise. You can praise students when they learn a new sound, when they read lists of words, or when

they read a story without making any errors. You can also praise students when they behave well and when they work particularly hard.

Praise should be simple and positive. You can say things such as, "Great. You read the entire list without making any mistakes." or "Good talking. I could hear everybody." Students are especially reinforced when you confirm a correct answer, such as, "Yes, that word is **am**."

Praise should be an integral part of your presentation, but don't overdo it. Every statement of praise should clearly result from a specific student action. If praise is indiscriminate and undeserved, it will lose meaning for students. Generally, students in the lower grades of the program will require more praise than students in the upper grades.

Correcting Mistakes

Reading Mastery includes correction procedures for many of the mistakes that students are likely to make. These mistakes fall into two categories: general and specific. General mistakes include not paying attention and not answering on signal. Specific mistakes include misidentifying words and giving the wrong answers to questions.

General Mistakes

General mistakes are most likely to occur when students are beginning the program. Correct these mistakes as soon as they occur to prevent students from falling into bad habits.

In Grades K and 1, students must always pay attention when you are pointing to letters or words in the *Presentation Book.* If a student is not paying attention, use the following procedure:

1. Look at the student.

2. Say, "Watch my finger. Let's try it again."

3. Repeat the question as soon as the student is paying attention.

4. Return to the beginning of the exercise.

Variations of this procedure can be used whenever a student is not paying attention. Always look at the student, tell the student to pay attention, repeat the question, and then return to the beginning of the exercise.

If a student is paying attention but does not answer a question, use the following procedure:

1. Look at the student.
2. Say, "I have to hear everybody."
3. Repeat the question.
4. Return to the beginning of the exercise.

Every student must answer exactly on signal. A student who does not answer on signal may begin to depend on other students for the correct answers. The following correction procedure shows students that you expect everyone to answer on signal:

1. Look at the student.
2. Say, "You're early" or "You're late."
3. Repeat the question until all students answer on signal.
4. Return to the beginning of the exercise.

By requiring a simultaneous response, you eliminate the problem of one student leading and the others following. When students answer simultaneously, they have to think for themselves, and they will pay closer attention to you.

For all correction procedures, you first correct the mistake and then return to the beginning of the exercise. By repeating the exercise, you demonstrate to students that mistakes will not be ignored. Students must work on an exercise from beginning to end until they get it right. If general mistakes are properly corrected during the early lessons, students will make far fewer mistakes in later lessons.

Specific Mistakes

When students misidentify a word or give a wrong answer, they are making a specific mistake. Many of the exercises in the Presentation Books contain correction procedures for specific mistakes. There are two basic procedures: the *model-lead-test-retest* procedure and the *process-test-retest* procedure.

The following example of the *model-lead-test-retest* procedure occurs in Grade K, when students are learning to read the letter **a.**

To correct:

If the children do not say *aaa*:

Model	1.	aaa.
Lead	2.	**(Touch the first ball of the arrow.)** Say it with me. Get ready. **(Move quickly to the second ball of the arrow. Hold for two seconds. Say aaa with the children.)** *aaa*.
Test	3.	**(Touch the first ball of the arrow.)** Your turn. Get ready. **(Move quickly to the second ball of the arrow. Hold for two seconds.)** *aaa*.

In step 1, you *model* the correct answer. In step 2, you *lead* students by saying the correct answer with them. (Sometimes, the *lead* step is not used.) In step 3, you *test* students by having them say the correct answer by themselves. At a later point in the lesson, you *retest* students by presenting the exercise again.

The following example of the *process-test-retest* procedure also occurs in Grade K, when students are learning to read the word **am**.

To correct:

1. Everybody, sound out the word. **(Touch each sound as the children sound out the word.)** *Aaammm.*

2. What word? **(Signal.)** *Am.*

In step 1, students use the *process* of sounding out to correct their mistake. In step 2, you *test* students by asking, "What word?" At a later point in the lesson, you *retest* the students by presenting the exercise again.

Specific correction procedures typically appear when a new skill is introduced because that is when students are most likely to make mistakes. If students are properly corrected when a skill is introduced, they are unlikely to make mistakes when the skill appears in subsequent exercises. Nevertheless, you should memorize the correction procedure for a particular skill so it can be administered at any time.

Teaching to Mastery

Every skill in *Reading Mastery* should be taught to mastery. When a skill is taught to mastery, every student in the group is able to perform the skill independently, without making any mistakes.

Teaching to mastery is of critical importance because students are constantly applying each new skill. When a skill is taught to mastery, students are able to apply the skill and are prepared to learn related skills. By teaching every skill to mastery, you ensure that each student is able to succeed throughout the program.

Practice Scripts

This section contains representative teacher presentation scripts from the Reading strand of *Reading Mastery Signature Edition*. You should practice the appropriate scripts before presenting the program to your students. You can practice these scripts on your own, with another teacher, or at a staff development session conducted by an experienced leader. (To view all the scripts for a particular lesson, turn to the Sample Lessons section on page 100.)

To practice a script or a lesson, first read each script carefully and become familiar with it. Then present the script aloud several times, with only brief glances at the actual text. During these presentations, you should execute the proper signals and develop a rapid pace. Finally, present the script to another person, who will play the role of student. This "student" can answer on your signal and can also make intentional errors that you have to correct.

You should practice the scripts that are relevant to the level you will be teaching. The table in the next column shows the practice scripts that are relevant to each level (K, 1, Fast Cycle, Transition, 2, 3, 4, 5). There are four types of practice scripts: sound reading, word reading, story reading, and skill exercise.

If time permits, practice some of the remaining scripts as well. This additional practice will give you a valuable perspective on the entire Reading strand.

Practice Scripts

Script	Type	K	1	FC	Tr	2	3	4	5
1	sound reading	◆		◆					
2	sound reading	◆		◆					
3	sound reading	◆	◆	◆					
4	word reading	◆		◆					
5	word reading	◆	◆	◆					
6	word reading		◆	◆	◆	◆	◆	◆	◆
7	story reading	◆	◆	◆					
8	story reading		◆	◆					
9	story reading				◆	◆	◆	◆	◆
10	skill exercise					◆	◆	◆	◆

Practice Script 1

The following sound-reading script appears in Lesson 4 of Grade K. The script introduces the continuous sound **mmm**.

SOUNDS
EXERCISE 5

Introducing the new sound **mmm** as in **mat**

---

a. (Touch the first ball of the arrow.) Here's a new sound. My turn to say it. When I move under the sound, I'll say it. I'll keep on saying it as long as I touch under it. Get ready. (Move quickly to the second ball of the arrow. Hold for two seconds.) *mmm.*

b. (Touch the first ball of the arrow.) My turn again. Get ready. (Move quickly to the second ball of the arrow. Hold for two seconds.) **mmm.**

c. (Touch the first ball of the arrow.) My turn again. Get ready. (Move quickly to the second ball of the arrow. Hold for two seconds.) **mmm.**

d. (Touch the first ball of the arrow.) Your turn. When I move under the sound, you say it. Keep on saying it as long as I touch under it. Get ready. (Move quickly to the second ball of the arrow. Hold for two seconds.) *mmm.* Yes, **mmm.**

To Correct

(If the children do not say *mmm:*)

1. **mmm.**
2. (Touch the first ball of the arrow.) Say it with me. Get ready. (Move quickly to the second ball of the arrow. Hold for two seconds. Say mmm with the children.) *mmm.*
3. (Touch the first ball of the arrow.) Your turn. Get ready. (Move quickly to the second ball of the arrow. Hold for two seconds.) *mmm.*

---

e. (Touch the first ball of the arrow.) Again. Get ready. (Move quickly to the second ball of the arrow. Hold for two seconds.) *mmm.* Yes, **mmm.**

f. (Repeat *e* until firm.)

g. (Call on individual children to do *d*.)

h. Good saying **mmm.**

Description

In steps a–c, you model the correct way to say the sound. In step d, you test students by having them say the sound. Step d also includes a correction procedure. In steps e and f, you continue to test students until all of them have mastered the sound. Finally, in step g, individual students take turns saying the sound.

Teaching Techniques

Hold the Presentation Book so all students can see the sound. Hold the book with one hand and point with the other hand. Use the following procedure to present the sound:

1. Touch the large ball of the arrow and say, "Your turn. Get ready."

2. Pause for one second.

3. Quickly move your finger to the second ball of the arrow. This movement acts as a signal for the group to say the sound.

4. Touch the second ball for two seconds. Because **mmm** is a continuous sound, the group says the sound for as long as you touch the second ball.

When presenting this exercise, make sure you do not block students' view of the letter. Always touch the balls, not the letter. Also, make sure that your signal timing is consistent. Always pause for one second before moving to the second ball, and always point to the second ball for two seconds.

Step f requires you to repeat step e until all students are "firm." Students are firm when every one of them has mastered the sound. Every student must be able to say the sound for as long as you touch it.

In step g, you test individual students. You do not have to give an individual test to every student on every exercise. However, during the course of a lesson, every student should receive at least two or three individual tests. Try to give more individual tests to the lowest performers in the group to ensure that they master each exercise.

Corrections

To correct mistakes, use the specified correction procedure.

1. *Model* the correct sound.
2. *Lead* students by saying the sound with them.
3. *Test* students by having them say the sound by themselves.

After you complete the correction procedure, provide a *retest* by presenting the sound again at a later point in the lesson.

Practice Script 2

The following sound-reading script appears in Lesson 27 of Grade K. The script introduces the stop sound **d**.

SOUNDS
EXERCISE 2

Introducing the new sound **d** as in **dad**

a. (Touch the ball of the arrow for **d**.) We always have to say this sound fast. The little arrow under the sound tells me that I can't stop under this sound. My turn to say it fast. (Slash to the end of the arrow as you say d.) (Return to the ball.) My turn to say it fast again. (Slash to the end of the arrow as you say d.)

b. (Touch the ball of the arrow.) Your turn. Say it fast. (Slash to the end of the arrow.) *d*. Yes, **d**.

c. (Repeat *b* until firm.)

d. (Call on individual children to do *b*.)

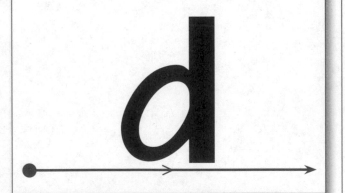

Description

This script is similar to Practice Script 1, except that the presentation has been streamlined and the correction procedure no longer appears. (Correction procedures are included only in the first few appearances of a skill, but they can still be used to correct student errors on subsequent appearances of the skill or on similar exercises.)

In step a, you model the correct way to say the sound. In step b, you test students by having them say the sound. In step c, you continue to test students until all of them have mastered the sound. Finally, in step d, individual students take turns saying the sound.

Teaching Techniques

Because **d** is a stop sound, you signal differently than for **mmm**.

1. Touch the large ball and say, "Your turn. Say it fast."

2. Pause for one second.

3. Slash your finger under the sound. This slash acts as a signal. When your finger passes under the sound, students "say it fast."

Corrections

To correct mistakes, use the *model-lead-test-retest* procedure.

1. *Model* the correct sound.

2. *Lead* students by saying the sound with the group.

3. *Test* students by having them say the sound by themselves.

4. *Retest* students by presenting the sound again at a later point in the lesson.

Practice Script 3

The following sound-reading script appears in Lesson 5 of Grade 1. The script reviews sounds that students have learned, including **u** as in *under,* **ch** as in *chat,* **d** as in *mad,* and **m** as in *ram.*

Description

In steps a–c, you test students by having them say each sound. Step c also includes a correction procedure. In step d, you retest students until you are sure that they have mastered each sound. Finally, you administer individual tests.

Teaching Techniques

Your presentation for Practice Script 3 is different from Practice Scripts 1 and 2 because there are no arrows under the sounds.

1. Point just below a sound, with your finger about an inch from the page.
2. Say, "Get ready."
3. Pause for one second.
4. Touch under the sound. Your touch acts as a signal. Always touch under the sound so that all students can see the symbol.

Students say the sound for as long as you touch under it. Touch continuous sounds, such as **u** and **m,** for two seconds; touch stop sounds, such as **ch, b** and **d,** for just an instant.

Corrections

To correct mistakes, use the specified correction procedure.

1. *Model* the correct answer by saying the sound.
2. *Lead* students by saying the sound with them. (You may need to repeat this step several times.)
3. *Test* students by having them say the sound by themselves.
4. *Retest* by proceeding to step d.

SOUNDS
EXERCISE 1

Sounds firm-up

a. (Point to the sounds.) Get ready to tell me these sounds.

b. When I touch it, you say it. Keep on saying it as long as I touch it.

c. (Point to each sound.) Get ready. (Touch the sound.) (The children say the sound.)

• (Lift your finger.)

To Correct

1. (Immediately say the correct sound as you continue to touch it.)
• (Lift your finger.)
2. Say it with me. (Touch the sound and say it with children.)
• (Lift your finger.)
3. Again. (Repeat until firm.)
4. All by yourselves. Get ready. (Touch the sound.) (The children say the sound.)

d. (Repeat problem sounds until the children can correctly identify all sounds in order.)

Individual test

(Call on several children to identify one or more sounds.)

u b e

ch i a

d f o

m r sh

Practice Script 4

The following word-reading script appears in Lesson 46 of Grade K. The script introduces the word **meat**.

EXERCISE 9

Children sound out the word and say it fast

a. (Touch the first ball of the arrow for **mēat**.) Sound it out. Get ready. (Move quickly under each sound.) *Mmmēēēt.*

b. (Return to the first ball.) Again, sound it out. Get ready. (Move quickly under each sound.) *Mmmēēēt.*

c. (Repeat *b* until firm.)

d. (Return to the first ball.) Say it fast. (Slash.) *Meat.*

• Yes, what word? (Signal.) *Meat.*

• A hamburger is made of (pause) **meat.**

Description

In steps a–c, students sound out the word by saying each sound in sequence. Then, in step d, students read the word normally by "saying it fast."

Teaching Techniques

To present the word, follow this procedure:

1. Touch the large ball of the arrow for **meat** and say, "Sound it out. Get ready."

2. Pause for one second.

3. Quickly move your finger to the second ball of the arrow. Hold your finger on the second ball for about one second, as students say **mmm.**

4. Move your finger to the third ball. Hold your finger on the third ball for about one second as the students say **ēēē.**

5. Move your finger to the fourth ball and hold it there for just an instant as students say **t.**

Note that the small **a** does not have a ball under it. Students do not say any small silent letters; you simply move your finger past them.

After students are proficient at sounding out the word, they "say it fast." Use the following procedure.

1. Touch the large ball of the arrow for **meat** and say, "Say it fast."

2. Pause for one second.

3. Quickly slash under the word as students "say it fast." *Meat.*

Corrections

Some students may have trouble "saying it fast." To correct mistakes, use a *model-test-retest* procedure.

1. *Model* the correct answer by sounding out the word and saying it fast.

2. *Test* students by having them sound out the word and say it fast.

3. *Retest* students by presenting the exercise again at a later point in the lesson.

Practice Script 5

The following word-reading script appears in Lesson 11 of Grade 1. The script reviews words that students have already learned.

EXERCISE 10

Read the fast way

a. Read these words the fast way.

b. (Touch the ball for **another.** Pause two seconds.) Get ready. (Signal.) *Another.* Yes, **another.**

c. (Repeat *b* for **whȳ, when,** and **funny.**)

another
whȳ
when
funny

Description

Because this is a review exercise, students read all the words "the fast way" without first sounding them out.

Teaching Techniques

To present the words, follow this procedure:

1. Touch the ball of the arrow.
2. Pause for two seconds. This pause gives students time to examine the word.
3. Say, "Get ready."
4. Pause for one second.
5. Quickly slash under the word with your finger, as students read the word.
6. Reinforce students by repeating the word out loud.

Corrections

Correct mistakes by using a *sound out-test-retest* procedure.

1. Direct students to sound out the word.
2. *Test* students by asking them, "What word?"
3. *Retest* students by returning to the top of the column and presenting all the words in order.

Practice Script 6

The following word-reading script appears in Lesson 34 of Grade 2. In this script, you define words that students read and have students practice using the words in context.

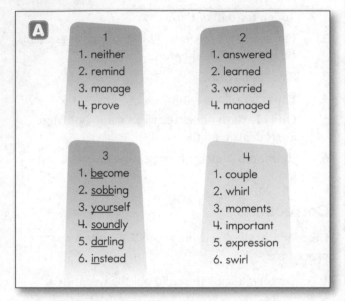

A

1	2
1. neither	1. answered
2. remind	2. learned
3. manage	3. worried
4. prove	4. managed

3	4
1. become	1. couple
2. sobbing	2. whirl
3. yourself	3. moments
4. soundly	4. important
5. darling	5. expression
6. instead	6. swirl

EXERCISE 2

Reading Words

Column 1

a. **Find lesson 34 in your textbook.** ✔
- Touch column 1. ✔
- (Teacher reference:)

1. neither	3. manage
2. remind	4. prove

b. Word 1 is **neither.** What word? (Signal.) *Neither.*
- Spell **neither.** Get ready. (Tap for each letter.) *N-E-I-T-H-E-R.*
c. Word 2 is **remind.** What word? (Signal.) *Remind.*
- Spell **remind.** Get ready. (Tap for each letter.) *R-E-M-I-N-D.*
d. Word 3 is **manage.** What word? (Signal.) *Manage.*
- Spell **manage.** Get ready. (Tap for each letter.) *M-A-N-A-G-E.*
- When you work hard to do something, you manage to do it. Here's another way of saying **He worked hard to keep swimming: He managed to keep swimming.**

- Your turn. What's another way of saying **He worked hard to keep swimming?** (Signal.) *He managed to keep swimming.*
- What's another way of saying **The baby worked hard to walk?** (Signal.) *The baby managed to walk.*
e. Word 4 is **prove.** What word? (Signal.) *Prove.*
- Spell **prove.** Get ready. (Tap for each letter.) *P-R-O-V-E.*
- When you prove something, you show that it is true. When you prove that you can stand up, you show it's true that you can stand up.
- What would you have to do to prove that they are serving spaghetti for lunch? (Call on a student. Idea: *Show it's true that they are serving spaghetti for lunch.*)
- What would you have to do to prove that it is raining outside? (Call on a student. Idea: *Show it's true that it's raining outside.*)
f. Let's read those words again, the fast way.
- Word 1. What word? (Signal.) *Neither.*
- (Repeat for words 2–4.)
g. (Repeat step f until firm.)

Description

In steps a–c, you direct students as they read and spell the first two words, *neither* and *remind.* In step d, after students read and spell the next word, *manage,* you define the word and model how to use it in context. Then you test the students by asking them to use *manage* in a different context. In step e, after students read and spell the last word, *prove,* you define the word. Then you call on different students to answer questions involving the new word. Finally, in steps f and g, you read all four words "the fast way."

Teaching Techniques

When presenting the word list, you need to use audible signals—such as taps, claps, or finger snaps—because students are looking at their books, not at you. Listen carefully as students spell each word. Give a series of audible signals—one for each letter.

When presenting the word meanings, you will either call on the group or on individual students. When the group is tested in step d, for example, students must answer in unison. When you call on individual students in step e, answers may vary. Accept sentences that express the correct meaning. Rephrase by referring to the sentence in the script, for example: "Yes, you show it's true that they are serving spaghetti for lunch."

Corrections

Some students may have trouble using the vocabulary words in context. For example, in step d they may say, "He worked hard to keep swimming," instead of "He managed to keep swimming." Use a *model-test-retest* procedure to correct mistakes.

1. *Model* the correct answer: He managed to keep swimming.

2. *Test* the group by repeating the question: What's another way of saying **He worked hard to keep swimming?** (Signal.) *He managed to keep swimming.*

3. *Retest* students by repeating the question at a later point in the lesson.

Practice Script 7

The following story-reading script appears in Lesson 14 of Grade 1. The script shows the first of two basic story-reading procedures used in *Reading Mastery*. (Practice Script 8 shows the second procedure.)

The first procedure is used in Grade K and the first half of Grade 1. Stories in these lessons appear in the special *Reading Mastery* font. Students read all or part of the story aloud and in unison.

Description

In Exercise 12, students read the title and the first part of the story aloud and in unison. In Exercise 13, students take turns reading the rest of the story aloud. You call on different students to read one sentence each, but you occasionally direct the group to read a sentence in unison. In Exercise 14, students take turns reading the story again as you present comprehension questions.

STORY 14
EXERCISE 12

First reading—title and three sentences

a. Keep your reader open to page 22. ✔

b. Everybody, touch the title. (Check to see that the children are touching under the first word of the title.)

c. I'll tap and you read each word in the title the fast way. Don't sound it out. Just tell me the word.

d. First word. ✔

• (Pause two seconds.) Get ready. (Tap.) *The.*

e. Next word. ✔

• (Pause two seconds.) Get ready. (Tap.) *Cow.*

f. (Repeat e for the remaining words in the title.)

g. Everybody, say the title. (Signal.) *The cow boy and the cow.*
Yes, **the cow boy and the cow.**

h. Everybody, get ready to read this story the fast way.

i. First word. ✔

• (Pause two seconds.) Get ready. (Tap.) *A.*

j. Next word. ✔

• (Pause two seconds.) Get ready. (Tap.) *Cow boy.*

k. (Repeat j for the remaining words in the first three sentences. Have the children reread the first three sentences until firm.)

EXERCISE 13

Remaining sentences

a. I'm going to call on individual children to read a sentence. Everybody, follow along and point to the words. If you hear a mistake, raise your hand.

b. (Call on a child.) Read the next sentence.

c. (Call on another child.) Read the next sentence.

d. (Repeat c for most of the remaining sentences in the story.)

e. (Occasionally have the group read a sentence. When the group is to read, say:) Everybody, read the next sentence. (Pause two seconds. Tap for each word in the sentence. Pause at least two seconds between taps.)

> the cow boy and the cow[1]
> a cow boy was sad. hē did
> not havₑ a hŏrsₑ.[2] the other cow
> boys said, "hō, hō, that funny
> cow boy has nō hŏrsₑ."
>
> a cow cāmₑ up to the cow
> boy. the cow said, "if you arₑ a
> cow boy, you nēēd a cow. I am
> a cow."
>
> the cow boy said, "do not bē
> funny. cow boys do not rIdₑ on
> cows."
>
> the cow said, "but I can run
> as fast as a hŏrsₑ.[3] and I can
> jump better than a hŏrsₑ."[4]
>
> the cow boy said, "I will
> givₑ you a trȳ. but I will fēēl
> very funny rIdiñg on a cow." sō
> the cow boy got on the cow.[5]
>
> then the other cow boys
> cāmₑ up the rōₐd. "hō, hō," they
> said. "look at that funny cow
> boy.[6] hē is trȳiñg to rIdₑ a cow."
>
> stop[7]

EXERCISE 14

Second reading—sentences and questions

a. You're going to read the story again. This time I'm going to ask questions.

b. Starting with the first word of the title. ✔ Get ready. (Tap as the children read the title.)

c. (Call on a child.) Read the first sentence.

┌─ **To Correct** ─────────────────────────
│ **word-identification errors (from, for example)**
│ 1. That word is **from.** What word? *From.*
│ 2. Go back to the beginning of the
│   sentence and read the sentence again.
└──────────────────────────────────────

d. (Call on another child.) Read the next sentence.

e. (Repeat *d* for most of the remaining sentences in the story.)

f. (Occasionally have the group read a sentence.)

g. (After each underlined sentence has been read, present each comprehension question specified below to the entire group.)

[1] What's this story going to be about? (Signal.) *The cow boy and the cow.*
What do cow boys usually ride on? (Signal.) *Horses.*

[2] Why was this cow boy sad? (Signal.) *He did not have a horse.*

[3] What did the cow say? (Signal.) *But I can run as fast as a horse.*

[4] Do you think the cow can really jump better than a horse? (The children respond.)

- We'll see.

[5] Is the cow boy going to give the cow a try? (Signal.) *Yes.*

[6] Why did the other cow boys make fun of him? (The children respond.)

[7] Is this the end of the story? (Signal.) *No.*

- Next time we'll read more about the cow boy and the cow.

Teaching Techniques

Use the following procedure to conduct the reading:

1. Direct students to touch under each word by saying, "First word" or "Next word."

2. Pause two seconds. This pause gives students time to examine the word.

3. Say, "Get ready."

4. Pause for one second.

5. Tap your hand as students read the word in unison.

Comprehension questions are cued by superscript numbers in your copy of the story. When students read up to a number, you present the question(s) for that number. Sentences that end with superscript numbers are always underlined. (The student version of the story does not contain any superscript numbers or underlines.)

Students should be looking at you when you present the questions, but they should continue to touch the current word in the story. For questions that require precise answers, you will need to use a *hand-drop signal,* as follows:

1. Hold out one hand as if you were stopping traffic.

2. Present the question.

3. Pause for one second.

4. Quickly drop your hand. Your hand-drop acts as a signal.

5. Listen carefully to students' answers and correct any mistakes.

Some comprehension questions are open-ended and do not require precise answers. You simply present these questions to individual students and accept all reasonable answers.

Corrections

Students will make two basic types of mistakes during the group reading: word-identification errors and comprehension errors. To correct word-identification errors, follow the procedure specified in Exercise 14.

1. *Model* the correct answer by saying the word.
2. *Test* the student by having the student say the word.
3. *Retest* the student by having the student reread the sentence.

Comprehension errors tend to fall into two groups. For some questions, students will give the right answer but will word it incorrectly. For other questions, students will simply give the wrong answer.

When students do not word the answer correctly, use the following procedure:

1. *Model* the correct answer by saying the answer correctly.
2. *Test* students by having them say the answer correctly.
3. *Retest* students by repeating the question.

If a comprehension question is clearly answered by a sentence in the story, use the following procedure:

1. Demonstrate a *process* for answering the question by rereading the appropriate sentence.
2. *Test* students by repeating the question.
3. *Retest* students by repeating the question again at a later time in the lesson.

If the question is not clearly answered by a sentence in the story, use the following procedure:

1. *Model* the correct answer by saying the correct answer.
2. *Test* students by having them say the correct answer.
3. *Test* students again by repeating the question.
4. *Retest* students by repeating the question at a later time in the lesson.

Practice Script 8

The following story-reading script appears in Lesson 95 of Grade 1. The script shows the second of two basic story-reading procedures used in *Reading Mastery*. (Practice Script 7 shows the first procedure.)

The second procedure is used in the second half of Grade 1 and in Grades 2–5. Stories in these lessons appear in traditional font, not the special font used in Grade K and the first half of Grade 1.

Instead of reading aloud and in unison, individual students take turns reading all or part of the story aloud, while staying within a decoding error limit.

Description

In steps a–d, you have students open to the story and remind them that if they make no more than five decoding errors by the time they reach the circled 5, they can read the rest of the story. (If students make more than five decoding errors before reaching the circled 5, they have to reread the first part until they can stay within the error limit.)

In steps e–g, individual students take turns reading the story. (The story appears on the next page.)

Once students read the first part of the story within the decoding error limit, you reread the first part aloud and ask comprehension questions. Then students read the rest of the story as you ask more comprehension questions.

The comprehension questions are cued by superscript numbers in your copy of the story. When students read up to a number, you present the question(s) for that number. Sentences that contain numbers are always underlined. (The student version of the story does not contain any superscript numbers or underlines.)

STORY 95
EXERCISE 5

Reading—decoding

a. (Pass out Storybook 2.)

b. Everybody, open your reader to page 34.

c. Remember, if the group reads all the way to the red 5 without making more than five errors, we can go on.

d. Everybody, touch the title of the story. ✔

e. If you hear a mistake, raise your hand. Remember, children who do not have their place lose their turn. (Call on individual children to read two or three sentences. Do not ask comprehension questions. Tally all errors.)

To Correct

word-identification errors (**from,** for example)
1. That word is **from.** What word? *From.*
2. Go back to the beginning of the sentence and read the sentence again.

f. (If the children make more than five errors before they reach the red 5: when they reach the 5 return to the beginning of the story and have the children reread to the 5. Do not ask comprehension questions. Repeat step *f* until firm, and then go on to step *g*.)

g. (When the children read to the red 5 without making more than five errors: read the story to the children from the beginning to the 5. Ask the specified comprehension questions. When you reach the 5, call on individual children to continue reading the story. Have each child read two or three sentences.

Ask the specified comprehension questions.)

Dan the Teacher[1]

A girl named Ann had a dog. The dog was named Dan.[2] One day Dan went to school with Ann.

The teacher said, "Ann, take that dog out of this school.[3] Schools are for boys and girls. Schools are not for dogs."

Ann said, "But this dog is very smart. He likes to read and he likes to add."[4]

The teacher said, "I will let that dog stay, but if he makes a sound, I will make him leave."

So the dog sat down to read a book to himself. The boys and girls worked with the teacher.

But then the teacher was called out of the room.

One boy said, "We do not have a teacher ★ now."[5]

Dan walked up and said, "I will be your teacher."

So he began to teach.[6] He was one of the best teachers the boys and girls had ever seen. ⑤He helped the children read a very hard book. And he helped them spell hard words.[7]

At the end of the day, some of the children went up to the dog and gave him a big kiss. They said, "We hope that Dan will be our teacher from now on."[8]

More to come

[1] What's the title of this story? (Signal.)
Dan the teacher.
[2] What was the name of the girl? (Signal.)
Ann.
• What was the name of the dog? (Signal.)
Dan.
[3] What did the teacher say? (Signal.)
Ann, take that dog out of this school.
[4] What does Dan like to do? (Signal.)
Read and add.
[5] What did the boy say? (Signal.)
We do not have a teacher now.
• Why didn't they have a teacher?
(The children respond.)
• Yes, the teacher was called out of the room.
[6] Who began to teach? (Signal.) *Dan the dog.*
[7] What did he help them do? (Signal.)
Spell hard words.
• What else? *Read a very hard book.*
[8] Do you think Dan will keep on being their teacher? (The children respond.)
• Next time we'll find out.

Teaching Techniques

Students should follow along with their finger or a marker as you read. Encourage students to look up when you ask a question but to "keep their place" with their finger or marker.

One of your major goals in reading the story to students is to model inflection, appropriate responses to story content, *and* rate. Adjust your rate so that you read to students a little faster—but only a little faster—than you expect them to read on their individual checkouts. (That time is specified in the checkouts.) A good way to know if you're reading at an appropriate rate is to watch students' fingers as they follow along. If their fingers are not in place, you're probably reading too fast. Never read to them as fast as you would if you were reading a story aloud during library time.

Corrections

Students will make two basic types of mistakes during the group reading: word-identification errors and comprehension errors. To correct **word-identification errors,** follow the same procedure specified in Practice Script 7.

1. *Model* the correct word.
2. *Test* the student by having the student say the word.
3. *Retest* the student by having the student reread the sentence.

To correct **comprehension errors** when students do not answer correctly, follow the same procedure specified in Practice Script 7.

1. *Model* the correct answer.
2. *Test* by having the student say the answer correctly.
3. *Retest* the student by repeating the question.

Corrections of other comprehension errors are handled in different ways for different levels of the program. Detailed descriptions of correction procedures appear in the Reading Presentation Books and Teacher's Guide for each level. In general, if the comprehension task involves a new skill or strategy, you should model a *process* for answering the question, as shown in Practice Script 7. If the comprehension task involves a familiar skill or strategy, you should use a *model-test-retest* procedure by either modeling the correct answer yourself or calling on a student to model the answer. For example:

1. *Model* the correct answer by calling on another student to give the correct answer.
2. *Test* the student who gave an incorrect answer by repeating the question.
3. *Retest* the student by repeating the question at a later time in the lesson.

The following story-reading script appears in Lesson 6 of Grade 4. Unlike practice scripts 7 and 8, this script is for a Story Background passage that precedes the main story for the lesson. Students take turns reading the passage, and there is no decoding error limit.

READING

EXERCISE 6

Story Background

1. Everybody, find part B. ✔
2. (Call on individual students to read two or three sentences each.)
3. (After students complete each section, ask the questions for that section.)

Today you will start reading a famous novel called *The Wonderful Wizard of Oz*. The version you will read is a little shorter than the original book, but the story remains the same.

The *Wonderful Wizard of Oz* begins in the state of Kansas more than a hundred years ago. At that time, people had almost none of the machines that we use today. They didn't have cars or televisions. They didn't have radios or CD players, computers or telephones. They used candles to light their houses, and they kept warm in the winter by building fires in their fireplaces.

- Name some things that people didn't have one hundred years ago. (Ideas: *Cars, televisions, radios, CD players, computers, telephones.*) (ND)
- What did people use to light their houses? (Ideas: *Candles, fires.*) (ND)
- How did people stay warm in the winter? (Idea: *By building fires.*) (ND)

The map on page 26 shows where Kansas is located. Kansas is a prairie, which is a flat grassland with almost no trees.

- Everybody, touch Kansas on the map. ✔
- Kansas is surrounded by four states.
- Which state borders Kansas on the north? (Response: *Nebraska.*) (VA)
- Which state borders Kansas on the south? (Response: *Oklahoma.*) (VA)
- Which state borders Kansas on the east? (Response: *Missouri.*) (VA)
- Which state borders Kansas on the west? (Response: *Colorado.*) (VA)
- What is a prairie? (Idea: *A flat grassland with few trees.*) (UCCM)
- If you lived on a prairie, would you have trouble building a wooden house? (Response: *Yes.*) (DI)
- Why? (Idea: *Because there are almost no trees.*) (DI)

More than a hundred years ago, many people moved to Kansas to become farmers. But life was hard for the early farmers in Kansas because the winters were cold and the summers were hot and dry. During the summer, the hot sun would turn the green grass gray, and the land would dry up and crack. The streams and ponds would also dry up, and the wind would blow great clouds of dust.

- What would the wind blow in the late summer? (Idea: *Great clouds of dust.*) (ND)
- Where would the dust come from? (Idea: *The dry land.*) (DI)

Comprehension Questions Abbreviations Guide

Access Prior Knowledge = (APK)   Author's Point of View = (APoV)   Author's Purpose = (AP)   Cause/Effect = (C/E)   Charts/Graphs/Diagrams/Visual Aids = (VA)

Classify and Categorize = (C+C)   Compare/Contrast = (C/C)   Determine Character Emotions, Motivation = (DCE)   Drawing Conclusions = (DC)   Drawing Inferences = (DI)

Fact and Opinion = (F/O)   Hypothesizing = (H)   Main Idea = (MI)   Making Connections = (MC)   Making Deductions = (MD)   Making Judgements = (MJ)

Narrative Elements = (NE)   Noting Details = (ND)   Predict = (P)   Reality/Fantasy = (R/F)   Recall Facts/Rules = (RF/R)   Retell = (R)   Sequence = (Seq)

Steps in a Process = (SP)   Story Structure = (SS)   Summarize = (Sum)   Understanding Dialogue = (UD)   Using Context to Confirm Meaning(s) = (UCCM)   Visualize = (V)

Description

In steps 1–3, students find the passage in their Textbooks and take turns reading it aloud. The sections that students read are reproduced in your Presentation Book. After students complete each section, you ask the comprehension questions for that section. (This arrangement is different from the *Presentation Books* for Grades K and 1, where questions are cued by superscript numbers in your copy of the story.)

Teaching Techniques

In this practice script, you present all the questions to individual students, so no signal is required. However, in other story-reading scripts for Grades 2–5, certain questions are presented to the entire group. Use a hand-drop signal for these questions. (The hand-drop signal is discussed in Practice Script 7.)

In Grade 4 and Grade 5, individual student answers to questions that require precise answers are preceded by the word "Response." Accept only the specified answer for these questions. For questions that do not require precise answers, possible answers are preceded by "Idea" or "Ideas." Accept any answers for these questions that express the same basic idea as the given answer(s).

Corrections

Students will make two basic types of mistakes during the group reading: word-identification errors and comprehension errors. To correct word-identification errors, follow the same procedure shown in Practice Script 7.

1. *Model* the correct word.
2. *Test* the student by having the student say the word.
3. *Retest* the student by having the student reread the sentence.

To correct comprehension errors when students do not word the answer correctly, follow the same procedure specified in Practice Script 7.

1. *Model* the correct answer.
2. *Test* by having the student say the answer correctly.
3. *Retest* the student by repeating the question.

Corrections for other comprehension errors are handled in different ways at different levels of the program. Detailed descriptions of correction procedures appear in the Presentation Books and Teacher's Guide for each level. In general, if the comprehension task involves a new skill or strategy, you should model a *process* for answering the question, as shown in Practice Script 7. If the comprehension task involves a familiar skill or strategy, you should use a *model-test-retest* procedure. For this procedure, you can either model the correct answer yourself or call on a student to model the answer. For example:

1. *Model* the correct answer by calling on another student to give the correct answer.
2. *Test* the student who gave an incorrect answer by repeating the question.
3. *Retest* the student by repeating the question at a later time in the lesson.

The following skill-exercise script appears in Lesson 49 of Grade 5. The script is for a Textbook skill exercise (metaphors) that appears after the story.

Description

Students take turns reading parts of the exercise aloud. After they complete each section, you present the questions specified in the Presentation Book. All the questions in this exercise are presented to individual students.

Teaching Techniques

Because all the questions are presented to individual students, no signals are used in this exercise. Call on a different student to answer each question. Lower-performing students should be called on more frequently so you can be sure they have mastered the skill.

Corrections

Use a *model-test-retest* procedure to correct mistakes.

D METAPHORS

Write the answers for items 1–6.

A metaphor is like a simile except it doesn't use the word *like*.

Here's an accurate statement: *The woman was very smart*. Here's a metaphor: *The woman was a walking encyclopedia.*
1. What two things are the same in that metaphor?
2. How could they be the same?
Here's another metaphor: *The man was a rattlesnake.*
3. What two things are the same in that metaphor?
4. How could they be the same?
Here's another metaphor: *Miss Minchin was a jailer.*
5. What two things are the same in that metaphor?
6. How could they be the same?

EXERCISE 3

Metaphors

1. Everybody, turn to part D at the end of today's story. ✔
- (Call on individual students to read several sentences each.)
- (At the end of each section, present the questions for that section.)

Write the answers for items 1–6.
A metaphor is like a simile except it doesn't use the word *like*.

- Name the kind of figurative language that is like a simile. (Response: *Metaphor.*)
- How is a metaphor different from a simile? (Idea: *It doesn't use the word like.*)

Here's an accurate statement: *The woman was very smart.* Here's a metaphor: *The woman was a walking encyclopedia.*
1. What two things are the same in that metaphor?

- What's the answer? (Response: *The woman, an encyclopedia.*)

2. How could they be the same?

- What's the answer? (Idea: *Both are full of information.*)

Here's another metaphor: *The man was a rattlesnake.*
3. What two things are the same in that metaphor?

- What's the answer? (Response: *The man, a rattlesnake.*)

4. How could they be the same?

- What's the answer? (Ideas: *Both are dangerous.*)
- You'll write the answers to the items later.

Scope and Sequence Chart

The following scope-and-sequence chart summarizes the skills taught in the Reading strands of *Reading Mastery Signature Edition.* The skills are divided into four principal areas: decoding skills, comprehension skills, literary skills, and study skills.

Decoding Skills

Reading Mastery uses a widely acclaimed phonics method that features step-by-step instruction for all decoding skills.

Phonemic Awareness (Decoding Readiness): Students learn blending, segmenting, rhyming, sequencing, and matching skills that prepare them for decoding.

Sound/Symbol Relationships (Sounds and Letters): Students learn letter sounds in a carefully programmed sequence. New letters are introduced every few lessons and then systematically reviewed.

Decoding and Word Recognition (Word Reading): Students learn how to sound out and read regularly spelled words and how to read irregularly spelled words.

Sentences and Stories: Students learn how to read sentences and stories. Individual fluency checkouts are used to monitor decoding rate and accuracy.

Comprehension Skills

Reading Mastery provides thorough instruction in reading comprehension. Oral questions, written questions, and skill exercises develop comprehension in five important areas.

Comprehension Readiness: Students learn how to follow directions and how to answer questions about pictures.

Vocabulary: Students learn how to identify word meanings and how to interpret definitions.

Literal Comprehension: Students learn how to understand the explicit meaning of a text.

Interpretive Comprehension: Students learn how to interpret the implicit meaning of a text.

Reasoning: Students learn how to analyze the underlying logic of a text.

Literary Skills

Reading Mastery stresses literary appreciation and interpretation. Students read a wide range of literature and carefully analyze content and style.

Characters and Settings: Students learn how to interpret complex characters and settings.

Literary Devices: Students learn how to interpret figurative language and other elements of literary style.

Types of Literature: Students learn about various types of literature and read examples of each type.

Study Skills

Reading Mastery teaches the writing and reference skills that are necessary for effective studying.

Writing: Students gradually develop writing skills, first by copying words and stories, then by writing answers to questions, and finally by writing whole paragraphs, stories, and poems.

Reference: Students learn how to interpret various reference materials, such as maps, diagrams, time lines, and graphs.

Decoding Skills

	K	1	Tr	2	3	4	5
Phonemic Awareness							
pronouncing individual sounds	◆						
sequencing from left to right	◆						
blending sounds orally	◆						
identifying rhyming sounds	◆						
Sound/Symbol Relationships							
reading short vowels	◆	◆					
reading long vowels	◆	◆					
reading voiced consonants	◆	◆					
reading unvoiced consonants	◆	◆					
reading sound combinations	◆	◆	◆	◆			
identifying vowel names		◆					
identifying consonant names		◆					
identifying alphabetical order		◆		◆			
Decoding and Word Recognition							
reading regularly spelled words	◆	◆	◆	◆	◆	◆	◆
reading irregularly spelled words	◆	◆	◆	◆	◆	◆	◆
recognizing rhyming words	◆		◆	◆		◆	◆
recognizing inflected endings	◆		◆		◆	◆	
recognizing compound words		◆	◆	◆	◆	◆	
reading word lists for accuracy		◆	◆	◆	◆	◆	
spelling difficult words		◆	◆	◆	◆		
prefixes and suffixes	◆	◆	◆	◆	◆	◆	◆
Sentences and Stories							
reading aloud	◆	◆	◆	◆	◆	◆	◆
reading silently	◆	◆	◆	◆	◆	◆	◆
reading aloud for rate and accuracy	◆	◆	◆	◆	◆	◆	◆
identifying punctuation marks	◆				◆	◆	

Comprehension Skills

	K	1	Tr	2	3	4	5
Comprehension Readiness							
following oral directions	◆	◆	◆	◆	◆	◆	◆
answering questions about pictures	◆	◆	◆	◆	◆	◆	◆
associating pictures with words	◆						
drawing pictures based on a story	◆						
repeating sentences	◆			◆	◆		
Vocabulary							
identifying the meanings of common words	◆	◆	◆	◆	◆	◆	◆
writing the names of pictured objects	◆	◆	◆				
comprehending vocabulary definitions				◆	◆	◆	◆
using vocabulary words in context				◆	◆	◆	◆
identifying homonyms and homographs					◆	◆	
comprehending contractions				◆			
using context to predict word meaning						◆	◆
Literal Comprehension							
answering literal questions about a text	◆	◆	◆	◆	◆	◆	◆
identifying literal cause and effect	◆	◆	◆	◆	◆	◆	◆
recalling details and events	◆	◆	◆	◆	◆	◆	◆
following written directions	◆	◆	◆	◆	◆	◆	◆
memorizing facts and rules		◆	◆	◆	◆		
sequencing narrative events				◆	◆	◆	◆
Interpretive Comprehension							
predicting outcomes	◆	◆	◆	◆	◆	◆	◆
relating titles to story content	◆	◆	◆	◆	◆	◆	
inferring causes and effects		◆	◆	◆	◆	◆	◆
inferring story details and events		◆	◆	◆	◆	◆	◆
making comparisons				◆	◆	◆	◆
inferring story morals				◆		◆	
inferring the main idea				◆	◆	◆	◆
inferring details relevant to a main idea					◆	◆	◆
outlining						◆	◆
Reasoning							
using rules to classify objects		◆		◆	◆		
completing written deductions		◆		◆			
drawing conclusions				◆	◆	◆	◆
using rules to predict outcomes				◆	◆		
evaluating problems and solutions					◆	◆	◆
identifying relevant evidence					◆		◆
identifying contradictions							◆
identifying inferential questions							◆
identifying logical fallacies							◆

Literary Skills

	K	1	Tr	2	3	4	5
Character and Settings							
interpreting a character's feelings	◆	◆	◆	◆	◆	◆	◆
pretending to be a character	◆	◆		◆	◆	◆	◆
inferring a character's point of view	◆	◆	◆	◆	◆	◆	◆
interpreting a character's motives		◆	◆	◆	◆	◆	◆
predicting a character's action				◆	◆	◆	◆
identifying features of a setting				◆	◆	◆	◆
identifying a character's traits				◆	◆	◆	◆
Literary Devices							
interpreting figurative language							◆
interpreting extended dialogues							◆
interpreting substitute words							◆
interpreting shortened sentences							◆
interpreting combined sentences							◆
interpreting literary irony							◆
Types of Literature							
reading realistic fiction	◆	◆	◆	◆	◆	◆	◆
reading fantasy	◆	◆	◆	◆	◆	◆	◆
reading factual articles		◆	◆	◆	◆	◆	◆
distinguishing between realism and fantasy				◆		◆	
distinguishing between fact and fiction					◆	◆	
reading poetry				◆	◆	◆	◆
reading drama				◆	◆		◆
reading biographies						◆	◆

Study Skills

	K	1	Tr	2	3	4	5
Writing							
copying letters	◆	◆					
copying words	◆						
copying sentences	◆	◆	◆				
writing answers to questions		◆	◆	◆	◆	◆	◆
completing writing assignments				◆	◆	◆	◆
organizing information					◆	◆	◆
Reference Materials							
interpreting maps				◆	◆	◆	◆
interpreting standard measurements				◆	◆		
interpreting diagrams				◆	◆	◆	◆
interpreting time lines				◆	◆	◆	
filling out forms				◆			◆
using reference sources				◆	◆	◆	◆
interpreting glossaries				◆	◆	◆	
interpreting indexes				◆	◆	◆	
interpreting graphs				◆	◆		◆

Placement Tests

You can use the following tests to determine each student's initial placement in the Signature Edition of *Reading Mastery*. (Placement tests also appear in the Teacher's Guide for each level of the program.) There is a separate test for each grade. The Placement Test for Grade K can be used to determine if students should be placed in Fast Cycle, and the test for Grade 2 can be used to determine if students should be placed in Transition.

Ideally, placement testing should be conducted at the beginning of the school year. Begin placement testing by giving students in Grades K–5 the placement test that corresponds with their grade level.

Grade K Placement Test

The Placement Test for Grade K is administered to individual students. You present test items aloud and tally the student's correct answers on a score sheet. You should administer the test in a place that is somewhat removed from the other students, so they will not overhear the testing.

The test items use several typefaces.

- ■ **This blue type indicates what you say.**
- ■ **(This type in parentheses indicates what you do.)**
- ■ *This italic type shows the student's answers.*

Some test items require you to point to the large letters that appear in this book. For these items, hold the book so the student can see the letters.

The score sheet appears on the next page. Make one copy of the score sheet for each student. To use the score sheet, simply circle 1 point or 2 points for each item the student answers correctly.

Placement Guidelines

Use the table below to determine placement for each student.

Part 1 Points	Placement
0–14 points	Grade K, Lesson 1
15–18 points	Grade K, Lesson 11
19–20 points	Give Part 2
Part 2 Points	**Placement**
0–7 points	Grade K, Lesson 11
8–10 points	Accelerated Schedule or Fast Cycle, if possible (see page 20).

Grade K Placement Test Scoring Sheet

Student's Name _____ Date_____

Circle 1 point or 2 points if the student answers correctly.

Part 1

Task 1	step b	0	1 point
	step c	0	1 point
Task 2	step b	0	1 point
		0	1 point
		0	1 point
		0	1 point
		0	1 point
	step d	0	1 point
		0	1 point
		0	1 point
		0	1 point
		0	1 point
Task 3	step b	0	2 points
	step c	0	2 points
Task 4	step b	0	2 points
	step d	0	2 points

Total Points ☐

Number of Points	Start At:
0-14	*Reading Mastery,* Grade K, Lesson 1
15-18	*Reading Mastery,* Grade K, Lesson 11 (Circle the lesson)
19-20	Continue testing in part 2 (Check box) ☐

Part 2

Task 1	step a	0	2 points
	step b	0	2 points
Task 2	step b	0	1 point
		0	1 point
	step c	0	1 point
		0	1 point
	step d	0	1 point
		0	1 point

Total Points ☐

Number of Points	Start At:
0-7	*Reading Mastery,* Grade K, Lesson 11
8-10	If possible, should be placed in Fast Cycle.

Part 1

Task 1   Total possible: 2 points

(Circle 1 point on the scoring sheet for each correct response at *b* and *c*.)

This is an oral task. For step *c,* say the sound **d,** not the letter name.

- **a.** You're going to say some sounds.
- **b.** **(test item)** Say (pause) **rrr.** *rrr.*
- **c.** **(test item)** Now say (pause) **d.** *d.*

Task 2   Total possible: 10 points

(Circle 1 point on the scoring sheet for each correct response at *b*.)

- **a.** (Point to the sounds.) **These are sounds.** (Point to the boxed **m.**) **This sound is** (pause) **mmm. What sound?** (Touch **m.**) *mmm.*
- **b.** **(test items)** (Point to each unboxed sound in the column. For each sound, ask:) **Is this** (pause) **mmm?**

(Circle 1 point on the scoring sheet for each correct response at step *d*.)

- **c.** (Point to the boxed **a.**) **This sound is** (pause) **ăăă. What sound?** (Touch **a.**) *ăăă.*
- **d.** **(test items)** (Point to each unboxed sound in the column. For each sound, ask:) **Is this** (pause) **ăăă?**

Task 3 Total possible: 4 points

(Circle 2 points on the scoring sheet for each correct response at *b* and *c*.)

a. Let's play Say It Fast. Listen. **Ice** (pause) **box.** I can say it fast. **Icebox.**
b. **(test item)** Listen. **Foot** (pause) **ball.** (Pause.) Say it fast. *Football.* Yes, **football.**
c. **(test item)** Here's another word. Listen. (Pause.) **Nnnōōōzzz.** (Pause.) Say it fast. *Nose.* Yes, **nose.**

Task 4 Total possible: 4 points

(Circle 2 points on the scoring sheet for each correct response at *b* and *d*.)

(This is an oral task. Do not stop between the sounds when saying *zzzoooo* or *wwwēēē*.)

a. First I'll say a word slowly. Then you'll say that word slowly. I'll say (Pause) **zoo** slowly. Listen. (Pause.) **Zzzoooo.**
b. **(test item)** Your turn. Say (pause) **zzzoooo.** *Zzzoooo.*
   (A child scores 2 points if he or she says the correct sounds without stopping between the sounds.)
c. Now I'll say (pause) **wē** slowly. Listen. (pause.) **Wwwēēē.**
d. **(test item)** Your turn. Say (pause) **wwwēēē.** (A child scores 2 points if he or she says the correct sounds without stopping between the sounds.)

Add the number of points the child earned on part 1. Note: Administer part 2 **only** to children who made 19 or 20 points on part 1.

Part 2

Task 1 Total possible: 4 points

(Circle 2 points on the scoring sheet for each correct response at *a* and *b*.)

a. **(test item)** Point to the boxed **m.**) Let's see if you remember this sound. (Pause.) What sound? (Touch **m.**) *mmm.*
b. **(test item)** Point to the boxed **a.**) Let's see if you remember this sound. (Pause.) What sound? (Touch **a.**) *ăăă.*

Task 2 Total possible: 6 points

(Circle 1 point on the scoring sheet for each correct response at *b*, *c*, and *d*.)

a. I'll say a word slowly. Then I'll say it fast. Listen. (Pause.) **Mmmaaannn.** (Pause.) I can say it fast. **Man.**
b. **(test item)** Your turn. Say (pause) **iiinnn.** *iiinnn.* **(test item)** Say it fast. *In.*
c. **(test item)** Your turn. Say (pause) **aaat.** *Aaat.* **(test item)** Say it fast. *At.*
d. **(test item)** Your turn. Say (pause) **sssiiit.** *Sssiiit.* **(test item)** Say it fast. *Sit.*

End of Placement Test

Grade 1 Placement Test

In the Placement Test for Grade 1, each student reads a story aloud as you count the student's decoding errors.

Make one copy of the story on the next page. You should administer the test in a place that is somewhat removed from the other students, so they will not overhear the testing.

Use the following procedures to administer the placement test:

1. Give the student a copy of the story.
2. Point to the story and say, "I want you to read this story out loud. Take your time. Start with the title and read the story as well as you can."
3. Time the student and make one tally mark for each error. Use the following guidelines when tallying errors.
   - If the student misreads a word, tell the student the word and mark one error.
   - If the student reads a word incorrectly and then correctly, mark one error.
   - If the student sounds out a word instead of reading it normally, mark one error. (Note: Correct the student the first time the student sounds out a word. Ask the student, "What word is that?" If the student reads the word correctly, do not mark an error. If the student sounds out the word, mark an error. Do not correct the student on any subsequent sounding-outs.)
   - If the student does not identify a word within four seconds, tell the student the word and mark one error.
   - If the student skips a word, point to the word. If the student does not read the word correctly, mark one error.
   - If the student skips a line, point to the line. If the student does not read the line correctly, mark one error.

4. After two and a half minutes, stop the student. Count every word not read as an error. For example, if the student is eight words from the end of the passage at the end of the time limit, count eight errors.
5. Total the student's errors.

Placement Guidelines

Use the table below to determine placement for each student.

Number of Errors	Placement
9 or more errors	Grade K*
4–8 errors	Grade 1, Lesson 1
0–3 errors	Grade 1, Lesson 11

* To determine an appropriate placement for students who made 9 or more errors, give them the individual rate-and-accuracy fluency checkouts from Grade K. Start with the checkout for Lesson 140. If the student passes the checkout, place the student in Lesson 141. If the student does not pass the checkout, present the checkout for Lesson 130. Continue working backward until the student passes a checkout. Place the student in the lesson that follows the checkout lesson.

the cow on the rōad

lots of men went down the rōad in a littlᵉ car.

a cow was sitting on the rōad. sō the men ran to the cow. "wē will lift this cow," they said.

but the men did not lift the cow. "this cow is sō fat wē can not lift it."

the cow said, "I am not sō fat. I can lift mē." then the cow got in the car.

the men said, "now wē can not get in the car." sō the men sat on the rōad and the cow went hōmᵉ in the car.

the end

Grade 2 and Transition Placement Test

The Grade 2 and Transition Placement Test consists of two parts. In part 1, individual students read a passage aloud as you count decoding errors. Part 2 is a group test that you administer to selected students after all students have completed Part 1.

Instructions for Part 1

Make one copy of the Grade 2 and Transition Placement Test on the next page for each student, and fill in the student's name. Also make a blank copy of the test. Then follow these steps:

1. (Call the student to a corner of the room, where the test will be given.)

2. (Give the blank copy of the test to the student. Use the student's copy to mark decoding errors.)

Vocabulary Reading

■ (Teacher reference:)

1.	expert
2.	clinic
3.	interest
4.	changes
5.	themselves
6.	people
7.	difference
8.	mirror
9.	through
10.	practicing
11.	questions

3. (Point to the column of words at the top of the test. Tell the student:) Touch word 1. (Pause.) That word is **expert.**

4. (Repeat step 3 for words 2–11.)

5. (Say:) Your turn to read those words.

6. Word 1. What word? (Student reads word.)

7. (Repeat step 6 for words 2–11.)

Passage Reading

8. (Point to the passage in Part 1.)

9. (Tell the student:) You're going to read this passage out loud. I want you to read it as well as you can. Don't try to read it so fast that you make mistakes. But don't read it so slowly that it doesn't make any sense. You have three minutes to read the passage. Go.

10. (Time the student, and make one tally mark for each error. If the student takes more than three seconds on a word, say the word, count it as an error, and permit the student to continue reading. Also count each of the following as an error:)

   • misreading a word.

   • omitting a word ending, such as *s* or *ed*.

   • reading a word incorrectly and then correctly.

   • sounding out a word instead of reading it normally.

   • skipping a word.

   • skipping a line. (Immediately show the student the correct line.)

   (If the student does not finish the passage within the time limit, count every word not read as an error. For example, if the student is eight words from the end of the passage at the end of the time limit, count eight errors.)

11. (Collect the test sheet.)

Criteria for Part 1

■ Students who made 5 errors or less **and** read the passage in two minutes or less should proceed to Part 2.

■ Students who made fewer than 8 errors **or** took between 2:01 and 3:00 minutes to read the passage should not proceed to Part 2. These students should be placed in the Transition program. (See Placement Criteria table on page 92.)

■ Students who made 8 or more errors should be placed in Grade 1.

Name _____

Part 1

1. expert
2. clinic
3. interest
4. changes
5. themselves
6. people
7. difference
8. mirror
9. through
10. practicing
11. questions

Bill tried to say things that would interest other people. He asked questions and tried to get people to talk about themselves. He said things that were funny. He talked faster and louder. He tried to smile more when he talked. But all those changes made no difference. After Bill was through speaking, everybody else was sleeping.

One day, Bill was at home. He was practicing in front of the mirror. He smiled, moved around a lot, and talked to the mirror.

Just then the door bell rang. Bill opened the door and saw a woman who said, "I am an expert at making people sleep. I work for the Sleep More Clinic. We help people who have trouble sleeping. I hear that you can make people sleep, too."

"Yes," Bill said. "If I speak for a while, people will sleep."

"That is interesting," the sleep expert said. "Can you explain why people sleep?"

"Yes, I can," Bill said.

Part 2

1. What was the first name of the man in the story?

   _____

2. Underline 4 things he did to try to be more interesting.
   - frown more
   - smile more
   - whisper
   - ask questions
   - answer questions
   - talk louder
   - talk softer
   - talk faster
   - talk slower

3. His problem was that he
   - was old • had five dogs • put people to sleep

4. He practiced in front of
   - his wife • the mirror • the TV

5. Who came over when he was practicing?
   - a sleeper • a dog expert • a sleep expert

6. Name the place where she worked.

   _____

Instructions for Part 2

Present Part 2 to students who meet the criteria specified above. Part 2 is a group test and should be administered no more than two hours after students complete Part 1. Follow these steps:

1. (Assemble students.)

2. (Give each student his or her copy of the placement test.)

3. (Give the group these instructions:) Follow along as I read the passage you read earlier.

> **Bill tried to say things that would interest other people. He asked questions and tried to get people to talk about themselves. He said things that were funny. He talked faster and louder. He tried to smile more when he talked. But all those changes made no difference. After Bill was through speaking, everybody else was sleeping.**
>
> **One day, Bill was at home. He was practicing in front of the mirror. He smiled, moved around a lot, and talked to the mirror.**
>
> **Just then the door bell rang. Bill opened the door and saw a woman who said, "I am an expert at making people sleep. I work for the Sleep More Clinic. We help people who have trouble sleeping. I hear that you can make people sleep, too."**
>
> **"Yes," Bill said. "If I speak for a while, people will sleep."**
>
> **"That is interesting," the sleep expert said. "Can you explain why people sleep?"**
>
> **"Yes, I can," Bill said.**

4. (After reading the passage, say:) At the bottom of the page are questions about the passage. Read the questions to yourself. Write or underline the answers. You have three minutes to finish.

5. (Time the students. Collect the test sheets after three minutes.)

Answer Key for Part 2

1. Bill

2.
   • smile more
   • ask questions
   • talk louder
   • talk faster

3. • put people to sleep

4. • the mirror

5. • a sleep expert

6. Sleep More Clinic

Placement Guidelines

Use the table below to determine placement for each student.

Part 1 Errors	Part 1 Time	Part 2 Errors	Placement
8 or more errors	3 minutes or less	NA	Grade 1
0–8 errors	2–3 minutes	NA	Transition
6 or 7 errors	2 minutes or less	NA	Transition
0–5 errors	2 minutes or less	2 or more	Transition
0–5 errors	2 minutes or less	0 or 1	Grade 2 or Transition

The Grade 3 Placement Test consists of two parts. In Part 1, individual students read a passage aloud as you count decoding errors. (You should administer Part 1 in a place that is somewhat removed from the other students, so they will not overhear the testing.) Part 2 is a group test that you administer after all students have completed Part 1.

Instructions for Part 1

Make one copy of the Grade 3 Placement Test on the next page for each student, and fill in the student's name. Also make a blank copy of the test. Then follow these steps:

1. (Call the student to a corner of the room, where the test will be given.)

2. (Give the blank copy of the test to the student. Use the student's copy to mark decoding errors.)

■ (Teacher reference:)

> 1. California
> 2. Pacific
> 3. lifeboat
> 4. Japan
> 5. loudspeaker

3. (Point to the column of words at the top of the test. Tell the student:) Touch word 1. (Wait.) That word is **California.**

4. (Repeat step 3 for words 2–5.)

5. (Say:) Your turn to read those words.

6. Word 1. What word? (Student reads word.)

7. (Repeat step 6 for words 2–5.)

8. (Point to the passage in Part 1.)

9. (Tell the student:) You're going to read this passage out loud. I want you to read it as well as you can. Don't try to read it so fast that you make mistakes. But don't read it so slowly that it doesn't make any sense. You have two minutes to read the passage. Go.

10. (Time the student, and make one tally mark for each error. If the student takes more than three seconds on a word, say the word, count it as an error, and permit the student to continue reading. Also count each of the following as an error:)

- misreading a word.
- omitting a word ending, such as *s* or *ed.*
- reading a word incorrectly and then correctly.
- sounding out a word instead of reading it normally.
- skipping a word.
- skipping a line. (Immediately show the student the correct line.)

(If the student does not finish the passage within the time limit, count every word not read as an error. For example, if the student is eight words from the end of the passage at the end of the time limit, count eight errors.)

11. (Collect the test sheet.)

Instructions for Part 2

Part 2 is a group test. After you've administered Part 1 to all students, present Part 2 to those students who made no more than 6 errors on Part 1. Follow these steps:

1. (Assemble students.)

2. (Give each student his or her copy of the placement test.)

3. (Make sure students have pencils.)

4. (Give the group these instructions:) These are questions about the passage that you read earlier. Write the answers. You have five minutes to finish.

5. (Collect the test sheets after five minutes.)

Answer Key for Part 2

1. Idea: *because the ship was on fire*
2. *Linda, Kathy*
3. *lifeboats*
4. *Linda*
5. *13*
6. *10*
7. *hand*
8. Idea: *in a lifeboat*
9. *Japan*
10. Idea: *to see their father*
11. *3 days*

Name _____

Part 1

"Fire! Fire!" a voice said over the loudspeaker. "The forward deck is on fire," the voice announced. "Everybody, leave the ship. Get into the lifeboats!"

Linda and her sister were on their way from the United States to Japan. Linda was thirteen years old, three years older than Kathy. Their father was in Japan, and they were on their way to visit him. Three days before, they had left California on a great ship called an ocean liner. They were now somewhere in the middle of the Pacific Ocean.

"Fire! Fire!" the voice shouted. "Everybody get into the lifeboats!"

People were running this way and that way on the deck of the ship. They were yelling and crying.

"Hold on to my hand," Linda said. The girls went to the lifeboats. People were all around them, shoving and yelling. People were not see much. She was afraid. Suddenly Linda could not see much. She was afraid. Suddenly she was no longer holding Kathy's hand.

Suddenly a strong pair of arms grabbed Linda. "In you go," a voice said. A big man picked Linda up and put her in the lifeboat.

"Where's my sister?" Linda asked. Linda looked but she couldn't see her younger sister.

1. California
2. Pacific
3. lifeboat
4. Japan
5. loudspeaker

Part 2

1. Why was everybody trying to leave the ship? _____

2. Name the two sisters that were on the ship. _____

3. People were trying to get into the _____.

4. Which sister was older? _____

5. How old was that girl? _____

6. How old was her sister? _____

7. Linda told Kathy, "Hold on to my _____."

8. When the big man picked up Linda, where did he put her? _____

9. What country were the girls going to? _____

10. Why were the girls going there? _____

11. How long had they been on the ship? _____

Placement Guidelines

Use the table below to determine placement for each student.

Number of Errors	Placement
7 or more errors on Part 1 **OR** 3 or more errors on Part 2	Grade 2 Placement Test
0–6 errors on Part 1 **AND** 0–2 errors on Part 2	Grade 3, Lesson 1

If you suspect that some students are too advanced for the program (students who score 0 or 1 on the placement test and who exhibit good comprehension skills), give them the placement test for Grade 4.

Grade 4 Placement Test

The Grade 4 Placement Test consists of two parts. In Part 1, individual students read a passage aloud as you count decoding errors. (You should administer Part 1 in a place that is somewhat removed from the other students, so they will not overhear the testing.) Part 2 is a group test that you administer after all students have completed Part 1.

Instructions for Part 1

Make one copy of the Grade 4 Placement Test on the next page for each student, and fill in the student's name. Also make a blank copy of the test. Then follow these steps:

1. (Call the student to a corner of the room, where the test will be given.)

2. (Give the blank copy of the test to the student. Use the student's copy to mark decoding errors.)

3. (Point to the passage and say:) You're going to read this passage out loud. I want you to read it as well as you can. Don't try to read it so fast that you make mistakes, but don't read it so slowly that it doesn't make any sense. You have two minutes to read the passage. Go.

4. (Time the student, and make one tally mark for each error. If the student takes more than three seconds on a word, say the word, count it as an error, and permit the student to continue reading. Also count each of the following as an error:)

   • Misreading a word.

   • Omitting a word ending, such as *s* or *ed*.

   • Reading a word incorrectly and then correctly.

   • Sounding out a word instead of reading it normally.

   • Skipping a word.

   • Skipping a line. (Immediately show the student the correct line.)

   (If the student does not finish the passage within the time limit, count every word not read as an error. For example, if the student is eight words from the end of the passage at the end of the time limit, count eight errors.)

5. (Collect the test sheet.)

Instructions for Part 2

After all students have finished Part 1, administer Part 2 to the entire group. Use the following procedure:

1. (Assemble students.)

2. (Give each student a copy of the test, and make sure students have pencils.)

3. (Say:) Here is the passage that you read earlier. Read the passage again silently; then answer the questions in Part 2. You have seven minutes. Go.

4. (Collect the test papers after seven minutes.)

5. (Total each student's errors, using the answer key.)

Answer Key for Part 2

1. Idea: *the Bermuda Islands*

2. Ideas: *to dive; to see the bottom of the ocean*

3. *warm*

4. *the guide*

5. Ideas: *partner; person*

6. Idea: *signal the guide*

7. Idea: *go to the surface of the water*

8. Idea: *The diver might get the bends.*

9. *pressure*

Placement Guidelines

Use the table below to determine placement for each student.

Number of Errors	Placement
7 or more errors on Part 1 **OR** 3 or more errors on Part 2	Grade 3 Placement Test
0–6 errors on Part 1 **AND** 0–2 errors on Part 2	Grade 4, Lesson 1
0–1 total errors	Grade 5 Placement Test

Grade 4 Placement Test

Name _____

Part 1

An Underwater World

The diving boat was anchored in a place where the water changed from light green to dark, dark blue. One by one, the divers went down the ladder on the side of the boat and entered the warm water. The boat was about 1,600 kilometers east of Florida. They were south of the Bermuda Islands. Darla was the last diver to go down the ladder and enter the warm water.

"Now stick together," the guide said as he floated with his mask tilted back on his forehead. "You've got your partners. Stay with your partner. If you see something you want to look at, signal me. If one person stops, we all stop or somebody's going to get lost."

The guide continued, "If you get separated, go to the surface of the water. Don't try to look for the rest of us. Just go to the surface. And remember, don't go up too fast. Take at least two minutes to go up, or you may get the bends."

The bends. Darla had read about the bends. She knew that a person gets them because of the great pressure of the water.

Part 2

1. Near which islands does this story take place?

   _____

2. Why was the group in this place?

   _____

3. Was the water warm or cold?

   _____

4. Who led the group?

   _____

5. Each diver was supposed to stay with a

   _____

6. What was a diver supposed to do if the diver wanted to stop to examine something?

   _____

7. What was a diver supposed to do if the diver got separated from the group?

   _____

8. What problem would the diver have if the diver went up to the surface too fast?

   _____

9. This problem was caused by the great

   _____ of the water.

Grade 5 Placement Test

The Grade 5 Placement Test consists of two parts. In Part 1, individual students read a passage aloud as you count decoding errors. (You should administer Part 1 in a place that is somewhat removed from the other students, so they will not overhear the testing.) Part 2 is a group test that you administer after all students have completed Part 1.

Instructions for Part 1

Make one copy of the Grade 5 Placement Test on the next page for each student, and fill in the student's name. Also make a blank copy of the test. Then follow these steps:

1. (Call the student to a corner of the room, where the test will be given.)

2. (Give the blank copy of the test to the student. Use the student's copy to mark decoding errors.)

3. (Point to the passage and say:) You're going to read this passage out loud. I want you to read it as well as you can. Don't try to read it so fast that you make mistakes, but don't read it so slowly that it doesn't make any sense. You have two minutes to read the passage. Go.

4. (Time the student, and make one tally mark for each error. If the student takes more than three seconds on a word, say the word, count it as an error, and permit the student to continue reading. Also count each of the following as an error:)

   • Misreading a word.

   • Omitting a word ending, such as *s* or *ed*.

   • Reading a word incorrectly and then correctly.

   • Sounding out a word instead of reading it normally.

   • Skipping a word.

   • Skipping a line. (Immediately show the student the correct line.)

   (If the student does not finish the passage within the time limit, count every word not read as an error. For example, if the student is eight words from the end of the passage at the end of the time limit, count eight errors.)

5. (Collect the test sheet.)

Instructions for Part 2

After all students have finished Part 1, administer Part 2 to the entire group. Use the following procedure:

1. (Assemble students.)

2. (Give each student a copy of the placement test.)

3. (Say:) Here is the passage that you read earlier. Read the passage again silently; then answer the questions in Part 2. You have seven minutes. Go.

4. (Collect the test papers after seven minutes.)

5. (Total each student's errors, using the answer key.)

Answer Key for Part 2

1. *a king*

2. *a princess*

3. Ideas: *his daughter; Marygold*

4. *gold*

5. Ideas: *his daughter; gold*

6. Idea: *They weren't gold.*

7. *roses*

8. *perfume*

9. Idea: *how much it would be worth if the roses were gold*

Placement Guidelines

Use the table below to determine placement for each student.

Number of Errors	Placement
7 or more errors on Part 1 OR 3 or more errors on Part 2	Grade 4 Placement Test
0–6 errors on Part 1 AND 0–2 errors on Part 2	Grade 5, Lesson 1

Grade 5 Placement Test

Part 1

The Golden Touch

Once upon a time in ancient Turkey there lived a rich king named Midas, who had a daughter named Marygold.

King Midas was very fond of gold. The only thing he loved more was his daughter. But the more Midas loved his daughter, the more he desired gold. He thought the best thing he could possibly do for his child would be to give her the largest pile of yellow, glistening coins that had ever been heaped together since the world began. So Midas gave all his thoughts and all his time to collecting gold.

When Midas gazed at the gold-tinted clouds of sunset, he wished they were real gold and that they could be herded into his strong box. When little Marygold ran to meet him with a bunch of buttercups and dandelions, he used to say, "Pooh, pooh, child. If these flowers were as golden as they look, they would be worth picking."

And yet, in his earlier days, before he had this insane desire for gold, Midas had shown a great love for flowers. He had planted a garden with the biggest and sweetest roses any person ever saw or smelled. These roses were still growing in the garden, as large, as lovely, and as fragrant as they were when Midas used to pass whole hours looking at them and inhaling their perfume. But now, if he looked at the flowers at all, it was only to calculate how much the garden would be worth if each of the rose petals was a thin plate of gold.

Part 2

1. *Circle the answer.* What kind of royal person was Midas?
   - an emperor
   - a king
   - a prince

2. *Circle the answer.* So his daughter was ▇▇▇.
   - an empress
   - a queen
   - a princess

3. What did Midas love most of all?

   _____

4. What did he love almost as much?

   _____

5. The more Midas loved _____,

   the more he desired _____.

6. Why did Midas think that dandelions were not worth picking?

   _____

7. What kind of flowers had Midas planted in his earlier days?

   _____

8. Midas used to inhale the _____ of those flowers.

9. What did Midas think about his garden now?

   _____

Sample Lessons

The following pages contain sample lessons from each level of *Reading Mastery,* including Transition. The lessons are reproduced in their entirety so you can practice the skills discussed in this Guide before presenting *Reading Mastery* to your students.

The following table shows the page on which each sample lesson begins.

Program	Lesson	Page
Grade K	108	100
Grade 1	76	109
Transition	6	119
Grade 2	71	130
Grade 3	21	143
Grade 4	76	155
Grade 5	57	166

Grade K—Lesson 108

The sample lesson for Grade K includes material from the following components:

- *Reading Presentation Book*
- *Storybook*
- *Workbook*
- *Spelling Presentation Book*

This sample lesson is basically the same as Lesson 54 of Fast Cycle. The lesson begins with sound-reading activities (exercises 1–6) in the Reading Presentation Book, followed by word-reading activities (exercises 7–19). Then students read the *Storybook* story aloud as you monitor their decoding and comprehension (exercises 20–23). Next you explain the Workbook tasks (exercises 24–29). As students complete their Workbooks independently, you administer rate and accuracy fluency checkouts to individual students (exercise 30). Sometime after the main lesson is over, you present activities from the *Spelling Presentation Book*.

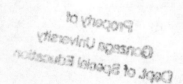

LESSON 108

SOUNDS

EXERCISE 1

Teaching **p** as in **pat**

a. (Point to **p.**) Here's a new sound. It's a quick sound.

b. My turn. (Pause. Touch **p** for an instant, saying:) **p.** (Do not say **puuh.**)

c. Again. (Touch **p** and say:) **p.**

d. (Point to **p.**) Your turn. When I touch it, you say it. (Pause.) Get ready. (Touch **p.**) *p.*

e. Again. (Touch **p.**) *p.*

f. (Repeat e until firm.)

EXERCISE 2

Individual test

(Call on individual children to identify **p.**)

EXERCISE 3

Sounds firm-up

a. Get ready to say the sounds when I touch them.

b. (Alternate touching **p** and **d.** Point to the sound. Pause one second. Say:) Get ready. (Touch the sound.) *The children respond.*

c. (When **p** and **d** are firm, alternate touching **p, g, d,** and **t** until all four sounds are firm.)

EXERCISE 4

Individual test

(Call on individual children to identify **p, g, d,** or **t.**)

EXERCISE 5

Sounds firm-up

a. (Point to **p.**) When I touch the sound, you say it.

b. (Pause.) Get ready. (Touch **p.**) *p.*

c. Again. (**Repeat b** until firm.)

d. Get ready to say all the sounds when I touch them.

e. (Alternate touching **k, v, u, ō, p, sh, h,** and **n** three or four times. Point to the sound. Pause one second. Say:) Get ready. (Touch the sound.) *The children respond.*

EXERCISE 6

Individual test

(Call on individual children to identify one or more sounds in exercise 5.)

108

READING VOCABULARY

EXERCISE 7

Children rhyme with **mop**

a. (Touch the ball for **mop.**) You're going to read this word the fast way. (Pause three seconds.) Get ready. (Move your finger quickly along the arrow.) *Mop.*

b. (Touch the ball for **cop.**) This word rhymes with (pause) **mop.** (Move to **c,** then quickly along the arrow.) *Cop.*
• Yes, what word? (Signal.) *Cop.*

c. (Touch the ball for **top.**) This word rhymes with (pause) **mop.** (Move to **t,** then quickly along the arrow.) *Top.*
• Yes, what word? (Signal.) *Top.*

EXERCISE 8

Children identify, then sound out an irregular word (was)

a. (Touch the ball for **was.**) Everybody, you're going to read this word the fast way. (Pause three seconds.) Get ready. (Move your finger quickly along the arrow.) *Was.* Yes, **was.**

b. Now you're going to sound out the word. Get ready. (Quickly touch **w, a, s** as the children say wwwaaasss.)

c. Again. (Repeat *b.*)

d. How do we say the word? (Signal.) *Was.* Yes, **was.**

e. (Repeat *b* and *d* until firm.)

EXERCISE 9

Individual test
(Call on individual children to do *b* and *d* in exercise 8.)

EXERCISE 10

Children read the fast way

(Touch the ball for **ōld.**) Get ready to read this word the fast way. (Pause three seconds.) Get ready. (Signal.) *Old.*

EXERCISE 11

Children read the words the fast way

(Have the children read the words on this page the fast way.)

EXERCISE 12

Individual test
(Call on individual children to read one word the fast way.)

108

EXERCISE 13

Children identify, then sound out an irregular word (**of**)

a. (Touch the ball for **of.**) Everybody, you're going to read this word the fast way. (Pause three seconds.) Get ready. (**Move your finger quickly along the arrow.**) *Of.* Yes, **of.**

b. Now you're going to sound out the word. Get ready. (Quickly touch **o, f** as the children say *ooofff.*)

c. Again. (Repeat *b.*)

d. How do we say the word? (Signal.) *Of.* Yes, **of.**

e. (Repeat *b* and *d* until firm.)

f. (Call on individual children to do *b* and *d.*)

EXERCISE 14

Children identify, then sound out an irregular word (**to**)

(Repeat the procedures in exercise 13 for **to.**)

EXERCISE 15

Children read the fast way

(Touch the ball for **that.**) Get ready to read this word the fast way. (Pause three seconds.) Get ready. (Signal.) *That.*

EXERCISE 16

Children sound out the word and tell what word

a. (Touch the ball for **cōat.**) Sound it out.

b. Get ready. (Touch **c, ō, t** as the children say *cōōōt.*)

• (If sounding out is not firm, repeat *b.*)

c. What word? (Signal.) *Coat.* Yes, **coat.**

EXERCISE 17

Children sound out the word and tell what word

a. (Touch the ball for **gōat.**) Sound it out.

b. Get ready. (Touch **g, ō, t** as the children say *gōōōt.*)

• (If sounding out is not firm, repeat *b.*)

c. What word? (Signal.) *Goat.* Yes, **goat.**

EXERCISE 18

Children read the words the fast way

(Have the children read the words on this page the fast way.)

EXERCISE 19

Individual test

(Call on individual children to read one word the fast way.)

of

to

that

cōₐt

gōₐt

STORYBOOK

STORY 108

EXERCISE 20

First reading—children read the story the fast way

(Have the children reread any sentences containing words that give them trouble. Keep a list of these words.)

a. (Pass out Storybook.)

b. Open your book to page 37 and get ready to read. ✔

c. We're going to read this story the fast way.

d. Touch the first word. ✔

e. Reading the fast way. First word. (Pause three seconds.) Get ready. (Tap.) *Thē.*

f. Next word. ✔
  • (Pause three seconds.) Get ready. (Tap.) *Old.*

g. (Repeat f for the remaining words in the first sentence. Pause at least three seconds between taps. The children are to identify each word without sounding it out.)

h. (Repeat d through g for the next two sentences. Have the children reread the first three sentences until firm.)

i. (The children are to read the remainder of the story the fast way, stopping at the end of each sentence.)

j. (After the first reading of the story, print on the board the words that the children missed more than one time. Have the children sound out each word one time and tell what word.)

k. (After the group's responses are firm, call on individual children to read the words.)

EXERCISE 21

Individual test

a. I'm going to call on individual children to read a whole sentence the fast way.

b. (Call on individual children to read a sentence. Do not tap for each word.)

EXERCISE 22

Second reading—children read the story the fast way and answer questions

a. You're going to read the story again the fast way and I'll ask questions.

b. First word. ✔
  • Get ready. (Tap.) *Thē.*

c. (Tap for each remaining word. Pause at least three seconds between taps. Pause longer before words that gave the children trouble during the first reading.)

d. (Ask the comprehension questions below as the children read.)

After the children read:	You ask:
The old goat had an old coat.	What did she have? (Signal.) *An old coat.*
The old goat said, "I will eat this old coat."	What did she say? (Signal.) *I will eat this old coat.*
So she did.	What did she do? (Signal.) *She ate the old coat.*
"That was fun," she said.	What did she say? (Signal.) *That was fun.*
"I ate the old coat."	What did the goat say? (Signal.) *I ate the old coat.*
"And now I am cold."	What did she say? (Signal.) *And now I am cold.*
Now the old goat is sad.	How does she feel? (Signal.) *Sad.* • Why? (Signal.) *The children respond.*

EXERCISE 23

Picture comprehension

a. What do you think you'll see in the picture? *The children respond.*

b. Turn the page and look at the picture.

c. (Ask these questions:)

1. How does that goat feel? *The children respond.*
  • Cold and sad.
2. Why is she out in the cold without a coat? *The children respond.*
  • Because she ate her coat.
3. Did you ever go outside without a coat when it was cold? *The children respond.*

WORKSHEET 108

SUMMARY OF INDEPENDENT ACTIVITY

EXERCISE 24

Introduction to independent activity

a. (Pass out Worksheet 108 to each child.)

b. Everybody, you're going to do this worksheet on your own. (Tell the children when they will work the items.)

• Let's go over the things you're going to do.

Sentence copying

a. (Hold up side 1 of your worksheet and point to the first line in the sentence-copying exercise.)

b. Everybody, here's the sentence you're going to write on the lines below.

c. Get ready to read the words in this sentence the fast way. First word. ✔

• Get ready. (Tap.) *Thē.*

d. Next word. ✔

• Get ready. (Tap.) *Goat.*

e. (Repeat *d* for the remaining words.)

f. After you finish your worksheet, you get to draw a picture about the sentence, **thē gōat āte thē cōat.**

Sound writing

a. (Point to the sound-writing exercise.) Here are the sounds you're going to write today. I'll touch the sounds. You say them.

b. (Touch each sound.) *The children respond.*

c. (Repeat the series until firm.)

Matching

a. (Point to the column of words in the Matching Game.)

b. Everybody, you're going to follow the lines and write these words.

c. Reading the fast way.

d. (Point to the first word. Pause.) Get ready. (Signal.) *The children respond.*

e. (Repeat *d* for the remaining words.)

f. (Repeat *d* and *e* until firm.)

Cross-out game

(Point to the boxed word in the Cross-out Game.) Everybody, here's the word you're going to cross out today. What word? (Signal.) *Not.* Yes, **not.**

Pair relations

a. (Point to the pair-relations exercise on side 2.) You're going to circle the picture in each box that shows what the words say.

b. (Point to the space at the top of the page.) After you finish, remember to draw a picture that shows **the gōat āte the cōat.**

★INDIVIDUAL CHECKOUT: STORYBOOK

EXERCISE 25

2½–minute individual fluency checkout: rate/accuracy—whole story

(Make a permanent chart for recording results of individual checkouts. See Teacher's Guide for sample chart.)

a. As you are doing your worksheet, I'll call on children one at a time to read the **whole story.** If you can read the whole story the fast way in less than two and a half minutes and if you make no more than three errors, I'll put two stars after your name on the chart for lesson 108.

b. If you make too many errors or don't read the story in less than two and a half minutes, you'll have to practice it and do it again. When you do read it in under two and a half minutes with no more than three errors, you'll get one star. Remember, two stars if you can do it the first time, one star if you do it the second or third time you try.

c. (Call on a child. Tell the child:) Read the whole story very carefully the fast way. Go. (Time the child. If the child makes a mistake, quickly tell the child the correct word and permit the child to continue reading. As soon as the child makes more than three errors or exceeds the time limit, tell the child to stop.) You'll have to read the story to yourself and try again later. (Plan to monitor the child's practice.)

d. (Record two stars for each child who reads appropriately. Congratulate those children.)

e. (Give children who do not earn two stars a chance to read the story again before the next lesson is presented. Award one star to each of those children who meet the rate and accuracy criterion.)

41 words/**2.5 min = 16 wpm [3 errors]**

END OF LESSON 108

STORY 108

38

STORY 108

thē ōld gōₐt had an ōld cōₐt.

thē ōld gōₐt said, "I will ēₐt this

ōld cōₐt." sō shē did.

"that was fun," shē said. "I āteₑ

thē ōld cōₐt. and now I am cōld."

now thē ōld gōₐt is sad.

37

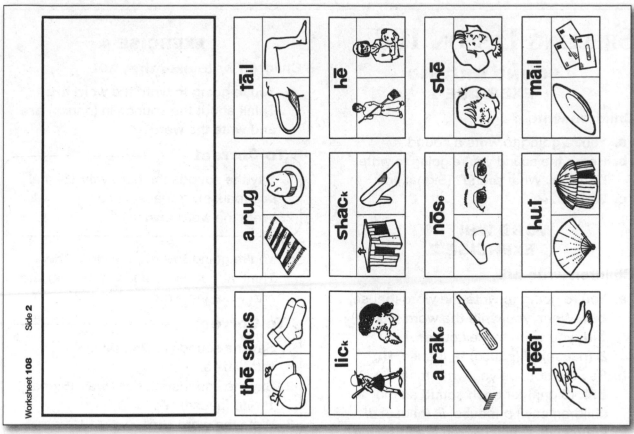

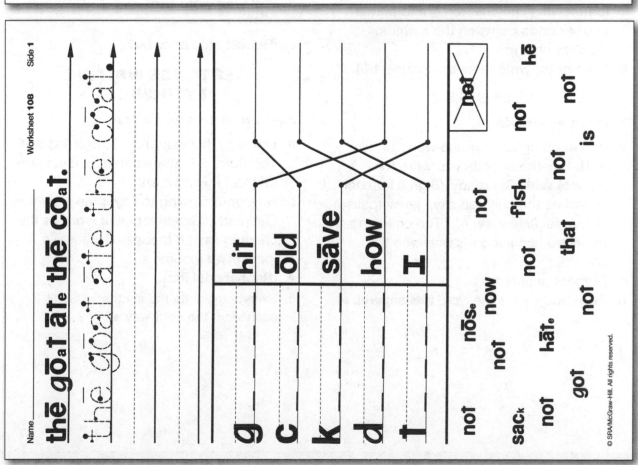

SPELLING LESSON 108

SOUND WRITING
EXERCISE 1

Children write **p**

a. You're going to write a sound.
b. Here's the sound you're going to write. Listen. **p.** What sound? (Signal.) *p.*
c. Write **p.** ✔

WORD WRITING
EXERCISE 2

Children write **bill**

a. You're going to write the word (pause) **bill.** When you write the word (pause) **bill,** you write these sounds. **B** (pause) **iii** (pause) **lll** (pause) **lll.**
b. Say the sounds you write for (pause) **bill.** (Signal for each sound as the children say:) *b* (pause) *iii* (pause) *lll* (pause) *lll.* (The children are to pause two seconds between the sounds.)
• (Repeat until firm.)
c. Everybody, write the word (pause) **bill.** ✔

EXERCISE 3

Children write **will**

a. You're going to write the word (pause) **will.** Say the sounds you write for (pause) **will.** Get ready. (Signal for each sound as the children say:) *www* (pause) *iii* (pause) *lll* (pause) *lll.* (The children are to pause two seconds between the sounds.)
• (Repeat until firm.)
b. Everybody, write the word (pause) **will.** ✔

EXERCISE 4

Children write **are, the, but**

a. You're going to write the word **are.** Think about the sounds in (pause) **are** and write the word. ✔

┌─ **To Correct** ──────────────────
1. Say the sounds the hard way. (Signal.) *aaa* (pause) *rrr* (pause) *ēēē.*
2. Write the word **are.** ✔
└──────────────────────────────────

b. You're going to write the word **thē.** Think about the sounds in (pause) **thē** and write the word. ✔

┌─ **To Correct** ──────────────────
1. Say the sounds in **thē.** (Signal.) *ththth ē ē ē.*
2. Say the sounds the hard way. (Signal.) *ththth* (pause) *ēēē.*
3. Write the word **thē.** ✔
└──────────────────────────────────

c. (Repeat step *b* for **but.**)

SENTENCE WRITING
EXERCISE 5

Children write a sentence

a. Listen to this sentence. **It is a fat ant.** Your turn. Say that sentence. Get ready. (Signal.) *It is a fat ant.*
b. Now you're going to say it the slow way. Get ready. (Signal for each word as the children say:) *It* (pause) *is* (pause) *a* (pause) *fat* (pause) *ant.*
• (Repeat until firm.)
c. Everybody, write the sentence. Spell each word the right way. ✔

67

Grade 1—Lesson 76

The sample lesson for Grade 1 includes material from the following components:

- *Reading Presentation Book*
- *Storybook*
- *Workbook*
- *Spelling Presentation Book*

This sample lesson is basically the same as Lesson 107 of Fast Cycle. The lesson begins with word-reading activities in the Reading Presentation Book (exercises 1–6). Then students read the Storybook story aloud as you monitor their decoding and comprehension (exercises 7–10). Next you explain the Workbook tasks (exercises 11–15), which students then complete independently. Sometime after the main lesson is over, you present activities from the *Spelling Presentation Book*.

LESSON 76

READING VOCABULARY

Do not touch small letters.

Get ready to read all the words on this page without making a mistake.

EXERCISE 1

Sound out first

best

a. (Touch the ball for **best.**) Sound it out. Get ready. (Quickly touch **b, e, s, t** as the children say:) *beeessst.*

b. What word? (Signal.) *Best.* Yes, **best.**

c. (Repeat exercise until firm.)

EXERCISE 2

ing words

ing

a. (Point to **ing.**) When these letters are together, they usually say **ing.** What do these letters usually say? (Signal.) *ing.* Yes, **ing.**
* (Repeat until firm.)

b. (Point to the words.) These are words you already know. See if you can read them when they look this way.

something

looking

rēading

d. (Point to **ing** in **something.**) What do these letters say? (Signal.) *ing.*

e. (Touch the ball for **something.**) Read the fast way. Get ready. (Signal.) *Something.* Yes, **something.**

f. (Repeat *d* and *e* for **looking** and **rēading.**)

g. (Repeat the series of words until firm.)

---

parts

EXERCISE 3

ar word

a. (Touch the ball for **parts.**) Read this word the fast way. (Pause two seconds.) Get ready. (Signal.) *Parts.* Yes, **parts.**

b. (Point to **ar** in **parts.**) Everybody, what do these letters say? (Signal.) *Are.* Yes, **are.**

c. (Touch the ball for **parts.**) Sound it out. Get ready. (Quickly touch **p, ar, t, s** as the children say:) *partsss.*

d. What word? (Signal.) *Parts.* Yes, **parts.**

e. (Repeat *c* and *d* until firm.)

kites

EXERCISE 4

Practice final-e rule

a. Read this word the fast way. Remember to look at the end of the word.

b. (Touch the ball for **kites.** Pause two seconds.) Get ready. (Signal.) *Kites.* Yes, **kites.**

c. (Touch the ball for **kites.**) Sound it out. Get ready. (Quickly touch **k, ī, t, s** as the children say:) *kīītsss.*

d. What word? (Signal.) *Kites.* Yes, **kites.**

e. (Repeat *b* through *d* until firm.)

(Repeat any troublesome words.)

Individual test

(Call on individual children. Each child reads a different word.)

76

Do not touch small letters.

Get ready to read all the words on this page without making a mistake.

EXERCISE 5

Read the fast way

a. Read these words the fast way.
b. (Touch the ball for **store**. Pause two seconds.) Get ready. (Signal.) *Store.* Yes, **store**.
c. (Repeat *b* for remaining words.)

how

home

store

from

pāper

what

make

began

when

makes

other

then

making

else

who

next

Individual test

(Call on individual children. Each child reads a different word.)

(Repeat any troublesome words.)

148 Lesson 76

STORYBOOK

STORY 76

EXERCISE 7

First reading—title and three sentences

a. (Pass out Storybook 1.)
b. Everybody, open your reader to page 200.
c. Everybody, touch the title of the story and get ready to read the words in the title.
d. First word. ✔
• Get ready. (Tap.) *Sam.*
e. (Tap for each remaining word in the title.)
f. Everybody, say the title. (Signal.)
Sam gets a kite kit.

76

Get ready to read all the words on this page without making a mistake.

EXERCISE 6

Long and short vowel words

a. Read these words the fast way. Remember to look at the end of the word.
b. (Touch the ball for **rode.** Pause two seconds.) Get ready. (Signal.) *Rode.* Yes, **rode.**
c. (Repeat b for **kite, sam, not, same, rod, note,** and **kit.**)

not

same

rod

note

kit

rode

kite

sam

Individual test

(Call on individual children to read a column of words from this lesson. If the column contains only one or two words, direct the child to read additional words from an adjacent column.)

76

g. Everybody, get ready to read this story. ✓

h. First word. ✓

• Get ready. (Tap.) *Sam.*

i. Next word. ✓

• Get ready. (Tap.) *Liked.*

j. (Repeat i for the remaining words in the first three sentences. Have the children reread the first three sentences until firm.)

EXERCISE 8

Remaining sentences

a. I'm going to call on individual children to read a sentence. Everybody, follow along and point to the words. If you hear a mistake, raise your hand.

b. (Call on a child.) Read the next sentence.

To Correct

word-identification errors (**from**, for example)

1. That word is **from**. What word? *From.*
2. Go back to the beginning of the sentence and read the sentence again.

c. (Call on another child.) Read the next sentence.

d. (Repeat c for most of the remaining sentences in the story.)

e. (Occasionally have the group read a sentence. When the group is to read, say:) Everybody, read the next sentence. (Tap for each word in the sentence.)

EXERCISE 9

Second reading—sentences and questions

a. You're going to read the story again. This time I'm going to ask questions.

b. Starting with the first word of the title. ✓

• Get ready. (Tap as the children read the title.)

150 Lesson 76

---

sam gets a kite kit[1]

sam liked to make things. he liked to make toy cars. so he went to the store and got a toy car kit.[2] his mom said, "that kit has the parts of a car. you have to rēad and fīnd out how to fit the parts so that they make a car."

sam said, "I will do that."

so sam began to rēad the pāper that came with the car kit.[3] then he began to fit the parts to make a car. soon he had a toy car.

his mom said, "that is a fīne car. you are good at rēading and at making things."[4]

sam did not like to make the same thing again. he said, "I will not make other cars. I will make something else."

so he went to the store and got a kite kit.[5] when he got home, he shōwed his mom the kite kit. his mom said, "that kit has a lot of parts in it. you will have to rēad the pāper that comes with the kit to fīnd out how to make the kite."[6]

---

c. (Call on a child.) Read the first sentence.

To Correct

word-identification errors (**from**, for example)

1. That word is **from**. What word? *From.*
2. Go back to the beginning of the sentence and read the sentence again.

d. (Call on another child.) Read the next sentence.

e. (Repeat d for most of the remaining sentences in the story.)

f. (Occasionally have the group read a sentence.)

g. (After each underlined sentence has been read, present each comprehension question specified below to the entire group.)

1
• What will Sam get? (Signal.) *A kite kit.*
• What is a kite kit? (The children respond.)
• Yes, in a kite kit you get all the parts to build a kite.

2
• What kind of kit did he get? (Signal.) *A toy car kit.*
• What is he going to make? (Signal.) *A toy car.*

3
• Why does he have to read the paper? (The children respond.)
• Right, the paper tells him how to make the car.

4
• Everybody, say that. (Signal.) *You are good at reading and at making things.*

5
• What did he get this time? (Signal.) *A kite kit.*

6
• Why does he have to read the paper? (The children respond.)
• Right, the paper tells him how to make the kite.

WORKSHEET 76

SUMMARY OF INDEPENDENT ACTIVITY

EXERCISE 11

Introduction to independent activity

a. (Pass out Worksheet 76 to each child.)

b. (Hold up side 1 of your worksheet.) Everybody, you're going to do this worksheet on your own. (Tell the children when they will work the items.)

• Let's go over the things you're going to do.

Story items

(Point to the story-items exercise.) Everybody, remember to write your answers in the blanks.

Following instructions

a. (Touch the sentence in the box.)

b. Everybody, first you're going to read the sentence in the box. Then you're going to read the instructions below the box and do what the instructions tell you to do.

Story-picture items

(Point to the story-picture items on side 2.) Remember to follow these instructions and look at the picture when you work these items.

Reading comprehension

(Point to the story.) You're going to read this story and then do the items. Remember to write the answers in the blanks.

END OF LESSON 76

EXERCISE 10

Picture comprehension

a. Look at the picture.

b. (Ask these questions:)

1. (Point to the toy car.) Who made that car? (Signal.) *Sam.*

2. Why did Sam make that car? (Signal.) *He likes to make things.*

3. (Point to the kite parts.) What is that stuff on the floor? (The children respond.) *Yes, those are the kite parts.*

4. Can you see a paper telling Sam how to make the kite? (Signal.) *No.*

• Why not? (The children respond.)

• Right, the paper is missing.

• I hope he can put all those parts together.

76

> sam looked inside the kit. then he said, "what pāper? there is no pāper in this kit."[7]
>
> sam's mom said, "that is too bad. how will you make the kite if there is no pāper in the kit?"
>
> sam said, "I will go back to the store and get a pāper that tells how to make a kite from these parts."
>
> when sam got to the store, the man in the store said, "I dŏn't have other pāpers that tell how to make kites."
>
> sam asked, "how can I make a kite if I dŏn't have the pāper?"[8]
>
> the man said, "you will have to do the best you can."[9]
>
> sam was not happy. he went home and looked at all the parts in the kite kit.
>
> more to come[10]

[7] Was there a paper in the kit? (Signal.) *No.*

• I wonder how he'll make the kite without that paper. (The children respond.)

• Let's read and find out.

[8] Everybody, say that question. (Signal.) *How can I make a kite if I don't have the paper?*

[9] Everybody, say the man's answer. (Signal.) *You will have to do the best you can.*

[10] We'll read more next time.

sam gets a kite kit

sam liked to make things. he liked to make toy cars. so he went to the store and got a toy car kit. his mom said, "that kit has the parts of a car. you have to rēad and fīnd out how to fit the parts so that they make a car."

sam said, "I will do that."

so sam began to rēad the pāper that came with the car kit. then he began to fit the parts to make a car. soon he had a toy car.

his mom said, "that is a fīne car. you are good at rēading and at making things."

sam did not like to make the same thing again. he said, "I will

not make other cars. I will make something else."

so he went to the store and got a kite kit. when he got home, he shōwed his mom the kite kit. his mom said, "that kit has a lot of parts in it. you will have to rēad the pāper that comes with the kit to fīnd out how to make the kite."

sam looked inside the kit. then he said, "what pāper? there is no pāper in this kit."

sam's mom said, "that is too bad. how will you make the kite if there is no pāper in the kit?"

sam said, "I will go back to the store and get a pāper that tells how to make a kite from these parts."

STORY 76

203

STORY 76

When sam got to the store, the man in the store said, "I dōn't have other pāpers that tell how to make kites."

sam asked, "how can I make a kite if I dōn't have the pāper?"

the man said, "you will have to do the best you can."

sam was not happy. he went home and looked at all the parts in the kite kit.

more to come

202

Worksheet 76   Side 2

look at the picture on page 203 of your reader.

1. is sam reading a paper? _____

2. do you see sam's toy car? _____

bob got a kit for making a toy duck. the kit had a lot of parts. bob worked hard. at last, he said, "that duck looks real." the duck ate a hole in the wall. then he ate some grass. the duck went to the pond and swam away.

1. who got a kit for making a toy duck? _____

2. the duck ate a hole in the _____.

3. then he ate some _____.

4. where did he go for a swim? _____

Name _____   Worksheet 76   Side 1

1. who made a toy car from a car kit? _____

2. who said, "you are good at reading and at making things"? his _____

3. what kit did sam get after he made a car? a
   • car kit   • cat kit   • kite kit   • log kit

4. what was missing from the kit? a
   • paper   • kite part   • car part   • kit

5. where did sam go to get a paper? _____
   • to the lake   • to the store
   • because he needed it   • told him

6. did the man at the store have another paper? _____

tim went to the park.

1. circle the word that tells who went to the park.

2. make a line over the words that tell where tim went.

3. make a line over the circle.

LESSON 76

WORD WRITING
EXERCISE 1

Say the sounds, write **her, win, said, where, has**

a. You're going to write the word (pause) **her.** Say the sounds in **her.** Get ready. (Tap for each sound as the children say:) *h* (pause) *er.*
- (Repeat until firm.)
b. Everybody, write the word (pause) **her.** ✔
c. (Repeat steps *a* and *b* for **win, said, where,** and **has.**)

EXERCISE 2

Write **bark, stop, ever, sing, of, dish**

a. You're going to write the word (pause) **bark.** Think about the sounds in **bark** and write the word. ✔
b. (Repeat step *a* for **stop, ever, sing, of,** and **dish.**)

SENTENCE WRITING
EXERCISE 3

Write three sentences

a. Listen to this sentence. **That man went with him.** Say that sentence. Get ready. (Signal.) *That man went with him.*
b. Now you're going to say that sentence the slow way. Get ready. (Signal for each word as the children say:) *That* (pause) *man* (pause) *went* (pause) *with* (pause) *him.*
c. Everybody, write the sentence. Spell each word the right way. ✔
d. (Repeat steps *a–c* for **The men are in the barn** and **He has a ball.**)

50

Transition—Lesson 6

The sample lesson for Transition includes material from the following components:

- *Presentation Book*
- *Textbook*
- *Workbook*

The lesson begins with word-reading activities in the Presentation Book (exercises 1–6). Then students read the Storybook story aloud as you monitor their decoding and comprehension (exercises 7 and 8). Next you explain the Workbook tasks (exercise 9), which students then complete independently.

Textbook

EXERCISE 1

Reading Words

a. Open your textbook to lesson 6. Find the letter **L.** ✔
- (Teacher reference:)

1. <u>sound</u>ed	4. <u>valley</u>s
2. <u>follow</u>ing	5. <u>any</u>where
3. <u>mountain</u>s	6. <u>paint</u>ing

- You'll tell me the underlined part of each word and then tell me the whole word.
b. Word 1. What's the underlined part? (Signal.) *sound.*
- What's the whole word? (Signal.) *Sounded.*
c. Word 2. What's the underlined part? (Signal.) *follow.*
- What's the whole word? (Signal.) *Following.*
d. Word 3. What's the underlined part? (Signal.) *mountain.*
- What's the whole word? (Signal.) *Mountains.*
e. Word 4. What's the underlined part? (Signal.) *valley.*
- What's the whole word? (Signal.) *Valleys.*
f. Word 5. What's the underlined part? (Signal.) *any.*
- What's the whole word? (Signal.) *Anywhere.*
g. Word 6. What's the underlined part? (Signal.) *paint.*
- What's the whole word? (Signal.) *Painting.*
h. Let's read those words again the fast way.
- Word 1. What word? (Signal.) *Sounded.*
- (Repeat for remaining words: **following, mountains, valleys, anywhere, painting.**)

EXERCISE 2

Reading Words

a. Find the letter **A.** ✔
- (Teacher reference:)

1. phone	4. lovely
2. of course	5. robot
3. moving	

b. Word 1 is **phone.** What word? (Signal.) *Phone.*
Yes, answer the **phone.**
- **Phone** has a very strange spelling. Spell word 1. Get ready. (Tap 5 times.) *P-H-O-N-E.*
- What word? (Signal.) *Phone.*
c. The words for number 2 are **of course.** What words? (Signal.) *Of course.*
Of course, you know that.
- Spell **of.** Get ready. (Tap 2 times.) *O-F.*
- Spell **course.** Get ready. (Tap 6 times.) *C-O-U-R-S-E.*
- What words did you spell? (Signal.) *Of course.*
d. Spell word 3. Get ready. (Tap 6 times.) *M-O-V-I-N-G.*
- What word? (Signal.) *Moving.*
e. Spell word 4. Get ready. (Tap 6 times.) *L-O-V-E-L-Y.*
- What word? (Signal.) *Lovely.*
f. Spell word 5. Get ready. (Tap 5 times.) *R-O-B-O-T.*
- What word? (Signal.) *Robot.*
Yes, a **robot** is a machine that can do some of the things a human can do.
g. Let's read those words again the fast way.
- Word 1. What word? (Signal.) *Phone.*
- Number 2. What words? (Signal.) *Of course.*
- Word 3. What word? (Signal.) *Moving.*
- Word 4. What word? (Signal.) *Lovely.*
- Word 5. What word? (Signal.) *Robot.*

EXERCISE 3

Reading Words

Words with O-I

a. Find the letter **M.** ✔
- (Teacher reference:)

1. p<u>oi</u>nt	3. b<u>oi</u>l
2. v<u>oi</u>ce	

b. You'll spell each word and then tell me the word.
c. Spell word 1. Get ready. (Tap 5 times.) *P-O-I-N-T.*
- What word? (Signal.) *Point.*
d. Spell word 2. Get ready. (Tap 5 times.) *V-O-I-C-E.*
- What word? (Signal.) *Voice.*
e. Spell word 3. Get ready. (Tap 4 times.) *B-O-I-L.*
- What word? (Signal.) *Boil.*
f. Let's read those words again the fast way.
- Word 1. What word? (Signal.) *Point.*
- (Repeat for remaining words: **voice, boil.**)

EXERCISE 4

Reading Words

a. Find the letter **R.** ✔
- (Teacher reference:)

1. spoke	4. together
2. wash	5. merry
3. awful	6. music

b. Word 1 is **spoke.** What word? (Signal.) *Spoke.*
Yes, she **spoke** in a very low voice.
c. Word 2 is **wash.** What word? (Signal.) *Wash.*
Yes, **wash** your hands and face.
d. Word 3 is **awful.** What word? (Signal.) *Awful.*
e. Word 4 is **together.** What word? (Signal.) *Together.*
f. Word 5 is **merry.** What word? (Signal.) *Merry.*
g. Word 6 is **music.** What word? (Signal.) *Music.*

h. Let's read those words again the fast way.
- Word 1. What word? (Signal.) *Spoke.*
- (Repeat for remaining words: **wash, awful, together, merry, music.**)

EXERCISE 5

Reading Words

Rhyming Words

a. Find the letter **S.** ✔
- (Teacher reference:)

1. sneak	4. gray
2. speak	5. nice
3. ray	6. mice

- These words are in rhyming pairs.
b. Spell word 1. Get ready. (Tap 5 times.) *S-N-E-A-K.*
- What word? (Signal.) *Sneak.*
c. Word 2 rhymes with **sneak.** What word? (Signal.) *Speak.*
d. Spell word 3. Get ready. (Tap 3 times.) *R-A-Y.*
- What word? (Signal.) *Ray.*
e. Word 4 rhymes with **ray.** What word? (Signal.) *Gray.*
Yes, the sky was **gray.**
f. Spell word 5. Get ready. (Tap 4 times.) *N-I-C-E.*
- What word? (Signal.) *Nice.*
g. Word 6 rhymes with **nice.** What word? (Signal.) *Mice.*
h. Let's read those words again the fast way.
- Word 1. What word? (Signal.) *Sneak.*
- (Repeat for remaining words: **speak, ray, gray, nice, mice.**)

EXERCISE 6

Reading Words

a. Find the letter **P.** ✔
- (Teacher reference:)

1. sl<u>i</u>ces	3. perfect
2. people	4. toaster

- These are new words. You'll spell each word and then tell me the word.

b. Spell word 1. Get ready. (Tap 6 times.)
S-L-I-C-E-S.
- What word? (Signal.) *Slices.*
Yes, **slices** of bread.

c. Spell word 2. Get ready. (Tap 6 times.)
P-E-O-P-L-E.
- What word? (Signal.) *People.*
Yes, there were lots of **people** at the store.

d. Spell word 3. Get ready. (Tap 7 times.)
P-E-R-F-E-C-T.
Yes, she was a **perfect** reader.

e. Spell word 4. Get ready. (Tap 7 times.)
T-O-A-S-T-E-R.
- What word? (Signal.) *Toaster.*
Put bread in the **toaster.**

f. Let's read those words again the fast way.
- Word 1. What word? (Signal.) *Slices.*
- (Repeat for remaining words: **people, perfect, toaster.**)

Individual Turns

```
1. sounded
2. following
3. mountains
4. valleys
5. anywhere
6. painting

1. phone
2. of course
3. moving
4. lovely
5. robot

1. point
2. voice
3. boil

1. spoke
2. wash
3. awful
4. together
5. merry
6. music

1. sneak
2. speak
3. ray
4. gray
5. nice
6. mice

1. slices
2. people
3. perfect
4. toaster
```

- (Call on individual students to read one or two of the words on the page.)

EXERCISE 7

Story Reading

a. (Write on the board:)

> **six**

- Everybody, tell me how many reading mistakes for this story. (Signal.) *Six.*

b. Find the story. ✔
- You'll read the title of the story. Get ready. (Tap for each word.) *Rolla . . . Slows . . . Down.*
- What happens in this story? (Call on a student. Idea: *Rolla slows down.*)

c. (Call on individual students to read one or two sentences each.)

Rolla was very happy. She was horse number 1 on a merry-go-round. She went up and down with the music. The children were happy, and their mothers were happy.

Things went on like this for weeks. But then one day, something happened. Rolla said to herself, "I am number 1, but I am right behind number 8." Rolla thought that she should be far away from number 8. Then it would look as if she was the leader and the other horses were following her.

Rolla said, "I will get far from horse 8." To do that, Rolla slowed down. She went slower, and slower, and slower. But of course her plan didn't work. When she went slower, all the other horses went slower. The music slowed down and sounded awful. The mothers were unhappy. One of them said, "This merry-go-round is so slow you can't tell if it's going or if it has stopped."

d. Next page. ✔

The other horses were not happy with Rolla. Horse 2 kept shouting at Rolla, "Come on, Rolla. Let's get this merry-go-round moving." But Rolla tried as hard as she could to slow down.

At the end of the day, horse 8 was still there, right in front of her.

That evening, horse number 3 asked, "What are you trying to do?"

When Rolla told them, some of the horses started to laugh. Then horse number 5 said, "Rolla, would you be happy if you could not see horse 8?"

"Yes," Rolla said. "If I could not see that horse, I would not feel like I was following it. I would feel like the leader."

e. Next page. ✔

> So the other horses got together and did a lot of talking. When they were done, they smiled and told Rolla they would fix things up.
> The next day when Rolla woke up, she looked in front of her and saw mountains and valleys. They were lovely. She couldn't see another horse anywhere in front of her. After a while, she found out that the other horses had made a painting and put it between her and horse 8. But Rolla didn't care. She felt wonderful leading the other horses into the mountains.
> So everything is fine now. The horses are happy. The music sounds good. And the mothers and children like the merry-go-round even more than before.
> The end.

- (For no more than 6 errors, go to **Comprehension.**)
- (For 7 or 8 errors in the entire story, direct the rereading of the sentences in which mistakes occurred. Then go to **Comprehension.**)
- (For 9 or more errors, direct the rereading of the entire story. Then go to **Comprehension.**)

EXERCISE 8

Comprehension

- (Call on individuals to read one or two sentences each.)
- (Call on individuals to answer each question.)

a. Now you'll read the story again, and I'll ask questions.
b. Touch the title. ✔

Rolla Slows Down

> Rolla was very happy. She was horse number 1 on a merry-go-round. She went up and down with the music. The children were happy, and their mothers were happy.

- How did Rolla feel? [Idea: *Very happy.*]
- What made her feel happy? [Idea: *She was number 1.*]

> Things went on like this for weeks. But then one day, something happened. Rolla said to herself, "I am number 1, but I am right behind number 8." Rolla thought that she should be far away from number 8. Then it would look as if she was the leader and the other horses were following her.

- What is bothering Rolla? [Idea: *She is right behind number 8.*]
- What horse is right in front of her? [Idea: *Number 8.*]
- Where does she want that horse to be? [Idea: *Far away.*]

> Rolla said, "I will get far from horse 8." To do that, Rolla slowed down. She went slower, and slower, and slower. But of course her plan didn't work. When she went slower, all the other horses went slower. The music slowed down and sounded awful. The mothers were unhappy. One of them said, "This merry-go-round is so slow you can't tell if it's going or if it has stopped."

- What did Rolla do to try to get far from horse 8? [Idea: *Slowed down.*]
- Did her plan work? *[No.]*
- What did the other horses do? [Idea: *Went slower.*]
- What did the music do? [Idea: *Slowed down.*]
- How did that sound? [Idea: *Awful.*]

- Look at the picture. Rolla is slowing down. Is she getting far from horse 8? *[No.]*
- What's the mother saying? *[I can't tell if we are moving.]*
- That doesn't look like a lot of fun.

c. Next page. ✔

> The other horses were not happy with Rolla. Horse 2 kept shouting at Rolla, "Come on, Rolla. Let's get this merry-go-round moving." But Rolla tried as hard as she could to slow down.
>
> At the end of the day, horse 8 was still there, right in front of her.
>
> That evening, horse number 3 asked, "What are you trying to do?"
>
> When Rolla told them, some of the horses started to laugh. Then horse number 5 said, "Rolla, would you be happy if you could not see horse 8?"
>
> "Yes," Rolla said. "If I could not see that horse, I would not feel like I was following it. I would feel like the leader."

- What did horse 5 ask Rolla? [Idea: *Rolla, would you be happy if you could not see horse 8?*]
- Would Rolla be happy if she could not see horse 8? *[Yes.]*

- Look at the picture. What is Rolla saying? *[I don't feel like the leader.]*
- She looks pretty sad. Do the other horses look sad? *[No.]*
- What are they thinking? *[Rolla is silly.]*

d. Next page. ✔

> So the other horses got together and did a lot of talking. When they were done, they smiled and told Rolla they would fix things up.
>
> The next day when Rolla woke up, she looked in front of her and saw mountains and valleys. They were lovely. She couldn't see another horse anywhere in front of her. After a while,

> she found out that the other horses had made a painting and put it between her and horse 8. But Rolla didn't care. She felt wonderful leading the other horses into the mountains.
>
> So everything is fine now. The horses are happy. The music sounds good. And the mothers and children like the merry-go-round even more than before.
>
> The end.

- What did the other horses make for Rolla? [Idea: *A painting.*]
- Where did they put it? [Ideas: *Between her and horse 8; in front of her.*]

- Look at the picture. Everybody looks pretty happy. What is that mother saying? *[What a lovely merry-go-round.]*
- Look at Rolla. Can she see horse 8? *[No.]*
- What is Rolla thinking? *[I am the leader.]*

Lined Paper

INDEPENDENT WORK

Passage Reading
a. Find the passage. ✔
b. Later you'll read this passage and complete the items.

Workbook

Story Items
a. Open your workbook to lesson 6. Find the story items. ✔
b. Later you'll complete the items.

Character Matching Game

> *Note:* Instruct students who have not read Grade 1 stories to skip the blue words and blue pictures.

- I am king of all the animals.

- I am so strong I can move big ships.

- I can't take the vow of a genie.

- I want to find out more rules so I can get out of here.

- I changed a frog into a king.

a. Find the character matching game. ✔
b. Later you'll draw lines to match the sentences with the pictures.

Writing Words for Pictures

a. Find the box of words. ✔
b. The first word in the box is **love.** Find the picture that shows love and write **love** under it.
   (Observe students and give feedback.)
c. Later you'll write the rest of the words under the pictures.

Independent Work Summary:

- Passage reading.
- Story items.
- Character matching game.
- Writing words for pictures.

END OF LESSON 6

Rolla Slows Down

Rolla was very happy. She was horse number 1 on a merry-go-round. She went up and down with the music. The children were happy, and their mothers were happy.

Things went on like this for weeks. But then one day, something happened. Rolla said to herself, "I am number 1, but I am right behind number 8." Rolla thought that she should be far away from number 8. Then it would look as if she was the leader and the other horses were following her.

Rolla said, "I will get far from horse 8." To do that, Rolla slowed down. She went slower, and slower, and slower. But of course her plan didn't work. When she went slower, all the other horses went slower. The music slowed down and sounded awful. The mothers were unhappy. One of them said, "This merry-go-round is so slow, you can't tell if it's going or if it has stopped."

28   Lesson 6

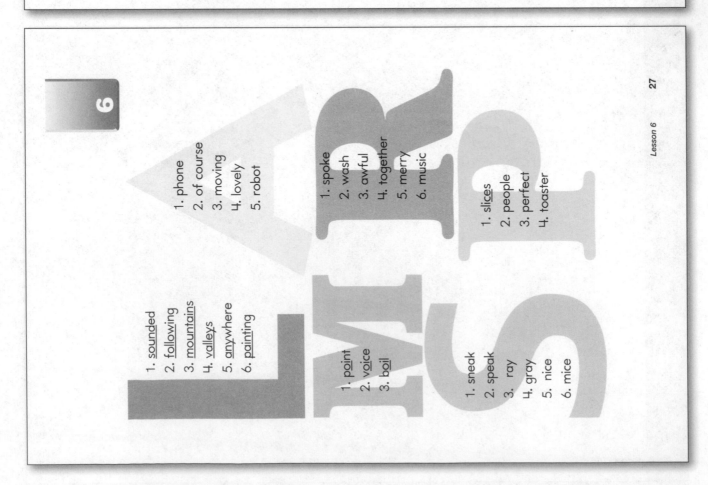

1. sounded
2. following
3. mountains
4. valleys
5. anywhere
6. painting

1. phone
2. of course
3. moving
4. lovely
5. robot

1. point
2. voice
3. boil

1. spoke
2. wash
3. awful
4. together
5. merry
6. music

1. sneak
2. speak
3. ray
4. gray
5. nice
6. mice

1. slices
2. people
3. perfect
4. toaster

Lesson 6   27

Lesson 6

"I don't feel like the leader."

"Rolla is silly."

The other horses were not happy with Rolla. Horse 2 kept shouting at Rolla, "Come on, Rolla. Let's get this merry-go-round moving." But Rolla tried as hard as she could to slow down.

At the end of the day, horse 8 was still there, right in front of her.

That evening, horse number 3 asked, "What are you trying to do?"

When Rolla told them, some of the horses started to laugh. Then horse number 5 said, "Rolla, would you be happy if you could not see horse 8?"

"Yes," Rolla said. "If I could not see that horse, I would not feel like I was following it. I would feel like the leader."

Lesson 6   29

Lesson 6

"What a lovely merry-go-round."

"I am the leader."

So the other horses got together and did a lot of talking. When they were done, they smiled and told Rolla they would fix things up.

The next day when Rolla woke up, she looked in front of her and saw mountains and valleys. They were lovely. She couldn't see another horse anywhere in front of her. After a while, she found out that the other horses had made a painting and put it between her and horse 8. But Rolla didn't care. She felt wonderful leading the other horses into the mountains.

So everything is fine now. The horses are happy. The music sounds good. And the mothers and children like the merry-go-round even more than before.

The end.

30   Lesson 6

Lesson 6

A boy named Ted was always thinking. He would think in the morning. He would think when he ate lunch. He would think in school and at home. One day, his sister said to him, "Why do you spend so much time thinking?"

Ted said, "I don't know. Let me think about that."

So Ted thought about why he thought. This went on for five days.

Then he told his sister, "I don't know why I think so much. But I think I'm tired of thinking. Let's do something else."

So they went bike riding.

1. Who always thought?
2. He thought at home and in ____.
3. Who asked him why he thought so much?
4. Did Ted know why he thought so much?
5. What did Ted and his sister do after Ted got tired of thinking?

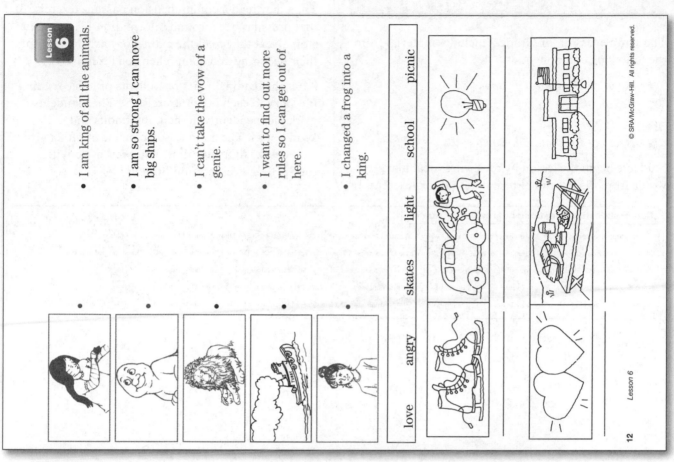

Lesson 6

- I am king of all the animals.
- I am so strong I can move big ships.
- I can't take the vow of a genie.
- I want to find out more rules so I can get out of here.
- I changed a frog into a king.

love   angry   skates   light   school   picnic

12

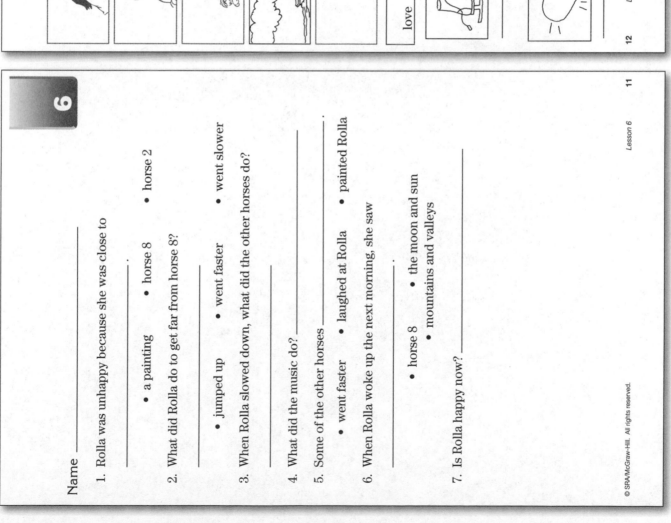

6

Name _____

1. Rolla was unhappy because she was close to
   - a painting
   - horse 8
   - horse 2

2. What did Rolla do to get far from horse 8?
   - jumped up
   - went faster
   - went slower

3. When Rolla slowed down, what did the other horses do? _____

4. What did the music do? _____

5. Some of the other horses
   - went faster
   - laughed at Rolla
   - painted Rolla

6. When Rolla woke up the next morning, she saw
   - horse 8
   - the moon and sun
   - mountains and valleys

7. Is Rolla happy now? _____

Grade 2—Lesson 71

The sample lesson for Grade 2 includes material from the following components:

- *Reading Presentation Book*
- *Textbook*
- *Workbook*
- *Spelling Presentation Book*

Students begin the lesson by reviewing vocabulary words from the Reading Presentation Book (exercise 1) and reading word lists in their Textbooks (exercise 2). Then they read a comprehension passage (exercise 3) that provides background information for the main story. Next they read the main story as you monitor their decoding and comprehension (exercise 4).

After the reading, pairs of students practice reading the story to each other (exercise 5). Then students work independently in their Textbooks and Workbooks. The main lesson concludes with a group workcheck. At a later time, you present activities from the Spelling Presentation Book.

Comprehension Questions Abbreviations Guide

Access Prior Knowledge = (APK) Author's Point of View = (APoV) Author's Purpose = (AP) Cause/Effect = (C/E) Charts/Graphs/Diagrams/Visual Aids = (VA)

Classify and Categorize = (C+C) Compare/Contrast = (C/C) Determine Character Emotions, Motivation = (DCE) Drawing Conclusions = (DC) Drawing Inferences = (DI)

Fact and Opinion = (F/O) Hypothesizing = (H) Main Idea = (MI) Making Connections = (MC) Making Deductions = (MD) Making Judgements = (MJ)

Narrative Elements = (NE) Noting Details = (ND) Predict = (P) Reality/Fantasy = (R/F) Recall Facts/Rules = (RF/R) Retell = (R) Sequence = (Seq)

Steps in a Process = (SP) Story Structure = (SS) Summarize = (Sum) Understanding Dialogue = (UD) Using Context to Confirm Meaning(s) = (UCCM) Visualize = (V)

LESSON 71

EXERCISE 1

Vocabulary Review

a. You learned a sentence that tells how long she survived.
- Everybody, say that sentence. Get ready. (Signal.) *She survived until she was rescued*.
- (Repeat until firm.)

b. You learned a sentence that tells what the soldiers did.
- Say that sentence. Get ready. (Signal.) *The soldiers protected their equipment*.
- (Repeat until firm.)

c. Here's the last sentence you learned: Lawyers with talent normally succeed.
- Everybody, say that sentence. Get ready. (Signal.) *Lawyers with talent normally succeed*.
- (Repeat until firm.)

d. Everybody, what do we call people who help us when we have questions about the law? (Signal.) *Lawyers*.
- What's another word for **usually?** (Signal.) *Normally*.
- What word refers to the special skills a person has? (Signal.) *Talent*.
- What word means the opposite of **fail?** (Signal.) *Succeed*.

e. Once more. Say the sentence that tells about lawyers with talent. Get ready. (Signal.) *Lawyers with talent normally succeed*.

EXERCISE 2

Reading Words

Column 1

a. **Find lesson 71 in your textbook.** ✔
- Touch column 1. ✔
- (Teacher reference:)

1. Mr. Daniels	4. medicine
2. recognize	5. guess
3. elevator	6. dozen

b. Number 1 is the name **Mr. Daniels.** What name? (Signal.) *Mr. Daniels*.

c. Word 2 is **recognize.** What word? (Signal.) *Recognize*.

- When you **recognize** something that you see or feel, you know what it is. Here's another way of saying **She knew what the smell was: She recognized the smell.**

d. Your turn. What's another way of saying **She knew what the smell was?** (Signal.) *She recognized the smell*.
- (Repeat step d until firm.)

e. What's another way of saying **She knew who the person was?** (Signal.) *She recognized the person*.

f. Word 3 is **elevator.** What word? (Signal.) *Elevator*.
- Spell **elevator.** Get ready. (Tap for each letter.) *E-L-E-V-A-T-O-R*.

g. Word 4 is **medicine.** What word? (Signal.) *Medicine*.
- Spell **medicine.** Get ready. (Tap for each letter.) *M-E-D-I-C-I-N-E*.

h. Word 5 is **guess.** What word? (Signal.) *Guess*.
- Spell **guess.** Get ready. (Tap for each letter.) *G-U-E-S-S*.

i. Word 6 is **dozen.** What word? (Signal.) *Dozen*.
- Spell **dozen.** Get ready. (Tap for each letter.) *D-O-Z-E-N*.

j. Let's read those words again, the fast way.
- Number 1. What words? (Signal.) *Mr. Daniels*.

k. Word 2. What word? (Signal.) *Recognize*.
- (Repeat for words 3–6.)

l. (Repeat steps j and k until firm.)

Column 2

m. Find column 2. ✔
- (Teacher reference:)

1. silently	4. approached
2. watering	5. fairly
3. heater	

- All these words have endings.

n. Word 1. What word? (Signal.) *Silently*.
- (Repeat for words 2–5.)

o. (Repeat step n until firm.)

Column 3

p. Find column 3. ✔
- (Teacher reference:)

1. clues	**4. drugs**
2. doctors	**5. typists**
3. offices	**6. lawyers**

- All these words end with the letter **S**.

q. Word 1. What word? (Signal.) *Clues*.
- (Repeat for words 2–6.)

r. (Repeat step q until firm.)

Column 4

s. Find column 4. ✔
- (Teacher reference:)

1. cock your head	**4. refinery**
2. equipment	**5. friendly**
3. motorcycle	**6. unfriendly**

t. Number 1. What words? (Signal.) *Cock your head*.
- When you cock your head, you tilt it. Everybody, show me how you cock your head. ✔

u. Word 2. What word? (Signal.) *Equipment*.
- (Repeat for words 3–6.)

v. Let's read those words again.
- Number 1. What words? (Signal.) *Cock your head*.

w. Word 2. What word? (Signal.) *Equipment*.
- (Repeat for words 3–6.)

x. (Repeat steps v and w until firm.)

Column 5

y. Find column 5. ✔
- (Teacher reference:)

1. explain	**4. crude**
2. insist	**5. fifth**
3. honest	

z. Word 1. What word? (Signal.) *Explain*.
- When you **explain** something, you **tell about it.** Here's another way of saying **She told about her talent: She explained her talent.**

a. Your turn. What's another way of saying **She told about her talent?** (Signal.) *She explained her talent*.
- (Repeat step a until firm.)

b. What's another way of saying **He told about his plan?** (Signal.) *He explained his plan*.

c. Word 2. What word? (Signal.) *Insist*.
- (Repeat for words 3–5.)

d. Let's read those words again.
- Word 1. What word? (Signal.) *Explain*.
- (Repeat for words 2–5.)

e. (Repeat step d until firm.)

Column 6

f. Find column 6. ✔
- (Teacher reference:)

1. narrow	**4. several**
2. prison	**5. pipeline**
3. polite	

g. Word 1. What word? (Signal.) *Narrow*.
- (Repeat for words 2–5.)

h. (Repeat step g until firm.)

Individual Turns

(For columns 1–6: Call on individual students, each to read one to three words per turn.)

EXERCISE 3

Story Background

a. Find part B in your textbook. ✔
- You're going to read the next story about Bertha. First you'll read the information passage. It gives some facts about wells.

b. Everybody, touch the title. ✔
- (Call on a student to read the title.) *[Oil Wells.]*
- Everybody, what's the title? (Signal.) *Oil Wells*. ⓃⒹ

c. (Call on individual students to read the passage, each student reading two or three sentences at a time. Ask the specified questions as the students read.)

Oil Wells

A well is a deep hole in the ground. The well has pipe in it so the hole stays open.

- Why does the well have a pipe in it? (Call on a student. Idea: *So the hole stays open*.) ⓃⒹ

There are different types of wells.
- Some wells are fresh-water wells. These wells pump fresh water from under the ground.

- What do fresh-water wells do? (Call on a student. Idea: *Pump fresh water from under the ground*.) (RF/R)

- Some wells are oil wells. These wells pump crude oil from under the ground.

- What do oil wells do? (Call on a student. Idea: *Pump crude oil from under the ground*.) (RF/R)

Picture 1 shows a machine that is drilling a hole for a well.

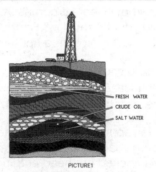

FRESH WATER
CRUDE OIL
SALT WATER

PICTURE1

- Everybody, touch the underground pipe in picture 1 and show how far down the well is already dug. ✔

If the machine keeps drilling, what type of liquid will it reach first?

- Everybody, touch the liquid it will reach first. ✔
- What kind of liquid is that? (Signal.) *Fresh water*. (VA)

If the machine keeps drilling past the fresh water, what kind of liquid will it reach next?

- Everybody, touch the liquid it will reach next. ✔
- What kind of liquid is that? (Signal.) *Crude oil*. (VA)

If the machine keeps drilling, what will it reach after the oil?

- Everybody, touch the liquid it will reach next. ✔ ,
- What kind of liquid is that? (Signal.) *Salt water*. (VA)
- If you dig a well deep enough, you'll always hit salt water.

If the well is an oil well, it pumps crude oil from the ground. Crude oil is a dark liquid that can be changed to make things like gasoline, motor oil, and plastic.

- What can be made from crude oil? (Call on a student.) *Gasoline, motor oil, plastic*. (RF/R)

The crude oil is pumped from the well. Then it goes into a pipeline.

- Everybody, where does the crude oil go from the well? (Signal.) *Into a pipeline*. (RF/R)

The pipeline goes along the ground and carries the crude oil many miles to a refinery.

- Everybody, where does the pipeline take the crude oil? (Signal.) *To a refinery*. (RF/R)
- Is the refinery usually right next to the well? (Signal.) *No*. (RF/R)

The refinery is a large place with strange-looking equipment and large tanks for holding oil.
The refinery changes crude oil into gasoline and other things.

PICTURE 2

- What does the refinery do? (Call on a student. Idea: *Changes crude oil into gasoline and other things*.) (RF/R)
- Everybody, touch the crude oil underground in picture 2. ✔
- Now follow it up the pipe to the surface of the ground. ✔
- Now follow it in the pipeline to the other end of the pipeline. ✔

- What's the other end? (Signal.) *The refinery*. (VA)
- What does that refinery do to the crude oil? (Call on a student. Idea: *Changes it into gasoline and other things*.) (RF/R)
- The oil company that you're reading about is a refinery.

EXERCISE 4

Story Reading

a. Find part C in your textbook. ✔
- The error limit for this story is 9. Read carefully.

b. Everybody, touch the title. ✔
- (Call on a student to read the title.) *[Maria Tests Bertha's Talent.]*
- What's going to happen in this story? (Call on a student. Idea: *Maria will test Bertha's talent*.) (P)

c. (Call on individual students to read the story, each student reading two or three sentences at a time. Ask questions marked **1.**)

- (**Correct errors:** Tell the word. Direct the student to reread the sentence.)
- (If the group makes more than 9 errors, direct the students to reread the story.)

---

d. (After the group has read the selection making no more than 9 errors, read the story to the students and ask questions marked **2.**)

Maria Tests Bertha's Talent

Bertha had a plan for helping Maria figure out where the water came from. You probably know what her plan was.

1. What do you think it was? (Call on a student. Idea: *Get water from the oil company and have Bertha smell it to see whether it came from the creek or water wells*.) (P)

Although Bertha didn't know too much about oil wells and refineries, she did know that she could smell the difference between water taken from the creek and water taken from water wells.

2. Everybody, where was the company supposed to be taking water from? (Signal.) *Wells*. (APK)

2. Where did Maria think it was coming from? (Signal.) *The creek*. (APK)

Bertha was sitting on Maria's porch. She said, "Maria, it's easy for me to tell if the water comes from the creek or from the well. I'll just smell it."

Maria looked slowly at Bertha and made a face. "What are you talking about?"

1. Everybody, show me the kind of face Maria probably made. ✔

1. What was Maria thinking about Bertha? (Call on a student. Idea: *That she was strange or crazy*.) (DCE)

Bertha said, "Take me with you and I'll tell you where the water comes from."

Maria made another face. "How will you know where it comes from?"

"I told you. I'll smell it," Bertha said. Then she explained her talent.

1. How would she do that? (Call on a student. Idea: *By telling Maria how she used her sense of smell*.) (P)

"I can tell about anything by smelling it. Honest I can."

Maria cocked her head and looked at Bertha.

2. Everybody, show me how you cock your head. ✔ (V)

"What is this, a joke?" Maria asked.

Bertha said, "Give me a test. Get glasses of water from different places. I'll tell you where you got each glass of water." At first Maria didn't want to do it. "This is crazy," she kept saying. But Bertha kept insisting on the test.

2. What would she say to keep insisting on the test? (Call on a student. Idea: *Get glasses of water from different places and I'll tell you where each one came from*.) (DI)

Finally Maria went into her house and came back with three glasses of water. She said, "You can't feel them, or you may get some clues about where I got them."

2. What kind of clues could you get by feeling the water glasses? (Call on a student. Idea: *Clues about temperature*.) (APK)

> Bertha said, "I don't have to feel them. The one on the left is from your water heater.

2. What's a water heater? (Call on a student. Idea: *A machine that makes cold water get hot*.) (APK)

> The middle glass is from a watering can or something like that.

2. What do you do with a watering can? (Call on a student. Idea: *Water plants and flowers*.) (APK)

> That water has been sitting out for a couple of days. The water in the last glass came from a water jug or something in your refrigerator. It's been in the refrigerator for a long time, and it probably doesn't taste very good."
>
> "I don't believe this," Maria said, and she tasted the water from the last glass. She made a face. "Oh, you're right. It's bad."

2. Everybody, show me the kind of face she made when she tasted the water. ✔ (V)

> Suddenly Maria laughed, turned around, and looked at Bertha. She said, "I don't believe this." Then she said, "I don't believe this," three or four more times. "You're amazing. You are amazing. You are the most amazing person I have ever seen."
>
> She kept talking very fast. She told about some of the amazing things that she had seen—a cow with two heads and a building over 3 hundred meters high. Finally, she said, "I once saw a man jump a motorcycle over twenty cars and that was amazing, but you are five times as amazing."

2. Maria is really excited. I'll read that part again. Listen to how she talks on and on.

> Suddenly Maria laughed, turned around, and looked at Bertha. She said, "I don't believe this." Then she said, "I don't believe this," three or four more times. "You're amazing. You are amazing. You are the most amazing person I have ever seen."
>
> She kept talking very fast. She told about some of the amazing things that she had seen—a cow with two heads and a building over 3 hundred meters high. Finally, she said, "I once saw a man jump a motorcycle over twenty cars and that was amazing, but you are five times as amazing."

> "Can I go with you?" Bertha asked. "Yes, yes, yes, yes, yes," Maria said. "This will be great."
> MORE NEXT TIME

1. Go back to the beginning of the story. Follow along while I read.
2. What do you think is going to happen? (Call on a student. Idea: *Maria will get Bertha to smell the water the oil company uses; etc.*) (P)

EXERCISE 5

Paired Practice

You're going to read aloud to your partner. Today the **B** members will read first. Then the **A** members will read from the star to the end of the story.
(Observe students and give feedback.)

End-of-Lesson Activities

INDEPENDENT WORK

Now finish your independent work for lesson 71. Raise your hand when you're finished.
(Observe students and give feedback.)

WORKCHECK

a. (Direct students to take out their marking pencils.)
• We're going to check your independent work. Remember, if you got an item wrong, make an **X** next to the item. Don't change any answers.

b. (For each item: Read the item. Call on a student to answer it. If the answer is wrong, say the correct answer. Refer to the Answer Key for the correct answers.)

c. Now use your marking pencil to fix up any items you got wrong. Remember, all mistakes must be fixed up before you hand in your independent work.

SPELLING

(Present Spelling lesson 71 after completing Reading lesson 71. See *Spelling Presentation Book*.)

71

A

1
1. Mr. Daniels
2. recognize
3. elevator
4. medicine
5. guess
6. dozen

2
1. silently
2. watering
3. heater
4. approached
5. fairly

3
1. clues
2. doctors
3. offices
4. drugs
5. typists
6. lawyers

4
1. cock your head
2. equipment
3. motorcycle
4. refinery
5. friendly
6. unfriendly

5
1. explain
2. insist
3. honest
4. crude
5. fifth

6
1. narrow
2. prison
3. polite
4. several
5. pipeline

B

Oil Wells

A well is a deep hole in the ground. The well has pipe in it so the hole stays open. There are different types of wells.

• Some wells are fresh-water wells. These wells pump fresh water from under the ground.

Lesson 71   173

• Some wells are oil wells. These wells pump crude oil from under the ground.

Picture 1 shows a machine that is drilling a hole for a well.

If the machine keeps drilling, what type of liquid will it reach first?

If the machine keeps drilling past the fresh water, what kind of liquid will it reach next?

If the machine keeps drilling, what will it reach after the oil?

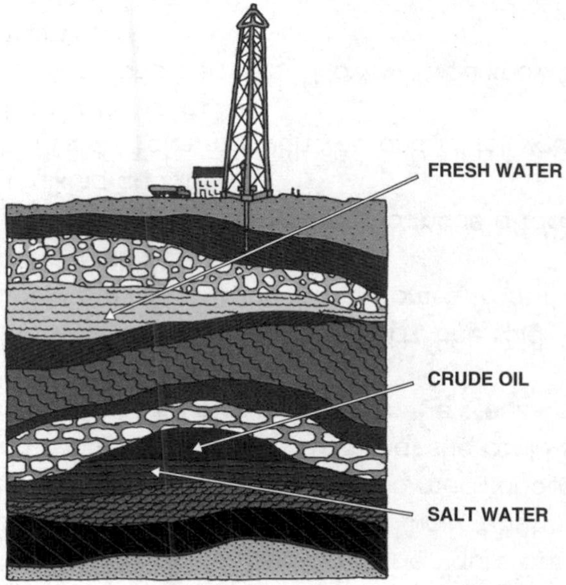

FRESH WATER

CRUDE OIL

SALT WATER

PICTURE 1

174   *Lesson 71*

If the well is an oil well, it pumps crude oil from the ground. Crude oil is a dark liquid that can be changed to make things like gasoline, motor oil, and plastic.

The crude oil is pumped from the well. Then it goes into a pipeline. The pipeline goes along the ground and carries the crude oil many miles to a refinery.

The refinery is a large place with strange-looking equipment and large tanks for holding oil.

The refinery changes crude oil into gasoline and other things.

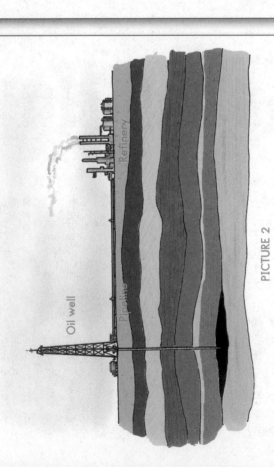

Oil well

Pipeline

Refinery

PICTURE 2

Lesson 71   **175**

C Maria Tests Bertha's Talent

Bertha had a plan for helping Maria figure out where the water came from. You probably know what her plan was. Although Bertha didn't know too much about oil wells and refineries, she did know that she could smell the difference between water taken from the creek and water taken from water wells.

Bertha was sitting on Maria's porch. She said, "Maria, It's easy for me to tell if the water comes from the creek or from the well. I'll just smell it."

Maria looked slowly at Bertha and made a face. "What are you talking about?"

Bertha said, "Take me with you and I'll tell you where the water comes from."

Maria made another face. "How will you know where it comes from?"

"I told you. I'll smell it," Bertha said. Then she explained her talent. "I can tell about anything by smelling it. Honest I can."

Maria cocked her head and looked at Bertha. "What is this, a joke?" Maria asked.

Bertha said, "Give me a test. Get glasses of water from different places. I'll tell you where you got each glass of water." At first Maria didn't want to do it. "This is crazy," she kept saying. But Bertha kept insisting on the test. Finally Maria went into her house and came back with three

176   *Lesson 71*

glasses of water. She said, "You ✳ can't feel them, or you may get some clues about where I got them."

Bertha said, "I don't have to feel them. The one on the left is from your water heater. The middle glass is from a watering can or something like that. That water has been sitting out for a couple of days. The water in the last glass came from a water jug or something in your refrigerator. It's been in the refrigerator for a long time, and it probably doesn't taste very good."

"I don't believe this," Maria said, and she tasted the water from the last glass. She made a face. "Oh, you're right. It's bad."

Suddenly Maria laughed, turned around, and looked at Bertha. She said, "I don't believe this." Then she said, "I don't believe this," three or four more times. "You're amazing. You are amazing. You are the most amazing person I have ever seen."

She kept talking very fast. She told about some of the amazing things that she had seen—a cow with two heads and a building over 3 hundred meters high. Finally, she said, "I once saw a man jump a motorcycle over twenty cars and that was amazing, but you are five times as amazing."

"Can I go with you?" Bertha asked.

"Yes, yes, yes, yes," Maria said. "This will be great."
MORE NEXT TIME

D **Number your paper from 1 through 19.**

Skill Items

Lawyers with talent normally succeed.

1. What word means the opposite of **fail?**
2. What word names people who help us when we have questions about the law?
3. What word means **usually?**
4. What word refers to the special skills a person has?

Review Items

5. You can see drops of water on grass early in the morning. What are those called?

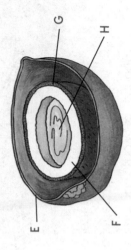

6. Which letter shows the coconut milk?
7. Which letter shows the inner shell?
8. Which letter shows the coconut meat?
9. Which letter shows the outer shell?

15. Write the letter that shows a tugboat.
16. Write two letters that show ships.
17. Write two letters that show docks.

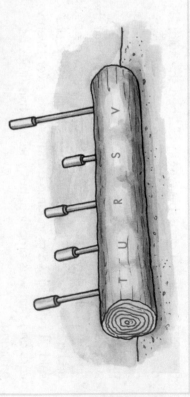

18. The place that is called Troy is now part of what country?

  • Greece   • Italy   • Turkey

19. Write the letters of the **4** kinds of weapons that soldiers used when they had battles with Troy.

a. bows   c. arrows   e. spears   g. planes
b. swords   d. rockets   f. guns   h. tanks

10. All machines make it easier for someone to ███.

11. You would have the most power if you pushed against one of the handles. Which handle is that?

12. Which handle would give you the least amount of power?

13. When people have very high fevers, how do they feel?

14. They may see and hear things that are not ███.

71

Name _____

A

1. Name two kinds of wells. _____

Write these names on the picture to show where each liquid is: **crude oil, fresh water, salt water.**

5. Fill in the boxes with the names for the **crude oil, pipeline, and refinery.**

6. Draw an arrow at A to show which way the crude oil is moving.

7. Draw an arrow at B to show which way the crude oil is moving.

B Story Items

8. Gasoline comes from a liquid called _____.

9. When Bertha first told Maria about her talent, did Maria believe her? _____

10. How many glasses of water did Maria use to test Bertha's talent? _____

11. **Underline** the items that tell where the water came from.
- fish bowl
- bath tub
- jug in refrigerator
- sink
- water heater
- frog pond
- watering can

12. Did Bertha pass Maria's test? _____

13. After the test, did Maria believe what Bertha said about her talent? _____

14. Bertha will help Maria by telling where ▇.
- the oil wells are
- the water came from
- the snow was

Review Items

15. The arrow by the handle shows which way it turns. Which arrow shows the way the log moves?

16. Which arrow shows the way the vine moves?

GO TO PART D IN YOUR TEXTBOOK.

LESSON 71

EXERCISE 1

Patterns

a. You're going to write words with endings. Some of the words are spelled with the letters **A-W.** Number your paper from 1 through 5. ✔

b. Word 1 is **fastest.** Who can run the **fastest?** What word? (Signal.) *Fastest.*
• Write the word **fastest.** ✔

c. Word 2 is **roomful.** We had a **roomful** of flowers. What word? (Signal.) *Roomful.*
• Write the word **roomful.** ✔

d. Word 3 is **awful.** I felt **awful.** What word? (Signal.) *Awful.*
• Write the word **awful.** ✔

e. Word 4 is **crawling.** The baby was **crawling** across the floor. What word? (Signal.) *Crawling.*
• Write the word **crawling.** ✔

f. Word 5 is **clearly.** We could see the ship **clearly.** What word? (Signal.) *Clearly.*
• Write the word **clearly.** ✔

g. Check your work. Make an **X** next to any word you got wrong.

h. Word 1. Spell **fastest.** Get ready. (Tap for each letter.) *F-A-S-T-E-S-T.*
• (Repeat for: **2. roomful, 3. awful, 4. crawling, 5. clearly.**)

EXERCISE 2

Phonemic Segmentation

a. Listen: **fast.** Say it. (Signal.) *Fast.*

b. I'll say the sounds in **fast:** fff . . . aaa . . . sss . . . t.
• Say the sounds in **fast.** Get ready. (Tap for each sound.) *fff . . .aaa . . . sss . . . t.*

> **To correct:**
> • (Return to step a.)

c. What's the first sound in **fast?** (Signal.) *fff.*

> **To correct:**
> • (Say the correct sound.)
> • (Return to step a.)

d. Next sound? (Signal.) *aaa.*

e. Next sound? (Signal.) *sss.*

f. Next sound? (Signal.) *t.*

g. Listen: **stop.** Say it. (Signal.) *Stop.*

h. I'll say the sounds in **stop:** sss . . . t . . . ooo . . . p.

i. Say the sounds in **stop.** Get ready. (Tap for each sound.) *sss. . . t . . . ooo . . . p.*

j. What is the first sound in **stop?** (Signal.) *sss.*

k. Next sound? (Signal.) *t.*

l. Next sound? (Signal.) *ooo.*

m. Next sound? (Signal.) *p.* Yes. Those are the sounds in **stop.**
• (Repeat steps g–m for **spot [sss . . . p . . . ooo . . . t], clap [c . . . lll . . . aaa . . . p].**)

n. (Call on individual students to say the sounds in: **fast, stop, spot, clap.**)

EXERCISE 3

Spelling Review

a. You're going to spell words.

b. Word 1 is **solid.** Spell **solid.** Get ready. (Signal.) *S-O-L-I-D.*

c. Word 2 is **claw.** Spell **claw.** Get ready. (Signal.) *C-L-A-W.*

d. Word 3 is **youthful.** Spell **youthful.** Get ready. (Signal.) *Y-O-U-T-H-F-U-L.*

e. Word 4 is **drawing.** Spell **drawing.** Get ready. (Signal.) *D-R-A-W-I-N-G.*

f. (Give individual turns on: **1. solid, 2. claw, 3. youthful, 4. drawing.**)

Lesson 71 **101**

Grade 3—Lesson 21

The sample lesson for Grade 3 includes material from the following components:

- *Reading Presentation Book*
- *Textbook*
- *Workbook*
- *Spelling Presentation Book*

Students begin the lesson by learning a new vocabulary sentence from the Reading Presentation Book (exercise 1) and reading word lists in their Textbooks (exercise 2). Then they read a comprehension passage (exercise 3) that provides background information for the main story. Next they read the main story as you monitor their decoding and comprehension (exercise 4).

After the reading, pairs of students practice reading the story to each other (exercise 5). Then students work independently in their Textbooks and Workbooks. The main lesson concludes with a group workcheck. At a later time, you present activities from the Spelling Presentation Book.

Comprehension Questions Abbreviations Guide

Access Prior Knowledge = (APK)   Author's Point of View = (APoV)   Author's Purpose = (AP)   Cause/Effect = (C/E)   Charts/Graphs/Diagrams/Visual Aids = (VA)

Classify and Categorize = (C+C)   Compare/Contrast = (C/C)   Determine Character Emotions, Motivation = (DCE)   Drawing Conclusions = (DC)   Drawing Inferences = (DI)

Fact and Opinion = (F/O)   Hypothesizing = (H)   Main Idea = (MI)   Making Connections = (MC)   Making Deductions = (MD)   Making Judgements = (MJ)

Narrative Elements = (NE)   Noting Details = (ND)   Predict = (P)   Reality/Fantasy = (R/F)   Recall Facts/Rules = (RF/R)   Retell = (R)   Sequence = (Seq)

Steps in a Process = (SP)   Story Structure = (SS)   Summarize = (Sum)   Understanding Dialogue = (UD)   Using Context to Confirm Meaning(s) = (UCCM)   Visualize = (V)

EXERCISE 1

Vocabulary

a. **Find page 352 in your textbook.** ✔
- Touch sentence 4. ✔
- This is a new vocabulary sentence. It says: The smell attracted flies immediately. Everybody, say that sentence. Get ready. (Signal.) *The smell attracted flies immediately.*
- Close your eyes and say the sentence. Get ready. (Signal.) *The smell attracted flies immediately.*
- (Repeat until firm.)

b. The smell **attracted** flies. If the smell attracted flies, the smell really interested the flies and pulled them toward the smell. Everybody, what word means **really interested** the flies? (Signal.) *Attracted.*

c. The sentence says the smell attracted flies **immediately. Immediately** means **right now.** Everybody, what word means **right now?** (Signal.) *Immediately.*

d. Listen to the sentence again: The smell attracted flies immediately. Everybody, say that sentence. Get ready. (Signal.) *The smell attracted flies immediately.*

e. What word means **really interested** the flies? (Signal.) *Attracted.*
- What word means **right now?** (Signal.) *Immediately.*

EXERCISE 2

Reading Words

Column 1

a. Find lesson 21 in your textbook. ✔
- Touch column 1. ✔
- (Teacher reference:)

1. mukluks	3. hailstone
2. wrist	4. playfully

b. Word 1 is **mukluks.** What word? (Signal.) *Mukluks.*
- Spell **mukluks.** Get ready. (Tap for each letter.) *M-U-K-L-U-K-S.*
- Mukluks are very warm boots that Eskimos wear.

c. Word 2 is **wrist.** What word? (Signal.) *Wrist.*
- Spell **wrist.** Get ready. (Tap for each letter.) *W-R-I-S-T.*
- Your wrist is the joint between your hand and your arm. Everybody, touch your wrist. ✔

d. Word 3. What word? (Signal.) *Hailstone.*

e. Word 4. What word? (Signal.) *Playfully.*

f. Let's read those words again, the fast way.
- Word 1. What word? (Signal.) *Mukluks.*
- (Repeat for words 2–4.)

g. (Repeat step f until firm.)

Column 2

h. Find column 2. ✔
- (Teacher reference:)

1. gulped	4. wavy
2. gently	5. kneeled
3. owed	6. dents

i. All these words have an ending.

j. Word 1. What word? (Signal.) *Gulped.*
- When you gulp something, you swallow it quickly. Here's another way of saying **She swallowed the water quickly: She gulped the water.**
- What's another way of saying **They swallowed their food quickly?** (Signal.) *They gulped their food.*
- Word 2. What word? (Signal.) *Gently.*
- Things that are gentle are the opposite of things that are rough. Everybody, what's the opposite of **a rough touch?** (Signal.) *A gentle touch.*
- What's the opposite of someone who behaves roughly? (Signal.) *Someone who behaves gently.*
- (Repeat until firm.)
- Word 3. What word? (Signal.) *Owed.*
- Something that you owe is something that you must pay. If you owe five dollars, you must pay five dollars. If you owe somebody a favor, you must pay that person a favor.

- Word 4. What word? (Signal.) *Wavy*.
- (Repeat for: **5. kneeled, 6. dents.**)

k. Let's read those words again, the fast way.
- Word 1. What word? (Signal.) *Gulped*.
- (Repeat for: **2. gently, 3. owed, 4. wavy, 5. kneeled, 6. dents.**)

l. (Repeat step k until firm.)

Column 3

m. Find column 3. ✔
- (Teacher reference:)

1. rose	**3. marble**
2. sight	**4. dove**

n. Word 1. What word? (Signal.) *Rose*.
- Something that moves up today rises. Something that moved up yesterday **rose.** Everybody, what do we say for something that moves up today? (Signal.) *Rises*.
- What do we say for something that moved up yesterday? (Signal.) *Rose*.
- Word 2. What word? *Sight*.
- A sight is something you see. A terrible sight is something terrible that you see. Everybody, what do we call something **wonderful** that you see? (Signal.) *A wonderful sight*.
- Word 3. What word? (Signal.) *Marble*.
- Word 4 rhymes with **stove.** What word? (Signal.) *Dove*.

o. Let's read those words again.
- Word 1. What word? (Signal.) *Rose*.
- (Repeat for words 2–4.)

p. (Repeat step o until firm.)

Individual Turns

(For columns 1–3: Call on individual students, each to read one to three words per turn.)

EXERCISE 3

Story Background

a. Find part B in your textbook. ✔
- You're going to read the next story about Oomoo and Oolak. First, you'll read the information passage. It gives some facts about clouds.

b. Everybody, touch the title. ✔
- (Call on a student to read the title.) [*Facts About Clouds.*]

- Everybody, what's the title? (Signal.) *Facts About Clouds*. ⓃⒹ

c. (Call on individual students to read the passage, each student reading two or three sentences at a time. Ask the specified questions as the students read.)

Facts About Clouds

You have read about a big storm cloud. Here are facts about clouds:
Clouds are made up of tiny drops of water.

- Everybody, say that fact. Get ready. (Signal.) *Clouds are made up of tiny drops of water*. ⓇⒻ/Ⓡ

In clouds that are very high, the water drops are frozen. Here is how those clouds look.

Picture 1   Picture 2

- Everybody, in what kind of clouds are the water drops frozen? (Signal.) *In clouds that are very high*. ⓇⒻ/Ⓡ
- Touch a high cloud. ✔ ⓋⒶ
- Those clouds are very pretty in the sunlight because the light bounces off the tiny frozen drops.

Some kinds of clouds may bring days of bad weather. These are low, flat clouds that look like bumpy blankets.

- Everybody, what kind of clouds may bring days of bad weather? (Signal.) *Low, flat clouds*. ⓇⒻ/Ⓡ
- Does that kind of cloud pass over quickly? (Signal.) *No*. ⓇⒻ/Ⓡ
- Touch a low, flat cloud. ✔ ⓋⒶ
- How long may that kind of cloud be around? (Call on a student. Idea: *Days*.) ⓇⒻ/Ⓡ

Some clouds are storm clouds. They are flat on the bottom, but they go up very high. Sometimes they are five miles high.

- Tell me how a storm cloud looks. (Call on a student. Idea: *It's flat on the bottom and it goes up very high*.) (RF/R)
- Everybody, how high is the top of a big storm cloud sometimes? (Signal.) *Five miles*. (RF/R)

The arrows in picture 3 show how the winds move inside a storm cloud. The winds move water drops to the top of the cloud.

- Everybody, touch the number **1** that is inside the cloud. ✔ (VA)
- That's where a drop of water starts. The wind blows it up to the top of the cloud. Everybody, follow the arrow to the top of the cloud and then stop. ✔ (VA)
- Tell me about the temperature of the air at the top of the cloud. Get ready. (Signal.) *It's freezing cold*. (APK)
- So what's going to happen to the drop? (Call on a student. Idea: *It will freeze*.) (DC)

The drops freeze. When a drop freezes, it becomes a tiny hailstone.

- Everybody, what do we call a drop when it moves up and freezes? (Signal.) *A tiny hailstone*. (RF/R)

The tiny hailstone falls to the bottom of the cloud.

- Everybody, touch the number **2** in the cloud. ✔ (VA)
- That's where the drop freezes. Now it falls down. Everybody, follow the arrow down. ✔ (VA)
- What's the temperature like at the bottom of the cloud? (Signal.) *It's warm*. (APK)

At the bottom of the cloud, the tiny hailstone gets covered with more water. Then it goes up again and freezes again.

- Everybody, when it gets to the top of the cloud, what's going to happen to the water that is covering it? (Signal.) *It will freeze*. (DC)

Now the hailstone is a little bigger. It keeps going around and around in the cloud until it gets so heavy that it falls from the cloud. Sometimes it is as big as a baseball. Sometimes it is smaller than a marble.

- Everybody, touch the number **1** in the cloud. ✔ (VA)
- Pretend that your finger is a drop. Show me a drop that goes around inside the cloud four times. Each time it goes through the top of the cloud, say: "It freezes." Go. ✔ (V)

If you want to see how many times a hailstone has gone to the top of the cloud, break the hailstone in half. You'll see rings.

- Everybody, what will you see inside the hailstone? (Signal.) *Rings*. (RF/R)

Each ring shows one trip to the top of the cloud. Count the rings and you'll know how many times the hailstone went through the cloud. Hailstone A went through the cloud three times.

- The rings are numbered. Everybody, count the rings in hailstone A out loud, starting with the center circle. Get ready. (Signal.) *One, two, three*. (VA)

How many times did Hailstone B go through the cloud?

- Everybody, figure out the answer. Remember to count the outside ring. (Wait.)
- How many times? (Signal.) *Seven*. (RF/R)

EXERCISE 4

Story Reading

a. Find part C in your textbook. ✔
- The error limit for group reading is 12 errors.
b. Everybody, touch the title. ✔
- (Call on a student to read the title.) *[The Killer Whales Wait.]*
- Everybody, what's the title? (Signal.) *The Killer Whales Wait*. (ND)

- Where were Oolak and Oomoo when we left them? (Call on a student. Idea: *Floating on an ice chunk*.) (APK)

c. (Call on individual students to read the story, each student reading two or three sentences at a time. Ask the specified questions as the students read.)

- **(Correct errors:** Tell the word. Direct the student to reread the sentence.)
- (If the group makes more than 12 errors, direct the students to reread the story.)

The Killer Whales Wait

Oomoo took off one of her boots. She kneeled down and slammed the boot against the surface of the ice.

- Why do you think she was doing that? (Call on a student. Idea: *She was trying to make noise so someone would hear her*.) (DI)
- Why didn't she yell? (Call on a student. Ideas: *She was losing her voice; nobody could hear her*.) (DI)

The boot made a loud spanking sound. Oolak watched for a moment, then took off one of his boots and slapped it against the surface of the ice. "Maybe they'll hear this," Oomoo said. "I hope they do," she added. But she knew that it was still raining a little bit and that the rain made noise. She also knew that she and Oolak were far from shore—too far. They were more than a mile from the tent. She guessed that the sounds they made with their boots were lost in the rain and the slight breeze that was still blowing from the south.

- Everybody, did she think that the people on the shore would hear the sounds? (Signal.) *No*. (ND)
- About how far away were these people? (Signal.) *Over a mile*. (ND)
- Why didn't she think they would hear the signal? (Call on a student. Idea: *Because the wind and rain were louder than the signal*.) (ND)

From time to time, Oomoo glanced to the ocean. She hoped that she would see the killer whales moving far away. She hoped that the sound

of the boots would scare them away. But each time she looked in their direction, she saw them moving back and forth, just past the top of the C-shaped ice floe.

- How do you think that made her feel? (Call on a student. Idea: *Afraid*.) (DCE)

Suddenly, Oolak tugged on Oomoo's shoulder and pointed toward the whales. His eyes were wide. He looked as if he was ready to cry. "I know," Oomoo said.

- What does she mean when she says, "I know?" (Call on a student. Idea: *She knew the whales were there*.) (DC)

Her voice was almost a whisper. "Just keep trying to signal," she said. "Maybe the people on the shore will hear us."

- Everybody, had Oolak noticed the whales before? (Signal.) *No*. (DC)
- Why did he look as if he was ready to cry? (Call on a student. Idea: *Because he was afraid of the killer whales*.) (DC)

As she pounded her boot against the surface of the ice, she stared toward the shore. She wanted to see a kayak moving silently through the rain. She wanted to hear the signal of a bell ringing. She wanted to. . . .

- She stopped thinking about those things. I wonder why.

Suddenly, she saw something white moving through the water.

- What do you think it is? (Call on individual students. Ideas: *Another ice chunk; a boat; an animal*; etc.) (P)

At first, she thought that it was a chunk of ice. But no, it couldn't be. It was not moving the way ice moves. It was very hard to tell what it was through the light rain. It wasn't a kayak. It wasn't a long boat. It was . . . Usk.

Usk ✳ was swimming directly toward the ice chunk. And he was moving very fast.

"Usk!" Oomoo yelled as loudly as she could. "Usk!" She stood up and waved her arms.

The huge polar bear caught up to the ice chunk when it was not more than a hundred meters away from the killer whales. "Will they go after Usk?" Oolak asked.

- Everybody, who does he think might go after Usk? (Signal.) *The killer whales.* Ⓓⓘ
- How close are they to the whales now? (Call on a student. Idea: *About 100 meters*.) ⓃⒹ

"They'll go after Usk if they're hungry," Oomoo replied. "We've got to get out of here fast."

The huge bear swam up to the ice chunk, put his huge paws on the surface, and started to climb onto it. When he tried that, he almost tipped it over.

- Why? (Call on a student. Idea: *Because he was so heavy.*) ⒹⒸ

"No," Oomoo said. "Stay down." She tried to push him back. He rolled into the water and made a playful circle. "Give me your laces," Oomoo said to Oolak. Oomoo and Oolak untied the laces from their boots. These laces were long, thick strips of animal skin. Oomoo tied all the laces together. Quickly, she glanced back. The ice chunk was less than a hundred meters from the killer whales.

She called Usk. He playfully swam around the ice chunk, rolling over on his back and slapping the water with his front paws.

- What does Usk want to do? (Call on a student. Idea: *Play.*) ⒹⒸ

Oomoo waited until Usk got close to the shore side of the ice chunk.

- Everybody, which side did he move to? (Signal.) *The shore side.* ⓃⒹ

- What do you think Oomoo's going to do? (Call on a student. Idea: *Get Usk to help them get back to shore.*) Ⓟ

Then she slipped the laces around his neck. "Hang on tight," she told Oolak, and handed him one end of the laces. She and Oolak sat down on the ice chunk and tried to dig their heels into dents in the surface of the ice.

"Play sled," she told Usk. "Play sled. Go home."

- Read the rest of the story to yourself. Find out two things. Find out what Usk did at first. Find out something he may have seen that made him stop being playful. Raise your hand when you're done.

At first, Usk just rolled over and almost got the laces tangled in his front paws. "Home," Oomoo repeated. "Play sled and go home."

Usk stayed next to the ice chunk, making a playful sound. "Home," Oomoo shouted again.

Then Usk seemed to figure out what he was supposed to do. Perhaps he saw the fins of the killer whales. He got low in the water and started to swim toward shore.

- (After all students have raised their hands:)
- What did Oomoo keep telling Usk to do? (Call on a student. Ideas: *Go home; play sled*.) ⓃⒹ
- Everybody, did Usk do that at first? (Signal.) *No.* ⓃⒹ
- What did he do? (Call on a student. Idea: *Rolled over*.) ⓃⒹ
- What may Usk have seen that made him stop being playful? (Call on a student. Idea: *The fins of the killer whales*.) ⓃⒹ
- What did Usk do then? (Call on a student. Idea: *Swam toward shore*.) ⓃⒹ
- Everybody, look at the picture. What are Oomoo and Oolak hanging on to? (Signal.) *The laces.* ⓋⒶ
- Point on the picture to show the direction Usk is moving. ✔ ⓋⒶ

EXERCISE 5

Paired Practice

You're going to read aloud to your partner. Today the **B** members will read first. Then the **A** members will read from the star to the end of the story.
(Observe students and give feedback.)

End-of-Lesson Activities

INDEPENDENT WORK

Now finish your independent work for lesson 21. Raise your hand when you're finished. (Observe students and give feedback.)

WORKCHECK

a. (Direct students to take out their marking pencils.)

• We're going to check your independent work. Remember, if you got an item wrong, make an **X** next to the item. Don't change any answers.

b. (For each item: Read the item. Call on a student to answer it. If the answer is wrong, say the correct answer. Refer to the Answer Key for the correct answers.)

c. Now use your marking pencil to fix up any items you got wrong. Remember, all mistakes must be fixed up before you hand in your independent work.

SPELLING

(Present Spelling lesson 21 after completing Reading lesson 21. See *Spelling Presentation Book.*)

ACTIVITIES

(Present Activity 2 after completing Reading lesson 21. See *Activities across the Curriculum.*)

> **Note:** A special project occurs after lesson 22. See page 128 for the materials you'll need.

21

A

1
1. mukluks
2. wrist
3. hailstone
4. playfully

2
1. gulped
2. gently
3. owed
4. wavy
5. kneeled
6. dents

3
1. rose
2. sight
3. marble
4. dove

B

Facts About Clouds

You have read about a big storm cloud. Here are facts about clouds:

• Clouds are made up of tiny drops of water.

• In clouds that are very high, the water drops are frozen. Here is how those clouds look.

Picture 1

• Some clouds are storm clouds. They are flat on the bottom, but they go up very high. Sometimes they are five miles high.

Picture 2

• Some kinds of clouds may bring days of bad weather. These are low, flat clouds that look like bumpy blankets.

freezing cold

warm

Picture 3

falls from the cloud. Sometimes it is as big as a baseball. Sometimes it is smaller than a marble.

The arrows in picture 3 show how the winds move inside a storm cloud. The winds move water drops to the top of the cloud. The drops freeze. When a drop freezes, it becomes a tiny hailstone. The tiny hailstone falls to the bottom of the cloud. At the bottom of the cloud, the tiny hailstone gets covered with more water. Then it goes up again and freezes again. Now the hailstone is a little bigger. It keeps going around and around in the cloud until it gets so heavy that it

If you want to see how many times a hailstone has gone to the top of the cloud, break the hailstone in half. You'll see rings. Each ring shows one trip to the top of the cloud. Count the rings and you'll know how many times the hailstone went through the cloud. Hailstone A went through the cloud three times.

How many times did Hailstone B go through the cloud?

Hailstone A   Hailstone B

C

The Killer Whales Wait

Oomoo took off one of her boots. She kneeled down and slammed the boot against the surface of the ice. The boot made a loud spanking sound. Oolak watched for a moment, then took off one of his boots and slapped it against the surface of the ice. "Maybe they'll hear this," Oomoo said. "I hope they do," she added. But she knew that it was still raining a little bit and that the rain made noise. She also knew that she and Oolak were far from shore—too far. They were more than a mile from the tent. She guessed that the sounds they made with their boots were lost in the rain and the slight breeze that was still blowing from the south.

From time to time, Oomoo glanced out to the ocean. She hoped that she would see the killer whales moving far away. She hoped that the sound of the boots would scare them away. But each time she looked in their direction, she saw them moving back and forth, just past the top of the C-shaped ice floe.

Suddenly, Oolak tugged on Oomoo's shoulder and pointed toward the whales. His eyes were wide. He looked as if he was ready to cry. "I know," Oomoo said. Her voice was almost a whisper. "Just keep trying to signal," she said. "Maybe the people on the shore will hear us."

As she pounded her boot against the surface of the ice, she stared toward the shore. She wanted to see a kayak moving silently through the rain. She wanted to hear the signal of a bell ringing. She wanted to . . . .

Suddenly, she saw something white moving through the water. At first, she thought that it was a chunk of ice. But no, it couldn't be. It was not moving the way ice moves. It was very hard to tell what it was through the light rain. It wasn't a kayak. It wasn't a long boat. It was . . . Usk.

Usk ⭐ was swimming directly toward the ice chunk. And he was moving very fast.

"Usk!" Oomoo yelled as loudly as she could. "Usk!" She stood up and waved her arms.

The huge polar bear caught up to the ice chunk when it was not more than a hundred meters away from the killer whales. "Will they go after Usk?" Oolak asked.

"They'll go after Usk if they're hungry," Oomoo replied. "We've got to get out of here fast."

The huge bear swam up to the ice chunk, put his huge paws on the surface, and started to climb onto it. When he tried that, he almost tipped it over.

"No," Oomoo said. "Stay down." She tried to push him back. He rolled into the water and made a playful circle. "Give me your laces," Oomoo said to Oolak. Oomoo and Oolak untied the laces from their boots. These laces were long, thick straps of animal skin. Oomoo tied all the laces together. Quickly, she glanced back. The ice chunk was less than a hundred meters from the killer whales.

She called Usk. He playfully swam around the ice chunk, rolling over on his back and slapping the water with his front paws. Oomoo waited until Usk got close to the shore side of the ice chunk. Then she slipped the laces around his neck. "Hang on tight," she told Oolak, and handed him one end of the laces. She and Oolak sat down on the ice chunk and tried to dig

their heels into dents in the surface of the ice.

"Play sled," she told Usk. "Play sled. Go home."

At first, Usk just rolled over and almost got the laces tangled in his front paws. "Home," Oomoo repeated. "Play sled and go home."

Usk stayed next to the ice chunk, making a playful sound. "Home," Oomoo shouted again.

Then Usk seemed to figure out what he was supposed to do. Perhaps he saw the fins of the killer whales. He got low in the water and started to swim toward shore.

D Number your paper from 1 through 12.

Story Items

1. What were Oomoo's boot laces made of?
2. What did Oomoo do with the laces after she tied them together?
3. What did she want Usk to do?
4. Did Usk immediately understand what he was supposed to do?
5. What did Usk start doing at the end of the story?

VOCABULARY SENTENCES

Lessons 1—70

1. The horses became restless on the dangerous route.
2. Scientists do not ignore ordinary things.
3. She actually repeated that careless mistake.
4. The smell attracted flies immediately.
5. The rim of the volcano exploded.
6. The new exhibit displayed mysterious fish.
7. She automatically arranged the flowers.
8. They were impressed by her large vocabulary.
9. He responded to her clever solution.
10. The patent attorney wrote an agreement.
11. The applause interrupted his speech.
12. She selected a comfortable seat.
13. Without gravity, they were weightless.
14. She demonstrated how animals use oxygen.
15. Lava erupted from the volcano's crater.
16. The incredible whales made them anxious.
17. The boring speaker disturbed the audience.

352   *Vocabulary Sentences*

Review Items

6. The map shows a route. What state is at the north end of the route?
7. What country is at the south end of the route?
8. About how many miles is the route?

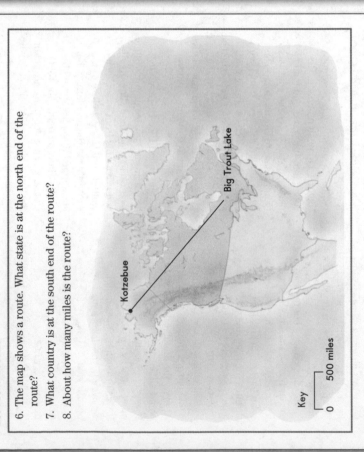

Big Trout Lake

Kotzebue

Key

0   500 miles

9. Female animals fight in the spring to protect █████.
10. Name 2 kinds of Alaskan animals that are dangerous in the spring.
11. Is it easier to fly alone or with a large flock?
12. Flying near the back of a large flock is like riding your bike ████.
    • with the wind   • against the wind

108   *Lesson 21*

21

Name _____

A

1. What are clouds made of? _____

2. What kind of cloud does picture A show? _____

3. Write the letter of the clouds that may stay in the sky for days at a time. _____

4. Write the letter of the storm clouds. _____

5. Write the letter of the clouds that have frozen drops of water. _____

6. Write the letter of the clouds that may be five miles high. _____

7. Look at cloud A. At which number does a drop of water start? _____

8. What happens to the drop at the number 2? _____

9. Draw 2 arrows on cloud A to show how a hailstone forms and returns to 1.

10. If you break a hailstone in half, what will you see inside the hailstone? _____

11. The picture shows half of a hailstone. How many times did the stone go through a cloud? _____

Lesson 21 37

B Story Items

12. Oomoo slapped her boot on the ice to make noise. Why did she want the people on shore to hear the noise? _____

13. Why did she want the killer whales to hear the noise? _____

14. Was Oomoo sure that someone would hear her? _____

15. About how far was the ice chunk from the tent? _____

16. About how far was the ice chunk from the killer whales? _____

Review Items

17. Write **north**, **south**, **east** and **west** in the correct boxes.

18. In which direction is ocean current **J** moving? _____

19. In which direction is ocean current **K** moving? _____

20. Which direction is the wind coming from? _____

21. Make an arrow above ice chunk **L** to show the direction the current will move the ice chunk.

22. Make an arrow above ice chunk **M** to show the direction the current will move the ice chunk.

GO TO PART D IN YOUR TEXTBOOK.

38   *Lesson 21*

LESSON 21

EXERCISE 1

Consonant Patterns

a. (Write on the board:)

> **-ack   -eck   -ick   -ock   -uck**

b. These are word endings that you need to pronounce correctly.
- I'll say each ending: **-ack, -eck, -ick, -ock, -uck.**
- Listen again: **-ack, -eck, -ick, -ock, -uck.**

c. Now read the endings one at a time.
- First ending? (Signal.) *-ack.*
- Next ending? (Signal.) *-eck.*
- Next ending? (Signal.) *-ick.*
- Next ending? (Signal.) *-ock.*
- Next ending? (Signal.) *-uck.*

d. (Call on individual students to read the endings.)

EXERCISE 2

Homonyms

a. Everybody, spell the word **meet** that refers to getting together with someone. Get ready. (Signal.) *M-E-E-T.*

b. Spell the word **meat** that refers to something you can eat. Get ready. (Signal.) *M-E-A-T.*

c. Spell the word **weak** that means **not strong.** Get ready. (Signal.) *W-E-A-K.*

d. Spell the word **week** that means **seven days.** Get ready. (Signal.) *W-E-E-K.*

EXERCISE 3

Spelling Review

*(Use context sentence for **meat.**)

a. You're going to write words on lined paper. Number your paper from 1 through 5. ✔

b. Word 1 is **thought.**
- Write the word **thought.** ✔

c. Word 2 is **meat*.**
- Write the word **meat.** ✔

d. Word 3 is **lightest.**
- Write the word **lightest.** ✔

e. Word 4 is **schools.**
- Write the word **schools.** ✔

f. Word 5 is **tough.**
- Write the word **tough.** ✔

g. Check your work. Make an **X** next to any word that is wrong. ✔

h. Word 1. Spell **thought.** Get ready. (Tap for each letter.) *T-H-O-U-G-H-T.*
- (Repeat for: **2. meat, 3. lightest, 4. schools, 5. tough.**)

Grade 4—Lesson 76

The sample lesson for Grade 4, includes material from the following components:

- *Reading Presentation Book*
- *Textbook*
- *Workbook*
- *Spelling Presentation Book*

Students begin the lesson by reading word lists in their Textbooks (exercise 1–5). Then they practice using context clues to determine word meaning (exercise 6).

Next they read a comprehension passage that provides information for the main story (exercise 7). Then they read the first part of the story aloud as you monitor their decoding and comprehension (exercise 8).

After students read the rest of the story silently, you ask more comprehension questions (exercise 9). Pairs of students then practice reading the story to each other (exercise 10). Next students work independently in their Textbooks and Workbooks and then participate in a group workcheck (exercises 11–12). At a later time, you present activities from the Spelling Presentation Book.

Comprehension Questions Abbreviations Guide

Access Prior Knowledge = (APK)   Author's Point of View = (APoV)   Author's Purpose = (AP)   Cause/Effect = (C/E)   Charts/Graphs/Diagrams/Visual Aids = (VA)

Classify and Categorize = (C+C)   Compare/Contrast = (C/C)   Determine Character Emotions, Motivation = (DCE)   Drawing Conclusions = (DC)   Drawing Inferences = (DI)

Fact and Opinion = (F/O)   Hypothesizing = (H)   Main Idea = (MI)   Making Connections = (MC)   Making Deductions = (MD)   Making Judgements = (MJ)

Narrative Elements = (NE)   Noting Details = (ND)   Predict = (P)   Reality/Fantasy = (R/F)   Recall Facts/Rules = (RF/R)   Retell = (R)   Sequence = (Seq)

Steps in a Process = (SP)   Story Structure = (SS)   Summarize = (Sum)   Understanding Dialogue = (UD)   Using Context to Confirm Meaning(s) = (UCCM)   Visualize = (V)

BEFORE READING

(Have students find lesson 76, part A, in their textbooks.)

EXERCISE 1

Hard Words

1. Everybody, find column 1. ✔
• The words in this column are hard words from your textbook stories.

1. soothe	5. conceal
2. persuade	6. dread
3. pirates	7. hasty
4. poverty	

2. Word 1 is **soothe.** Everybody, what word? (Signal.) *Soothe.*
• (Repeat for every word in the column.)
3. Let's read these words again.
4. Word 1. Everybody, what word? (Signal.) *Soothe.*
• (Repeat for every word in the column.)
5. (Repeat the column until firm.)

EXERCISE 2

Compound Words

1. Everybody, find column 2. ✔
• All these compound words consist of two short words.

1. shipwreck	4. halfway
2. horseback	5. courtyard
3. anybody	6. folktale

2. Word 1. Everybody, what's the first short word? (Signal.) *Ship.*
• Everybody, what's the compound word? (Signal.) *Shipwreck.*
• (Repeat for every word in the column.)
3. (Repeat the column until firm.)

EXERCISE 3

Word Practice

1. Everybody, find column 3. ✔
• We're going to practice these words.

1. ridicule	5. excuses
2. Beauty	6. ridiculed
3. cautious	7. countries
4. fatigue	8. furniture

2. Word 1. Everybody, what word? (Signal.) *Ridicule.*
• (Repeat for every word in the column.)
3. (Repeat the column until firm.)

EXERCISE 4

Vocabulary Review

1. Everybody, find column 4. ✔
• You've learned the meaning for all these words.

1. vanish	5. dimple
2. original	6. greedy
3. insane	7. victim
4. glossy	

2. Word 1. Everybody, what word? (Signal.) *Vanish.*
• (Repeat for every word in the column.)
3. (Repeat the column until firm.)
4. Now let's talk about what the words mean.

Word 1
1. Word 1 is **vanish.**
• What does **vanish** mean? (Idea: *Disappear.*)
2. Everybody, what's another way of saying **The mysterious stranger disappeared?** (Signal.) *The mysterious stranger vanished.*

Word 2
1. Word 2 is **original.**
• What is an **original?** (Idea: *Something that is not a copy of anything else.*)

Word 3

1. Word 3 is **insane**.
- What does **insane** mean? (Idea: *Crazy.*)
2. Everybody, what's another way of saying **He had a crazy desire for wealth?** (Signal.) *He had an insane desire for wealth.*

Word 4

1. Word 4 is **glossy**.
- What does **glossy** mean? (Idea: *Smooth and shiny.*)

Word 5

1. Word 5 is **dimple**.
- What is a **dimple**? (Idea: *A little dent in your cheek or chin.*)

Word 6

1. Word 6 is **greedy**.
- What does **greedy** mean? (Idea: *You are never satisfied with what you have.*)

Word 7

1. Word 7 is **victim**.
- What is a **victim**? (Idea: *A person who is harmed.*)

EXERCISE 5

Vocabulary Preview

1. Everybody, find column 5. ✔
- First we'll read the words in this column. Then we'll read the words in sentences.

1. desolate	4. selfish
2. persuade	5. soothe
3. terrify	6. poverty

2. Word 1. Everybody, what word? (Signal.) *Desolate.*
- (Repeat for every word in the column.)
3. (Repeat the column until firm.)

EXERCISE 6

Vocabulary From Context

1. Everybody, find part B. ✔
- These sentences use the words you just read.
2. We're going to use the rest of the sentence to figure out the meaning of the word in bold type.

Sentence 1

1. There was nothing within a hundred miles of this lonely, **desolate** place.

1. (Call on a student to read the sentence.)
- What could **desolate** mean? (Ideas: *Gloomy; barren; uninhabited.*)

Sentence 2

2. She was good at talking people into doing things, but she could not **persuade** anybody to go to the beach with her.

1. (Call on a student to read the sentence.)
- What could **persuade** mean? (Idea: *Convince.*)

Sentence 3

3. The old house was frightening, and the sounds within it **terrified** me.

1. (Call on a student to read the sentence.)
- What could **terrified** mean? (Idea: *Greatly frightened.*)

Sentence 4

4. She seemed to be kind, but she was really very **selfish** and thought of nobody but herself.

1. (Call on a student to read the sentence.)
- What could **selfish** mean? (Idea: *Concerned only with herself.*)

Sentence 5

5. He was so upset that nothing we could do would comfort or **soothe** him.

1. (Call on a student to read the sentence.)
- What could **soothe** mean? (Ideas: *Relax; make him feel better.*)

Sentence 6

6. At first he was wealthy, but then he lost all his wealth and found himself in **poverty**.

1. (Call on a student to read the sentence.)
- What could **poverty** mean? (Ideas: *Without money; the state of being poor.*)

READING

EXERCISE 7

Story Background

1. Everybody, find part C. ✔
2. (Call on individual students to read two or three sentences each.)
3. (After students complete each section, ask the questions for that section.)

Folktales

The next story you will read is a folktale called "Beauty and the Beast." Like myths, folktales are old stories that people told aloud before someone wrote them down. But folktales are usually much newer than myths. The myths you have just read, for example, take place about three thousand years ago. In comparison, "Beauty and the Beast" takes place just a few hundred years ago.

Another difference is that myths usually include gods and goddesses, but folktales do not. Instead, folktales often have witches, wizards, or other kinds of magic.

- Who were the gods in the myths you have read? (Ideas: *Zeus, Hermes; the stranger in "The Golden Touch."*) (APK)
- Who can name some folktales that have witches or wizards? (Ideas: *Cinderella; Sleeping Beauty; Snow White; Hansel and Gretel.*) (APK)

"Beauty and the Beast" is one of the most famous folktales of all time. Many movies have been made of the story, and many writers have retold it in their own words. The story comes from France, a large country in Europe.

- How many of you have seen a movie of "Beauty and the Beast"? (Have students raise their hands.) (APK)
- The version you will read is different from the movie versions.

EXERCISE 8

Reading Aloud

1. Everybody, find part D. ✔
   - The error limit for this lesson is 10.
2. (Call on individual students to read two or three sentences each.)

3. (After students complete each section, ask the questions for that section.)

Beauty and the Beast
Chapter 1

Once upon a time there lived a merchant who was enormously rich. The merchant had six sons and six daughters, and he would let them have anything they wanted.

- What do merchants do? (Idea: *Buy and sell things.*) (APK)
- How many children did the merchant have in all? (Response: *Twelve.*) (DC)
- How do you think those children might behave if they got everything they wanted? (Ideas: *They might be spoiled; they might be ungrateful.*) (H)

But one day their house caught fire and burned to the ground, with all the splendid furniture, books, pictures, gold, silver, and precious goods it contained. Yet this was only the beginning of their misfortune. Shortly after the fire, the merchant lost every ship he had upon the sea, either because of pirates, shipwrecks, or fire. Then he heard that the people who worked for him in distant countries had stolen his money. At last, he fell into great poverty.

- Name some things that went wrong for the merchant. (Ideas: *His house burned down; he lost all his ships; the people who worked for him stole his money.*) (R)
- How rich was the merchant after all this misfortune? (Ideas: *He wasn't rich; he was poor.*) (C/E)

All the merchant had after those misfortunes was a little cottage in a desolate place a hundred miles from the town in which he used to live. He moved into the cottage with his children. They were in despair at the idea of leading such a different life. The cottage stood in the middle of a dark forest, and it seemed to be the most dismal place on earth.

The children had to cultivate the fields to earn their living. They were poorly clothed, and they missed the comforts and amusements of their earlier life. Only the youngest daughter tried to be brave and cheerful. She had also been sad at first, but she soon recovered her good nature. She set to work to make the best of things. But when she tried to persuade her sisters to join her in dancing and singing, they ridiculed her and said that this miserable life was all she was fit for. But she was far prettier and more clever than they were. She was so lovely that she was called Beauty.

- Why do you think working was especially hard for these children? (Idea: *Because they were used to having servants do all the work.*) Ⓜ️Ⓙ
- What's the title of this story? (Response: *Beauty and the Beast.*) Ⓝ️Ⓔ
- Who do you think one of the main characters will be? (Response: *Beauty.*) ⓟ
- Who will the other main character be? (Response: *The Beast.*) ⓟ

After two years, their father received news that one of his ships, which he had believed to be lost, had come safely into port with a rich cargo. All the sons and daughters at once thought their poverty would be over, and they wanted to set out directly for the town. But their father was more cautious, so he decided to go by himself. Only Beauty had any doubt that they would soon be rich again. The other daughters gave their father requests for so many jewels and dresses that it would have taken a fortune to buy them. But Beauty did not ask for anything. Her father noticed her silence and said, "And what shall I bring for you, Beauty?"

"The only thing I wish for is to see you come home safely," she answered.

This reply angered her sisters, who thought she was accusing them of asking for costly things. But her father was pleased. Still, he told her to choose something.

"Well, dear Father," she said, "since you insist upon it, I want you to bring me a rose. I have not seen one since we came here, and I love them very much." ♦

- What did Beauty's sisters ask for? (Idea: *Jewels and dresses.*) Ⓝ️Ⓓ
- Why do you think Beauty asked for a rose? (Ideas: *Because she loved roses; because roses are beautiful; because roses don't cost much money.*) Ⓓ️Ⓒ️Ⓔ

EXERCISE 9

Silent Reading

1. Read the rest of the chapter to yourselves and be ready to answer some questions.

So the merchant set out on horseback and reached the town as quickly as possible. But when he got there, he found out that his partners had taken the goods the ship had brought. So he found himself poorer than when he had left the cottage. He had only enough money to buy food on his journey home. To make matters worse, he left town during terrible weather. The storm was so bad that he was exhausted with cold and fatigue before he was halfway home. Night came on, and the deep snow and bitter frost made it impossible for the merchant's horse to carry him any further.

The merchant could see no houses or lights. The only shelter he could find was the hollow trunk of a great tree. He crouched there all night long. It was the longest night he had ever known. In spite of his weariness, the howling of the wolves kept him awake. And when the day broke, he was not much better off, for falling snow had covered up every path, and he did not know which way to turn.

At last, he made out some sort of path, and he started to follow it. It was rough and slippery, so he kept falling down. But the path soon became easier, and it led him to a row of trees that ended at a splendid castle. It seemed very strange to the merchant that no snow had fallen in the row of trees. Stranger still, the trees were fruit trees, and they were covered with apples and oranges. ★

The merchant walked down the row of trees and soon reached the castle. He called, but nobody answered. So he opened the door and called again. Then he climbed up a flight of steps and walked through several splendid rooms. The pleasant warmth of the air refreshed him, and he suddenly felt very hungry; but there seemed to be nobody in this huge palace who could give him anything to eat.

The merchant kept wandering through the deep silence of the splendid rooms. At last, he stopped in a room smaller than the rest, where a bright fire was burning next to a couch. The merchant thought this room must be prepared for someone, so he sat down to wait. But very soon he fell into a heavy sleep.

His extreme hunger wakened him after several hours. He was still alone, but a good dinner had been set on a little table. The merchant had eaten nothing for an entire day, so he lost no time in beginning his meal, which was delicious. He wondered who had brought the food, but no one appeared.

After dinner, the merchant went to sleep again. He woke completely refreshed the next morning. There was still no sign of anybody, although a fresh meal of cakes and fruit was sitting on the little table at his elbow. The silence began to terrify the merchant, and he decided to search once more through the rooms. But it was no use. There was no sign of life in the palace. Not even a mouse could be seen.

- What bad news did the merchant discover when he reached the town? (Idea: *His partners had taken everything off the ship.*) (Seq)
- What was the weather like when he started back home? (Idea: *Cold and snowy.*) (V)
- Why did he have trouble finding his way in the morning? (Idea: *Snow had covered up the path.*) (C/E)
- What was unusual about the row of trees? (Ideas: *They had no snow on them; they had fruit on them.*) (R/F)
- What was unusual about the castle? (Ideas: *Nobody was there; a fire was burning by itself; food appeared while the merchant was sleeping.*) (R/F)
- Why did the merchant search through the palace the next day? (Ideas: *To see if anybody was there; to find the owner.*) (DCE)
- Who do you think the castle belongs to? (Ideas: *The Beast; a witch; a wizard.*) (H)

Paired Practice

1. Now you'll read in pairs.
- Whoever read second the last time will read first today.
- Remember to start at the diamond and switch at the star.
2. (Observe students and answer questions as needed.)

AFTER READING

Independent Work

1. Do all the items in your workbook and textbook for this lesson.
2. (The independent work in this lesson includes the following activities.)
- Story details
- Vocabulary
- Sequencing
- Related facts
- Story review
- Main idea
- Comprehension
- Writing

Workcheck

1. (Using the Answer Key, read the questions and answers for the workbook.)
2. (Have students read their answers for the textbook activities.)
3. (Have two or three students read their writing assignments aloud. Comment on each assignment.)
4. (Have students correct and turn in their work.)

(Present Spelling lesson 76 after completing Reading lesson 76. See *Spelling Presentation Book.*)

76

A WORD LISTS

1 Hard Words
1. soothe
2. persuade
3. pirates
4. poverty
5. conceal
6. dread
7. hasty

2 Compound Words
1. shipwreck
2. horseback
3. anybody
4. halfway
5. courtyard
6. folktale

3 Word Practice
1. ridicule
2. Beauty
3. cautious
4. fatigue
5. excuses
6. ridiculed
7. countries
8. furniture

4 Vocabulary Review
1. vanish
2. original
3. insane
4. glossy
5. dimple
6. greedy
7. victim

5 Vocabulary Preview
1. desolate
2. persuade
3. terrify
4. selfish
5. soothe
6. poverty

B VOCABULARY FROM CONTEXT

1. There was nothing within a hundred miles of this lonely, **desolate** place.
2. She was good at talking people into doing things, but she could not **persuade** anybody to go to the beach with her.
3. The old house was frightening, and the sounds within it **terrified** me.
4. She seemed to be kind, but she was really very **selfish** and thought of nobody but herself.
5. He was so upset that nothing we could do would comfort or **soothe** him.
6. At first he was wealthy, but then he lost all his wealth and found himself in **poverty.**

Lesson 76   75

C STORY BACKGROUND

Folktales

The next story you will read is a folktale called "Beauty and the Beast." Like myths, folktales are old stories that people told aloud before someone wrote them down. But folktales are usually much newer than myths. The myths you have just read, for example, take place about three thousand years ago. In comparison, "Beauty and the Beast" takes place just a few hundred years ago.

Another difference is that myths usually include gods and goddesses, but folktales do not. Instead, folktales often have witches, wizards, or other kinds of magic.

"Beauty and the Beast" is one of the most famous folktales of all time. Many movies have been made of the story, and many writers have retold it in their own words. The story comes from France, a large country in Europe.

D READING

Beauty and the Beast
Chapter 1

Once upon a time there lived a merchant who was enormously rich. The merchant had six sons and six daughters, and he would let them have anything they wanted.

But one day their house caught fire and burned to the ground, with all the splendid furniture, books, pictures, gold, silver, and precious goods it contained. Yet this was only the beginning of their misfortune. Shortly after the fire, the merchant lost every ship he had upon the sea, either because of pirates, shipwrecks, or fire. Then he heard that the people who worked for him in distant countries had stolen his money. At last, he fell into great poverty.

All the merchant had after those misfortunes was a little cottage in a desolate place a hundred miles from the town in which he used to live. He moved into the cottage with his children. They were in de-

76   Lesson 76

a good dinner had been set on a little table. The merchant had eaten nothing for an entire day, so he lost no time in beginning his meal, which was delicious. He wondered who had brought the food, but no one appeared.

After dinner, the merchant went to sleep again. He woke completely refreshed the next morning. There was still no sign of anybody, although a fresh meal of cakes and fruit was sitting on the little table at his elbow. The silence began to terrify the merchant, and he decided to search once more through the rooms. But it was no use. There was no sign of life in the palace. Not even a mouse could be seen.

up a flight of steps and walked through several splendid rooms. The pleasant warmth of the air refreshed him, and he suddenly felt very hungry; but there seemed to be nobody in this huge palace who could give him anything to eat.

The merchant kept wandering through the deep silence of the splendid rooms. At last, he stopped in a room smaller than the rest, where a bright fire was burning next to a couch. The merchant thought this room must be prepared for someone, so he sat down to wait. But very soon he fell into a heavy sleep.

His extreme hunger wakened him after several hours. He was still alone, but

spair at the idea of leading such a different life. The cottage stood in the middle of a dark forest, and it seemed to be the most dismal place on earth.

The children had to cultivate the fields to earn their living. They were poorly clothed, and they missed the comforts and amusements of their earlier life. Only the youngest daughter tried to be brave and cheerful. She had also been sad at first, but she soon recovered her good nature. She set to work to make the best of things. But when she tried to persuade her sisters to join her in dancing and singing, they ridiculed her and said that this miserable life was all she was fit for. But she was far prettier and more clever than they were. She was so lovely that she was called Beauty.

After two years, their father received news that one of his ships, which he had believed to be lost, had come safely into port with a rich cargo. All the sons and daughters at once thought their poverty would be over, and they wanted to set out directly for the town. But their father was more cautious, so he decided to go by himself. Only Beauty had any doubt that they would soon be rich again. The other daughters gave their father requests for so many jewels and dresses that it would have taken a fortune to buy them. But Beauty did not ask for anything. Her father noticed her silence and said, "And what shall I bring for you, Beauty?"

"The only thing I wish for is to see you come home safely," she answered.

This reply angered her sisters, who thought she was accusing them of asking for costly things. But her father was pleased. Still, he told her to choose something.

"Well, dear Father," she said, "since you insist upon it, I want you to bring me a rose. I have not seen one since we came here, and I love them very much." ◆

So the merchant set out on horseback and reached the town as quickly as possible. But when he got there, he found out that his partners had taken the goods the ship had brought. So he found himself poorer than when he had left the cottage. He had only enough money to buy food on his journey home. To make matters worse, he left town during terrible weather. The storm was so bad that he was exhausted with cold and fatigue before he was halfway home. Night came on, and the deep snow and bitter frost made it impossible for the merchant's horse to carry him any further.

The merchant could see no houses or lights. The only shelter he could find was the hollow trunk of a great tree. He crouched there all night long. It was the longest night he had ever known. In spite of his weariness, the howling of the wolves kept him awake. And when the day broke, he was not much better off, for falling snow had covered up every path, and he did not know which way to turn.

At last, he made out some sort of path, and he started to follow it. It was rough and slippery, so he kept falling down. But the path soon became easier, and it led him to a row of trees that ended at a splendid castle. It seemed very strange to the merchant that no snow had fallen in the row of trees. Stranger still, the trees were fruit trees, and they were covered with apples and oranges. ★

The merchant walked down the row of trees and soon reached the castle. He called, but nobody answered. So he opened the door and called again. Then he climbed

Grade 4 Textbook

E MAIN IDEA

For each paragraph, write a sentence that tells the complete main idea.

1. Saturday finally arrived. Janet took her camera out of her closet. Then she went outside to look for her friends. When she had found everybody, she told them to stand together on her porch. She looked through her camera and told everybody to stand closer together. Finally, she said, "Smile," and pressed the button on the camera. The camera went "click," and some of Janet's friends made faces.

2. William liked rowing boats. Last spring, William visited Swan Lake. He rented a rowboat for the whole day. He hopped into the boat and started to pull the oars. The boat started across the lake. William could see the boat rental place getting farther and farther away. William kept rowing. He looked at people fishing and at birds flying near the water. He had fun seeing how fast he could row. After a long time, he came to the opposite side of the lake.

F COMPREHENSION

Write the answers.

1. Why were most of the merchant's children greedy and spoiled?
2. Name at least three ways that Beauty was different from her sisters.
3. Why do you think Beauty asked her father for a rose?
4. Why did the merchant get lost on the way home?
5. Name at least three strange things about the palace.

G WRITING

What objects do you think are beautiful?
• Pick an object that you think is beautiful, such as a flower, a painting, or a river. Then write a poem about the object. Describe what the object looks like and tell why you think it's beautiful.

76

Name _____

A STORY DETAILS

Write the answers.

1. At the beginning of the story, how rich was the merchant?

2. How many children did the merchant have?

3. What happened to his house?

4. What kind of house did the family move into?

5. Before her father left for town, what did Beauty ask him to bring back?

6. What kinds of things did the other children ask for?

7. Where did the merchant sleep during the storm?

8. What was strange about the row of trees the merchant found?

9. Why was the palace so silent?

B VOCABULARY

Write the correct words in the blanks.

shrewd	calculate
witty	century
appetite	secure
inhabitant	sympathy
discontented	defeat

1. Lillian was so _____ with her job that she quit.

2. The wise man made many _____ decisions.

3. A _____ is a long time.

4. The experts could not _____ the number of stars in the sky.

5. She was glad to see the food because she had an enormous _____.

6. The cat was _____ from dogs as long as it stayed inside the house.

7. After the child fell, her mother held her and showed great _____.

C SEQUENCING

Put the following events in the correct order by numbering them from **1** to **5**.

_____ The merchant found a palace.

_____ The merchant spent the night in a tree.

_____ The merchant moved to a cottage.

_____ The merchant's house burned down.

_____ The merchant went back to the town.

D RELATED FACTS

Write which Greek god each statement describes. Choose **Hermes**, **Poseidon**, or **Zeus**.

1. The god of the sky

2. The god of the ocean

3. The god of travelers

E STORY REVIEW

Write whether each statement describes **The Miraculous Pitcher** or **The Golden Touch**.

1. Zeus appeared in this story.

2. The main character was a king.

3. One of the characters had a magic staff.

4. One of the characters was changed into a statue.

5. The story showed how evil greed can be.

6. The story showed why you should be kind to strangers.

GO TO PART E IN YOUR TEXTBOOK.

LESSON 76

EXERCISE 1

Word Introduction

> *Note:* Pronounce the sound /ē/ like the letter name **E**.

a. (Write on the board:)

> chief
> niece
> grief
> brief
> thief

b. Get ready to read these words.
- In each of these words, the sound /ē/ is spelled **i-e**.
- First word: **chief.** What word? (Signal.) *Chief.*

c. Next word: **niece.** What word? (Signal.) *Niece.*
- (Repeat for: **grief, brief, thief.**)

d. Now spell those words.
- Spell **chief.** Get ready. (Signal.) *C-H-I-E-F.*

e. Spell **niece.** Get ready. (Signal.) *N-I-E-C-E.*
- (Repeat for: **grief, brief, thief.**)

f. (Erase the board.)
- Spell the words without looking.

g. Spell **chief.** Get ready. (Signal.) *C-H-I-E-F.*

h. Spell **niece.** Get ready. (Signal.) *N-I-E-C-E.*
- (Repeat for: **grief, brief, thief.**)

EXERCISE 2

Word Building

a. (Write on the board:)

> 1. re + cover + ing =
> 2. re + cite + al =
> 3. slug + ish + ly =
> 4. waste + ful + ness =
> 5. dis + tract + ed =
> 6. mis + quote + ing =

b. You're going to write the words that go after the equal signs.
- Some of these words follow the final **e** rule. Be careful.
- Number your paper from 1 to 6. ✔

c. Word 1: Write **recovering** on your paper. ✔

d. Do the rest of the words on your own. ✔

e. Check your work. Make an **X** next to any word you got wrong.

f. Word 1. Spell **recovering.** Get ready. (Tap for each letter.) *R-E-C-O-V-E-R-I-N-G.*
- (Repeat for: **2. recital, 3. sluggishly, 4. wastefulness, 5. distracted, 6. misquoting.**)

EXERCISE 3

Prompted Review

a. (Write on the board:)

> 1. athlete
> 2. danger
> 3. studies
> 4. tensely
> 5. suddenly
> 6. recovering

b. Word 1 is **athlete.** Spell **athlete.** Get ready. (Signal.) *A-T-H-L-E-T-E.*

c. Word 2 is **danger.** Spell **danger.** Get ready. (Signal.) *D-A-N-G-E-R.*

d. (Repeat step *c* for: **3. studies, 4. tensely, 5. suddenly, 6. recovering.**)

e. (Erase the board.)
- Now spell those words without looking.

f. Word 1 is athlete. Spell **athlete.** Get ready. (Signal.) *A-T-H-L-E-T-E.*

g. Word 2 is danger. Spell **danger.** Get ready. (Signal.) *D-A-N-G-E-R.*

h. (Repeat step *g* for: **3. studies, 4. tensely, 5. suddenly, 6. recovering.**)

i. (Give individual turns on: **1. athlete, 2. danger, 3. studies, 4. tensely, 5. suddenly, 6. recovering.**)

Grade 5—Lesson 57

The sample lesson for Grade 5 includes material from the following components:

- *Reading Presentation Book*
- *Textbook*
- *Workbook*
- *Spelling Presentation Book*

Students begin the lesson by reading word lists in their Textbooks (exercises 1–3). Then they read definitions of words that will appear in their stories (exercise 4).

Next they review a Textbook skill exercise on inferential questions (exercise 5). After reading the focus question for the day's story (exercise 6), students have the option of reading the first part of the story aloud (exercise 7).

Students read the rest of the story silently, after which you present comprehension questions (exercise 8). Pairs of students then practice reading the story to each other (exercise 9). Next students work independently in their Textbooks and Workbooks and then participate in a group workcheck (exercises 10–11). At a later time, you present activities from the Spelling Presentation Book.

Comprehension Questions Abbreviations Guide

Access Prior Knowledge = (APK)   Author's Point of View = (APoV)   Author's Purpose = (AP)   Cause/Effect = (C/E)   Charts/Graphs/Diagrams/Visual Aids = (VA)

Classify and Categorize = (C+C)   Compare/Contrast = (C/C)   Determine Character Emotions, Motivation = (DCE)   Drawing Conclusions = (DC)   Drawing Inferences = (DI)

Fact and Opinion = (F/O)   Hypothesizing = (H)   Main Idea = (MI)   Making Connections = (MC)   Making Deductions = (MD)   Making Judgements = (MJ)

Narrative Elements = (NE)   Noting Details = (ND)   Predict = (P)   Reality/Fantasy = (R/F)   Recall Facts/Rules = (RF/R)   Retell = (R)   Sequence = (Seq)

Steps in a Process = (SP)   Story Structure = (SS)   Summarize = (Sum)   Understanding Dialogue = (UD)   Using Context to Confirm Meaning(s) = (UCCM)   Visualize = (V)

LESSON 57

BEFORE READING

(Have students find lesson 57, part A, in their textbooks.)

EXERCISE 1
Hard Words

1. Look at column 1.
- These are hard words from your textbook stories.

1. heron	4. wilderness
2. trio	5. gallant
3. Sylvia	6. pigeon

2. Word 1 is **heron**. Everybody, what word? (Signal.) *Heron.*
- (Repeat this procedure for every word in the column.)
3. Let's read the words again.
4. Word 1. Everybody, what word? (Signal.) *Heron.*
- (Repeat this procedure for every word in the column.)
5. (Repeat the column until firm.)

EXERCISE 2
Word Practice

1. Look at column 2.
- We're going to practice these words.

1. Circe	3. Scylla
2. Calypso	

2. Word 1. Everybody, what word? (Signal.) *Circe.*
- (Repeat this procedure for every word in the column.)
3. (Repeat the column until firm.)

EXERCISE 3
New Vocabulary

1. Look at column 3.
- First we'll read the words in this column. Then we'll read their definitions.

1. heron	5. gallant
2. foster parent	6. trio
3. huckleberry	7. game
4. bough	

2. Word 1. Everybody, what word? (Signal.) *Heron.*
- (Repeat this procedure for every word in the column.)
3. (Repeat the column until firm.)

EXERCISE 4
Vocabulary Definitions

1. Everybody, find part B. ✔
- These are definitions for the words you just read.
2. (For each word, call on a student to read the definition and the item. Then ask the student to complete the item.)

1. **heron**—*Herons* are birds that wade through water and eat frogs and fish. Herons usually have tall, thin legs and a long, S-shaped neck. The picture shows a *white heron.*
- Describe a heron.

- What's the answer? (Ideas: *It has tall, thin legs and a long, S-shaped neck; it wades through water and eats frogs and fish.*)

2. **foster parent**—A *foster parent* is somebody who brings up a child but is not the child's real parent.
- What do we call somebody who brings up a child but is not the child's real parent?

- What's the answer? (Response: *A foster parent.*)

3. **huckleberry**—A *huckleberry* is a small purple or black berry that grows on bushes.
- What is a huckleberry?

- What's the answer? (Idea: *A small purple or black berry that grows on bushes.*)

4. **bough**—A *bough* of a tree is a branch of the tree.
   - What is a branch of a tree?

   - What's the answer? (Response: *A bough.*)

5. **gallant**—Somebody who is *gallant* is brave and noble.
   - What's another way of saying *He was a noble warrior?*

   - What's the answer? (Response: *He was a gallant warrior.*)

6. **trio**—A *trio* is a group of three.
   - What's another way of saying *A group of three went to the river?*

   - What's the answer? (Response: *A trio went to the river.*)

7. **game**—Wild animals that are hunted are called *game.*
   - What do we call wild animals that are hunted?

   - What's the answer? (Response: *Game.*)

EXERCISE 5

Inference

1. Everybody, turn to part D at the end of today's story. ✔
   - (Call on individual students to read several sentences each.)
   - (At the end of each section, present the questions for that section.)

   Write the answers for items 1–8.
   You have to answer different types of questions about the passages you read. Some questions are answered by words in the passage. Other questions are *not* answered by words in the passage. You have to figure out the answer by making a deduction.

   - What do you use to answer the first kind of question? (Idea: *Words in the passage.*)
   - What do you use to answer the second kind of question? (Idea: *A deduction.*)

The following passage includes both types of questions.
More about Ecology
   Two hundred years ago, many people were not concerned with ecology. They believed there was no end to the different types of wildlife, so they killed wild animals by the hundreds of thousands. When we look back on these killings, we may feel shocked. But for the people who lived two hundred years ago, wild animals seemed to be as plentiful as weeds.
   Because of these killings, more than a hundred types of animals have become extinct since 1800. An animal is extinct when there are no more animals of that type.
   One type of extinct animal is the passenger pigeon. At one time, these birds were so plentiful that flocks of them used to blacken the sky. Now the passenger pigeon is gone forever. Think of that. You will never get to see a living passenger pigeon or any of the other animals that have become extinct. The only place you can see those animals is in a museum, where they are stuffed and mounted.

1. Are house cats extinct?

   - What's the answer? (Response: *No.*)

2. Is that question answered by **words** or a **deduction?**

   - What's the answer? (Response: *Deduction.*)
   - That's right, the passage does not contain this sentence: "House cats are not extinct." You figure out the answer by making a deduction.
   - Here's the deduction: **Animals are extinct when there are no more animals of that type. There are still many house cats. Therefore, house cats are not extinct.**

3. What extinct animal is mentioned in the passage?

   - What's the answer? (Response: *The passenger pigeon.*)

4. **Words** or **deduction?**

   - Is the question answered by **words** or by a **deduction?** (Response: *Words.*)

Lesson 57 **273**

- Read the sentence that contains words that answer the question. (Response: *One type of extinct animal is the passenger pigeon.*)

5. How many types of animals have become extinct since 1800?

- What's the answer? (Response: *More than a hundred.*)

6. **Words** or **deduction?**

- Is the question answered by **words** or by a **deduction?** (Response: *Words.*)
- Read the sentence that contains the words that answer the question. (Response: *Because of these killings, more than a hundred types of animals have become extinct since 1800.*)

7. The dodo bird is extinct. How many animals of that type are alive today?

- What's the answer? (Idea: *None.*)

8. **Words** or **deduction?**

- Is the question answered by **words** or by **deduction?** (Response: *Deduction.*)
- Here's the deduction: **Animals are extinct when there are no more animals of that type. The dodo bird is extinct. Therefore, there are no more animals of that type.**
- You'll write the answers later.

READING

EXERCISE 6
Focus Question

1. Everybody, find part C. ✔
2. What's the focus question for today's lesson? (Response: *How did Sylvia feel about living on her foster mother's farm?*)

EXERCISE 7
Reading Aloud (Optional)

1. We're going to read aloud to the diamond.
- (Call on individual students to read several sentences each.)

A White Heron
by Sarah Orne Jewett
Part 1
Focus Question: How did Sylvia feel about living on her foster mother's farm?

The woods were filled with shadows one June evening, but a bright sunset still glimmered faintly among the trunks of the trees. A girl named Sylvia was driving a cow from the pasture to her home. Sylvia had spent more than an hour looking for the cow and had finally found her hiding behind a huckleberry bush.

Sylvia and the cow were going away from the sunset and into the dark woods. But they were familiar with the path, and the darkness did not bother them.

Sylvia wondered what her foster mother, Mrs. Tilley, would say because they were so late. But Mrs. Tilley knew how difficult it was to find the cow. She had chased the beast many times herself. As she waited, she was only thankful that Sylvia could help her. Sylvia seemed to love the out-of-doors, and Mrs. Tilley thought that being outdoors was a good change for an orphan girl who had grown up in a town.

The companions followed the shady road. The cow took slow steps, and the girl took very fast ones. The cow stopped at the brook to drink, and Sylvia stood still and waited. She let her bare feet cool themselves in the water while the great twilight moths struck softly against her. She waded on through the brook as the cow moved away, and she listened to the waterbirds with pleasure.

There was a stirring in the great boughs overhead. They were full of little birds that seemed to be wide awake and going about their business. Sylvia began to feel sleepy as she walked along. However, it was not much farther to the house, and the air was soft and sweet.

She was not often in the woods so late as this. The darkness made her feel as if she were a part of the gray shadows and the moving leaves. She was thinking how long it seemed since she had first come to her foster mother's farm a year ago. Sylvia wondered if everything was still going on in the noisy town just the same as when she had lived there. ♦

EXERCISE 8

Silent Reading

1. Read the rest of the lesson to yourselves and be ready to answer some questions.

> It seemed to Sylvia that she had never been alive at all before she came to live at her foster mother's farm. It was a beautiful place to live, and she never wished to go back to the town. The thought of the children who used to chase and frighten her made her hurry along the path to escape from the shadows of the trees.
>
> Suddenly, she was horror-struck to hear a clear whistle not very far away. It was not a bird's whistle. It sounded more like a boy's. Sylvia stepped aside into the bushes, but she was too late. The whistler had discovered her, and he called out in a cheerful voice, "Hello, little girl, how far is it to the road?"
>
> Trembling, Sylvia answered quietly, "A long distance."
>
> She did not dare to look at the tall young man, who carried a gun over his shoulder. But Sylvia came out of the bushes and again followed the cow, while the young man walked alongside her.
>
> "I have been hunting for some birds," the stranger said kindly, "and I have lost my way. Don't be afraid," he added gallantly. "Speak up and tell me what your name is and whether you think I can spend the night at your house and go out hunting early in the morning." ★
>
> Sylvia was more alarmed than before. Would her foster mother blame her for this? She hung her head, but she managed to answer "Sylvia" when her companion again asked her name.
>
> Mrs. Tilley was standing in the doorway when the trio came into view. The cow gave a loud moo as if to explain the situation.
>
> Mrs. Tilley said, "Yes, you'd better speak up for yourself, you naughty old cow! Where'd she hide herself this time, Sylvia?" But Sylvia kept silent.
>
> The young man stood his gun beside the door and dropped a heavy gamebag next to it. Then he said good evening to Mrs. Tilley. He repeated his story and asked if he could have a night's lodging.
>
> "Put me anywhere you like," he said. "I must be off early in the morning, before day, but I am very hungry indeed. Could you give me some milk?"
>
> "Dear sakes, yes," said Mrs. Tilley. "You might do better if you went out to the main road, but you're welcome to what we've got. I'll milk the cow right now, and you make yourself at home. Now step round and set a plate for the gentleman, Sylvia!"
>
> Sylvia promptly stepped. She was glad to have something to do, and she was hungry herself.

- How did Sylvia feel about living on her foster mother's farm? (Ideas: *She loved being outdoors; the farm made her feel alive.*) (DCE)
- Why didn't Sylvia like the town? (Ideas: *The other children made fun of her; it was noisy and crowded.*) (DCE)
- Why do you think Sylvia didn't dare to look at the young man? (Ideas: *She was afraid of him; he was a stranger; she was shy.*) (DCE)
- How do you think Sylvia feels about hunting? Explain your answer. (Ideas: *She probably doesn't like hunting because she loves living things; she probably doesn't like hunting because guns are noisy.*) (DCE)
- What do you think will happen in the next part of the story? (Ideas: *The stranger will ask Sylvia to go hunting with him; the stranger will rob Sylvia and her foster mother.*) (P)

EXERCISE 9

Paired Practice (Optional)

1. Now you'll read in pairs.
- Whoever read second the last time will read first today.
- Remember to start at the diamond and switch at the star.
2. (Observe students and answer questions as needed.)

AFTER READING

EXERCISE 10

Independent Work

1. Do all the items in your workbook and textbook for this lesson.
2. (The independent work in this lesson includes the following activities.)

- Story details
- Vocabulary
- Figurative language
- Deductions
- Character traits
- Comparisons
- Inference
- Vocabulary review
- Comprehension
- Writing

EXERCISE 11

Workcheck

1. (Using the Answer Key, read the questions and answers for the workbook.)
2. (Have students read their answers for the textbook activities.)
3. (Have two or three students read their writing assignments aloud. Comment on each assignment.)
4. (Have students correct and turn in their work.)

SPELLING

(Present Spelling lesson 57 after completing Reading lesson 57. See *Spelling Presentation Book*.)

57

A WORD LISTS

1
Hard Words
1. heron
2. trio
3. Sylvia
4. wilderness
5. gallant
6. pigeon

2
Word Practice
1. Circe
2. Calypso
3. Scylla

3
New Vocabulary
1. heron
2. foster parent
3. huckleberry
4. bough
5. gallant
6. trio
7. game

B VOCABULARY DEFINITIONS

1. **heron**—*Herons* are birds that wade through water and eat frogs and fish. Herons usually have tall, thin legs and a long, S-shaped neck. The picture shows a *white heron*.
   • Describe a heron.

2. **foster parent**—A *foster parent* is somebody who brings up a child but is not the child's real parent.
   • What do we call somebody who brings up a child but is not the child's real parent?

3. **huckleberry**—A *huckleberry* is a small purple or black berry that grows on bushes.
   • What is a huckleberry?

4. **bough**—A *bough* of a tree is a branch of the tree.
   • What is a branch of a tree?

5. **gallant**—Somebody who is *gallant* is brave and noble.
   • What's another way of saying *He was a noble warrior?*

6. **trio**—A *trio* is a group of three.
   • What's another way of saying *A group of three went to the river?*

7. **game**—Wild animals that are hunted are called *game*.
   • What do we call wild animals that are hunted?

C READING

A White Heron
*by Sarah Orne Jewett**
Part 1

Focus Question: How did Sylvia feel about living on her foster mother's farm?

The woods were filled with shadows one June evening, but a bright sunset still glimmered faintly among the trunks of the trees. A girl named Sylvia was driving a cow from the pasture to her home. Sylvia had spent more than an hour looking for the cow and had finally found her hiding behind a huckleberry bush.

Sylvia and the cow were going away from the sunset and into the dark woods. But they were familiar with the path, and the darkness did not bother them.

Sylvia wondered what her foster mother, Mrs. Tilley, would say because they were so late. But Mrs. Tilley knew how difficult it was to find the cow. She had chased the beast many times herself. As she waited, she was only thankful that Sylvia could help her. Sylvia seemed to love the out-of-doors, and Mrs. Tilley thought that being outdoors was a good change for an orphan girl who had grown up in a town.

The companions followed the shady road. The cow took slow steps, and the girl took very fast ones. The cow stopped at the brook to drink, and Sylvia stood still and waited. She let her bare feet cool themselves in the water while the great twilight moths struck softly against her. She waded on through the brook as the cow moved away, and she listened to the waterbirds with pleasure.

There was a stirring in the great boughs overhead. They were full of little birds that seemed to be wide awake and going about their business. Sylvia began to feel sleepy as she walked along. However, it was not much farther to the house, and the air was soft and sweet.

She was not often in the woods so late as this. The darkness made her feel as if she were a part of the gray shadows and the moving leaves. She was thinking how long it seemed since she had first come to her foster mother's farm a year ago. Sylvia wondered if everything was still going on in the noisy town just the same as when she had lived there. ◆

It seemed to Sylvia that she had never been alive at all before she came to live at her foster mother's farm. It was a beautiful place to live, and she never wished to go back to the town. The thought of the children who used to chase and frighten her made her hurry along the path to escape from the shadows of the trees.

* *Adapted for young readers*

Suddenly, she was horror-struck to hear a clear whistle not very far away. It was not a bird's whistle. It sounded more like a boy's. Sylvia stepped aside into the bushes, but she was too late. The whistler had discovered her, and he called out in a cheerful voice, "Hello, little girl, how far is it to the road?"

Trembling, Sylvia answered quietly, "A long distance."

She did not dare to look at the tall young man, who carried a gun over his shoulder. But Sylvia came out of the bushes and again followed the cow, while the young man walked alongside her.

"I have been hunting for some birds," the stranger said kindly, "and I have lost my way. Speak up and tell me what your name is and whether you think I can spend the night at your house and go out hunting early in the morning." ★

Sylvia was more alarmed than before. Would her foster mother blame her for this? She hung her head, but she managed to answer "Sylvia" when her companion again asked her name.

Mrs. Tilley was standing in the door-way when the trio came into view. The cow gave a loud moo as if to explain the situation.

Mrs. Tilley said, "Yes, you'd better speak up for yourself, you naughty old cow! Where'd she hide herself this time, Sylvia?" But Sylvia kept silent.

The young man stood his gun beside the door and dropped a heavy gamebag next to it. Then he said good evening to Mrs. Tilley. He repeated his story and asked if he could have a night's lodging.

"Put me anywhere you like," he said. "I must be off early in the morning, before day, but I am very hungry indeed. Could you give me some milk?"

"Dear sakes, yes," said Mrs. Tilley. "You might do better if you went out to the main road, but you're welcome to what we've got. I'll milk the cow right now, and you make yourself at home. Now step round and set a plate for the gentleman, Sylvia!"

Sylvia promptly stepped. She was glad to have something to do, and she was hungry herself.

Lesson 57

323

Lesson 57

322

D INFERENCE

Write the answers for items 1–8.

You have to answer different types of questions about the passages you read. Some questions are answered by words in the passage. Other questions are *not* answered by words in the passage. You have to figure out the answer by making a deduction.

The following passage includes both types of questions.

More about Ecology

Two hundred years ago, many people were not concerned with ecology. They believed there was no end to the different types of wildlife, so they killed wild animals by the hundreds of thousands. When we look back on these killings, we may feel shocked. But for the people who lived two hundred years ago, wild animals seemed to be as plentiful as weeds.

Because of these killings, more than a hundred types of animals have become extinct since 1800. An animal is extinct when there are no more animals of that type.

One type of extinct animal is the passenger pigeon. At one time, these birds were so plentiful that flocks of them used to blacken the sky. Now the passenger pigeon is gone forever. Think of that. You will never get to see a living passenger pigeon or any of the other animals that have become extinct. The only place you can see those animals is in a museum, where they are stuffed and mounted.

1. Are house cats extinct?
2. Is that question answered by **words** or a **deduction?**
3. What extinct animal is mentioned in the passage?
4. **Words** or **deduction?**
5. How many types of animals have become extinct since 1800?
6. **Words** or **deduction?**
7. The dodo bird is extinct. How many animals of that type are alive today?
8. **Words** or **deduction?**
Write the answers about the deductions.

E DEDUCTIONS

Oliver believed that if he studied, he would pass the test. Oliver studied for the test.
1. So, what did Oliver believe would happen?

Nadia believed that if you ate an apple a day you would stay healthy. Nadia ate an apple every day.
2. So, what did Nadia believe would happen?

F VOCABULARY REVIEW

unprecedented
maneuver
devoted
spurn
endured
regard

For each item, write the correct word.
1. When you move skillfully, you ▮▮▮.
2. When you consider something, you ▮▮▮ it.
3. Something that has never occurred before is ▮▮▮.

G COMPREHENSION

Write the answers.
1. How did Sylvia feel about living on her foster mother's farm?
2. Why didn't Sylvia like the town?
3. Why do you think Sylvia didn't dare to look at the young man?
4. How do you think Sylvia feels about hunting? Explain your answer.
5. What do you think will happen in the next part of the story?

H WRITING

Where would you rather live, on a farm or in a town?
Write an essay that explains your answer. Try to answer the following questions:
• What are the advantages of living on a farm?
• What are the disadvantages of living on a farm?
• What are the advantages of living in a town?
• What are the disadvantages of living in a town?
• Where would you rather live? Why? Make your essay at least sixty words long.

57

Name _____

A STORY DETAILS

Write or circle the answers.

1. Sylvia was _____ who lived on a farm.
   • a vacationer • a farmhand • an orphan

2. Where had Sylvia lived before coming to the farm?

   _____

3. Sylvia thought she had never been _____ at all before coming to the farm.
   • scared • alive • punished

4. Which place did Sylvia enjoy more, the town or the farm?

   _____

5. How had the children in town treated Sylvia?

   _____

6. What was the young man doing in the woods?

   _____

7. Was Sylvia bold or shy?

   _____

8. What was the name of the person who owned the farm?

   _____

9. That person was Sylvia's _____.
   • employer • mother • foster parent

B VOCABULARY

Write the correct words in the blanks.

| regarded | suitable | humiliating |
| appealed | unprecedented | maneuvered |

1. The starving boy _____ to the sympathy of the crowd.

2. They _____ the criminal as a dangerous person.

3. He _____ the shopping cart past the fallen cans.

4. The pitcher made an _____ number of strikeouts.

C FIGURATIVE LANGUAGE

For each statement, write simile, metaphor, or exaggeration.

1. Her face was like a pale star.

   _____

2. The apartment was a prison.

   _____

3. The day was like a dream.

   _____

D DEDUCTIONS

Complete each deduction.

Every element has an atomic weight. Argon is an element.

1. What's the conclusion about argon?

   _____

   _____

Horses eat grass. A palomino is a horse.

2. What's the conclusion about a palomino?

   _____

   _____

E CHARACTER TRAITS

Write whether each phrase describes Sylvia, Mrs. Tilley, or the stranger.

1. Very shy

   _____

2. Whistled loudly

   _____

3. An orphan

   _____

4. Owned a farm

   _____

5. Felt like a part of the woods

   _____

6. Hunted for animals

   _____

F COMPARISONS

Write Odyssey if the event occurred in The Odyssey. Write Yarn if the event occurred in "Mystery Yarn."

1. Telemachus was one of the suitors.

   _____

2. Telemachus helped defeat the suitors.

   _____

3. The suitors took a test that involved unwinding string.

   _____

4. The suitors took a test that involved a bow and arrow.

   _____

█ GO TO PART D IN YOUR TEXTBOOK.

LESSON 57

EXERCISE 1

Word Introduction

a. (Write on the board:)

> tragic
> comic
> critic
> medic
> pulse
> magic

b. Get ready to read these words.
- First word: **tragic.** What word? (Signal.) *Tragic.*
c. Next word: **comic.** What word? (Signal.) *Comic.*
- (Repeat for: **critic, medic, pulse, magic.**)
d. Now spell those words.
- Spell **tragic.** Get ready. (Signal.) *T-R-A-G-I-C.*
e. Spell **comic.** Get ready. (Signal.) *C-O-M-I-C.*
- (Repeat for: **critic, medic, pulse, magic.**)
f. (Erase the board.)
- Spell the words without looking.
g. Spell **tragic.** Get ready. (Signal.) *T-R-A-G-I-C.*
h. Spell **comic.** Get ready. (Signal.) *C-O-M-I-C.*
- (Repeat for: **critic, medic, pulse, magic.**)
i. Get ready to write those words.
j. First word: **tragic.** Write it. ✔
- (Repeat for: **comic, critic, medic, pulse, magic.**)

EXERCISE 2

Word Building

a. (Write on the board:)

> 1. de + fer + ment = _____
> 2. pro + duct + ion = _____
> 3. style + ish + ly = _____
> 4. rhythm + s = _____
> 5. pro + tect + ive = _____
> 6. re + act + ive +ly = _____

b. You're going to write the words that go in the blanks.
- Number your paper from 1 to 6. ✔
c. Word 1. Write **deferment** on your paper. ✔
d. Do the rest of the words on your own. ✔
e. Check your work. Make an **X** next to any word you got wrong.
f. Word 1. Spell **deferment.** Get ready. (Tap for each letter.) *D-E-F-E-R-M-E-N-T.*
- (Repeat for: **2. production, 3. stylishly, 4. rhythms, 5. protective, 6. reactively.**)

EXERCISE 3

Spelling Review

a. Get ready to spell some words.
b. Word 1 is **thoughtlessly.**
- What word? (Signal.) *Thoughtlessly.*
- Spell **thoughtlessly.** Get ready. (Signal.) *T-H-O-U-G-H-T-L-E-S-S-L-Y.*
c. Word 2 is **stretcher.**
- What word? (Signal.) *Stretcher.*
- Spell **stretcher.** Get ready. (Signal.) *S-T-R-E-T-C-H-E-R.*
d. (Repeat step c for: **3. photographing, 4. retained, 5. reception, 6. music.**)
e. (Give individual turns on: **1. thoughtlessly, 2. stretcher, 3. photographing, 4. retained, 5. reception, 6. music.**)